IMAGINING QUEER METHODS

I0136227

Imagining Queer Methods

Edited by
Amin Ghaziani *and* Matt Brim

NEW YORK UNIVERSITY PRESS
New York

NEW YORK UNIVERSITY PRESS
New York
www.nyupress.org

© 2019 by New York University
All rights reserved

References to Internet websites (URLs) were accurate at the time of writing. Neither the author nor New York University Press is responsible for URLs that may have expired or changed since the manuscript was prepared.

Chapter 4 draws on material previously published in *Other, Please Specify: Queer Methods in Sociology*, edited by D'Lane Compton, Tey Meadow, and Kristen Schilt (Berkeley: University of California Press, 2018). Reprinted here with permission. Contributions from Kadji Amin, Petra L. Doan, Jessica Fields, Patrick R. Grzanka, E. Patrick Johnson, and Jane Ward draw on material previously published in the "Queer Methods" special double issue of *WSQ: Women's Studies Quarterly* 44 (3–4) (2016), edited by Matt Brim and Amin Ghaziani. Reprinted here with permission. The two introductions and chapter 8 have been significantly rewritten and expanded from their original form in that same issue.

Library of Congress Cataloging-in-Publication Data
Names: Ghaziani, Amin, editor. | Brim, Matt, editor.
Title: Imagining queer methods / edited by Amin Ghaziani and Matt Brim.
Description: New York : New York University Press, [2019] |
Includes bibliographical references and index.
Identifiers: LCCN 2018041800| ISBN 9781479821020 (cloth : alk. paper) |
ISBN 9781479829484 (pbk : alk. paper)
Subjects: LCSH: Queer theory—United States—Methodology. |
Gay and lesbian studies—United States—Methodology.
Classification: LCC HQ75.16.U6 I43 2019 | DDC 306.7601—dc23
LC record available at https://lccn.loc.gov/2018041800

New York University Press books are printed on acid-free paper, and their binding materials are chosen for strength and durability. We strive to use environmentally responsible suppliers and materials to the greatest extent possible in publishing our books.

Manufactured in the United States of America

10 9 8 7 6 5 4 3 2 1

Also available as an ebook

CONTENTS

INTRODUCTIONS

Methods/Mess

Queer Methods

Four Provocations for an Emerging Field

AMIN GHAZIANI AND MATT BRIM

Queer methods. Say the words out loud, and let them linger for a moment. The idea of distinctively queer methods is probably less familiar to you than its companion *queer theory*. Now say those words out loud. Do they sound any different? Feel any different?

Queer theory emerged at an academic conference in 1990 at the University of California, Santa Cruz. Teresa de Lauretis organized the gathering, and she coined the phrase "queer theory" for it. From the outset, the framework exploited an "antimethodological impulse" (Love 2016, 347). Queer theory was inspired by social movements of the day, especially ACT UP, which linked "deconstructive reading practices and grassroots activism together" (Freeman 2010, xv). A focus on methods, which direct techniques for gathering data, and methodologies, which pertain to the logics of research design, would have risked a confrontation with queer claims to interdisciplinarity, if not an antidisciplinary irreverence.

Although queer theorists have made great strides on the clarification of concepts like queerness, sexuality, gender, transgender, race, nationalism, discourse, fluidity, performativity, and normativity, among others, we have made much less progress on the application of these ideas in our research. In fact, scholars who use queer theory often proceed with "undefined notions of what they mean by 'queer research'" (Browne and Nash 2010a, 1). This isn't surprising, since queer theory frequently defines its object of study as "fluid, unstable, and perpetually becoming" (ibid.). How do we study ephemeral subjects and their worldmaking efforts using standard methodological procedures?

A movement has been growing in recent years inspired by questions of design, data, and analysis—a renaissance in queer methods, as we, your editors, like to call it. The turn toward methods makes visible "actual ways of working" (Mills 1959, 195), as scholars and students identify protocols that have been largely overshadowed by advances in theory. The 2010 volume *Queer Methods and Methodologies* (Browne and Nash 2010b) indexed this shift toward methods by reframing the well-rehearsed question "*What* is queer theory?" as the pioneering "*How* do we do queer theory?" Three years later, the Gender, Sexuality, and Women's Studies Program at the University of Pennsylvania hosted a two-day "Queer Method" conference where the panelists similarly asked: What does it mean to understand queer work as having a method, or to imagine method itself as queer?[1] In 2016, we edited a special issue of *WSQ: Women's Studies Quarterly* under the theme "Queer Methods." Two years after that, the University of California Press produced *Other, Please Specify: Queer Methods in Sociology* (Compton, Meadow, and Schilt 2018). We're back again and deliver for you a volume unlike any other. In these pages, we take the deepest dive yet, display the most cutting-edge innovations in the field of queer methods, and sample its intensely interdisciplinary flavor.

The enterprise on which we are embarking in this book has not come easily or inevitably for us. Questions of method incite heated discussions of disciplinarity, since our theories precede and largely determine the particular research strategies that we adopt in our work. Yet queer studies has staked its claim by working within, against, across, and even beyond disciplinary boundaries, thereby blurring distinctions between the field and its methods. Many humanists embrace a "suspicion of method" (Brim and Ghaziani 2016, 16) and assume that queer frameworks are incompatible with social science epistemologies. Scholars in the social sciences, their argument goes, emphasize the systematic, coherent, orderly, modal, normative, positivist, and generalizable while queer theorists in the humanities champion the fluid, flux, disruptive, transgressive, interpretivist, and local knowledges. Hence, conjoining "queer" with "method" can present a paradox. The former celebrates a "failure to adhere to stable classificatory systems or be contained by disciplinary boundaries" while the latter is "defined by orderly, discipline-specific, and easily reproducible techniques" (Ward 2016, 71). What productive avenues of inquiry exist between these orthogonal elements? What are the methodological implications and applications of queer theory in our research practices? Questions like these are impossible to answer unless we embrace an interdisciplinary imagination. We are pleased to be your curatorial guides as you adventure through the largely uncharted territory of queer methods. Page after page, our contributors shine a light on innovative ways of working and producing new knowledge as they collectively articulate the promises and pleasures of an emerging field.

Worldmaking and Livability

Queer methods are possible, despite the "apparent incommensurability" of the phrase (Brim and Ghaziani 2016, 16). Yes, the words do conjure "a classic odd couple, uptight *methods* attempting to impose order on the slovenly *queer*" (Love 2016, 346). But opposites attract—and often productively so. In the social sciences, the biggest obstacle for developing queer methods has been what political scientists Kevin Clarke and David Primo (2012) call "physics envy." To establish their legitimacy, sociologists, economists, and political scientists in particular mimic the "real" or "natural" sciences by using words like "theory," "experiments," and "laws." Science has a method, researchers in these areas insist, and to be scientific, we must adopt it. The scientific method proceeds from a theory from which researchers deduce one or more hypotheses that they can test against systematically collected data. This conventional approach to conducting research is called hypothetico-deductivism. "If your discipline does not operate by this method, then in the minds of many it's not scientific," Clarke and Primo explain in their thoughtful essay for the *New York Times*. Hypothetico-deductivism is a flawed rendering of how research actually occurs, however, since it ignores "everything messy and chaotic about scientific inquiry"—precisely the place where queerness thrives. The hegemony of this model has stymied social scientific efforts to build queer methods—until recently. A new generation of scholars sees generative possibilities where others felt blocked. Jane Ward (2016), a professor of gender and sexuality studies, writes words we previewed earlier and with which we very much agree: "To pair the terms 'queer' and 'methodology'—the former defined by its celebrated failure to adhere to stable classificatory systems or be contained by disciplinary boundaries, and the latter defined by orderly, discipline-specific, and easily reproducible techniques—produces something of an exciting contradiction, a productive oxymoron" (71–72).

Scholars in the humanities have encountered their own challenges by casting queer theory in the dual roles of method and method's foil. The late literary theorist Eve Sedgwick's "nonce taxonomy" created an early flashpoint for this conflation. Rather than embrace reproducibility as an emblem of methodological rigor, Sedgwick champions "the making and unmaking and remaking and redissolution of hundreds of old and new categorical meanings concerning all the kinds it may take to make up a world" (1990, 23). Humanities scholars have gravitated toward terms like "critical approaches" and "critical frameworks" to name their work. Such phrases imply that we create a lens through which to view our objects of analysis, and these in turn influence and direct how we see them.

Worldmaking matters, but a critical position doesn't always lend itself to a discussion of methodological specificity. Recent advances in queer, trans, non-Western, and queer of color scholarship respond to this elision of methods in our worldmaking efforts by featuring the resistant, mobile, and intimate practices by which knowledge is constructed. The cultural critic Phillip Brian Harper (2005, 108) identifies one way to re-engage with methods in the humanities at the millennial turn by promoting what he calls "speculative rumination," an approach that counts as evidence the "guesswork and conjecture" that accrues to the experience of eroticized blackness in the United States. Certainty and guesswork, knowability and conjecture mix quite easily in this framework. Consider as well the renewed discussions of reading that have emerged from scholars like the English professor Peter Coviello (2013), who advocates "ground-level explication" and "long exposure" to texts. These, he says, are "better served by a practice invested in detail, particularity, and unsystematizable variousness—all the specificities that literature proffers" (2013, 18). Citing the "descriptive turn" away from the literary, Heather Love (2013, 404), who generously writes an additional introduction to our volume, promotes "thin description," a practice that describes "patterns of behavior and visible activity but that do[es] not traffic in speculation about interiority, meaning, or depth." Her efforts at reworking research practices in the humanities show that any analysis of "layers of meaning" (407) is incomplete without also including "visible behavior[s]" and "physical act[s]" (406). Love rejects the assertion that empiricism is confined to the social sciences. Such a fallacy has "blocked humanities scholars from using a range of potentially useful tools" (419), including observations and descriptions, both of which are "an important part of reading" (427). Love offers an insight that a number of scholars in the social sciences and humanities have mutually proposed yet seldom said: what appears as an expression of pure theory also implies a methodological praxis.

With repercussions beyond the academy, and certainly beyond just one discipline, queer methods offer options for "making space for what is" (Love et al. 2012, 144). They "bring to the surface social worlds only dimly articulated hitherto—with, of course, the suggestion that there are more, many more, even more deeply hidden" (Plummer 2005, 368). To see them, we must resist the hypothetico-deductive urge to "fix objects in place" and instead "ask what we think we know and how we think we know it" (Morgensen 2015, 311). We thus envision a dual mandate for queer methods: *to outline the conditions of queer worldmaking* and *to clarify, but not overdetermine, the conditions that "make life livable,"* to borrow a lovely phrase from an interview with the gender theorist Judith Butler (Ahmed 2016b, 490).

The proposals and practices that we share with you in this volume are coherent and provisional, precise and protean, expansive and self-reflexive, timely and anticipatory, disciplinary and boundary-spanning. Unlike the first published volume on queer methods, which focused on the social sciences (Browne and Nash 2010b), or the next iteration that zoomed in on just one discipline (Compton, Meadow, and Schilt 2018), we offer an inclusive call to action that comes from all corners of the academy. We have brought together thinkers who have very different viewpoints on what methods mean and why they matter. In fact, we deliberately sweep from *verstehen*, pure interpretivism, reading, and ephemera to formal measurement, modeling, sampling, scaling, and statistics. This range represents the interface of scientific and humanistic modes of producing new knowledge, the place where qualitative, meaning-oriented approaches mix and mingle with formal, behavioral, and quantitative styles of knowing the world. No one else has attempted to do what we've done in this volume.

We asked our contributors to grapple with tough questions. If interdisciplinarity, multidisciplinarity, and antidisciplinarity are the defining features of queer theory, then what challenges emerge as especially urgent within a program of queer methods? What inferential and interpretive possibilities are afforded to us when we think about this as a program of study unto its own? What we present to you is a picture of queer methods as an emergent enterprise—hardly the last word. We want to stir and provoke you, not force a premature consensus and closure. Here you will find ways of holding multiple, opposed ideas in your mind while still retaining the ability to imagine queer methods as a new scholarly enterprise.

In the rest of this chapter, we offer four provocations to arouse your imagination: identifying new types of data; modifying existing protocols to better resonate with queer theoretical frameworks; challenging methodological norms of coherence, generalizability, and reliability; and eliciting the pedagogical implications of queer methods. These are not prescriptive, exhaustive, or mutually exclusive. Rather, we wish to identify some of the most exciting and useful possibilities of queer worldmaking and the conditions that make life livable.

The First Provocation: Queer Methods

Although they write from different backgrounds and different countries, English and comparative literature professor Jack Halberstam (1998) in the United States and emeritus sociology professor Ken Plummer (2005) from the United Kingdom both see in queer theory "a refusal of all orthodox methods—a certain disloyalty to conventional disciplinary methods" (Plummer 2005, 366). Implied in their argument is the possibility of something new, rather than a reworking of what we already have available to us in our existing portfolios. But how can we diversify our approaches beyond an "overwhelming" interest in "an analysis of texts—films, literature, television, opera, musicals" (ibid.)? How do we respond today to the earlier proposition that "almost everything that would be called queer theory is about ways in which texts—either literature or mass culture of language—shape sexuality" (Warner 1992, 19)? We know that sexuality is epistemologically distinct (Sedgwick 1990)—not to mention "complex, diffuse, and messy"—and existing methods tend to "make a mess of it" (Law 2004, 2). What are we to do?

Sociologists John Mohr and Amin Ghaziani (2014, 231–36) offer an example from the history of science that can help us. Scholars who developed a theory of measurement in the mid-century argued that its formal applications were possible only if the "axiom of additivity" (Stevens 1959, 21), or the ability to add or subtract numerical quantities, corresponded with how we manipulated objects. In other words, the applications of measurement theory required "quantitative estimates of sensory events" (Stevens 1975, 38). This standard was too stringent, however. The psychologist S. S. Stevens, who we know today as the founder of scales (nominal, ordinal, interval, and ratio), complained, "Only a few properties, such as length, weight, and electric resistance are measurable in this fundamental way" (1959, 21). The belief that true measurement was possible only when an experimenter could perform a physical or empirical addition—or locate a phenomenon in discrete categories and then count those categories—was "blocking progress in psychophysics," Stevens lamented. How do we measure subjective states like brightness or loudness, which escape "the requirement of empirical addition" (Stevens 1979, 50)? Stevens saw a need "to measure the previously unmeasured" since "procedures such as the counting and adding of beans do not suffice for the measurement of such concepts as the social status accorded a person" (1979, 46).

Like the scholars in our volume today, Stevens then sought to extend an existing theory into new domains. To clear a path forward, he resisted "old-style assumptions" about the singular application of measurement theory to "problems of counting" (Stevens 1959, 19). New developments were possible only under new conditions of the imagination: "the assignment of numerals to objects or events according to a rule—any rule" (ibid.), he supposed, not just the assignment of numerals by addition or subtraction alone. Provided that "a consistent rule is followed, some form of measurement is achieved" (ibid.). Procedural innovations are hard to devise because the approaches we adopt in our practice of a theory appear "ontologically real" (ibid.). Stevens explained how he maneuvered his way through the quagmire: "The best way out seemed to be to approach the problem from another point of view" (ibid., 23). To adopt the ever-elusive "another point of view" requires us to engage in an "ongoing and regular confrontation with the methodological assumptions of the field" (Mohr and Ghaziani 2014, 233). Only then can we reinvent our protocols and procedures. This process consists of conflict, differentiation, and split, and it produces a "fractal distinction" (Abbott 2001) at the end, or a new idea that upends entrenched conventions.

The development of queer and measurement theories have a surprising amount in common. Concepts within each framework structure how we experience reality and how we study it. The imagery of fractals is apt for queer conversations, as these structures can account for irregularly shaped objects and spatial nonuniformity in a way that Euclidean geometry cannot process.[2] The challenge for us is how to move from a place of conceptual innovation and experiential resonance to empirical expression and methodological diversification—the fractal distinction of queer methods. To do this, we replicate Stevens's logic below. We first present the hallmarks of queer theory that Arlene Stein and Ken Plummer (1994, 181–83) proposed—but we use them "to approach the problem from another point of view," that is, to outline the possibilities of distinctively queer methods.

1. REJECT UNCHANGING CATEGORIES. Terms like "heterosexual" and "homosexual" are not ahistorical (it is a fallacy to assert that sexuality is a biological expression exempt from historical forces) or transhistorical (it is equally misguided to believe that sexual meanings are stable across time). Sexuality has a history (Halperin 2002). One early example of this constructionist argument comes from the British sociologist and activist Mary McIntosh (1968), who argued that homosexuality is a "social role" that varies across societies, not an essential "condition" that has existed in all places at all times. The French philosopher Michel Foucault provides another influential redirection when he declared that "the homosexual as a species" was born around 1870 (1978, 43). In this tradition, we also find the American historian Jonathan Ned Katz, who notes that German sodomy-law reformer Karl Maria Kertbeny coined the terms *heterosexuality* and *homosexuality* in 1868. Unlike other scholars who focused on *homo*sexual history, Katz dives into the "sex cultures" (Ghaziani 2017) of *hetero*sexuality and challenges an idea that many people accept, even now, without second thought: heterosexuality is not as "old as procreation, ancient as the lust of Eve and Adam." Although many people mistake heterosexuality as "unchanging, universal, essential: ahistorical" (Katz 1990, 7), Katz proposed an alternative thesis: heterosexuality is a recent invention, located in specific moments in time, and it has organized

arrangements between men and women in ways that are culturally constructed. From this corpus of research flows four queer methodological principles: (a) embrace a logic of historical variation and social construction; (b) analyze how the meanings of sexuality change over time, especially their discursive character; (c) identify triggers of change (e.g., institutional agents such as psychiatrists and legal definitions); and (d) specify the contexts in which these definitions operate.

2. REJECT IMPERMEABLE CATEGORIES. A study by neuroscientist Simon LeVay showed that homosexuality may have a biological antecedent based on a controversial finding that gay men and straight women have a similarly sized hypothalamus. To this, psychologist John Money retorts, "Of course it [sexual orientation] is in the brain. The real question is, when did it get there? Was it prenatal, neonatal, during childhood, puberty? That we do not know."[3] Searching for the origins of sexual orientation— asking what "makes one" a lesbian or if she was "born that way," for example—has been afforded an outsized and obsessive role in sexuality studies. Underlying the raging nature/nurture debates are assumptions about identity and difference, continuity and change. According to history professor David Halperin, sexuality scholars need a "strategy for accommodating the aspects of sexual life that seem to persist through time as well as the dramatic differences between historically documented forms of sexual experience" (2000, 88). Such a procedure begins with the "methodological suspension of modern categories" (90) so that we can locate them at different points in time (to Kertbeny, for example, who coined homosexuality and heterosexuality). Halperin calls this a "genealogical analysis" (ibid.), and queer researchers can use it to investigate the cultural contradictions of categories (does heterosexuality require the absolute negation of homosexual encounters?) and their allegedly unified meaning (is heterosexuality as timeless as the lust of Eve and Adam?). We can use ongoing arguments about sexuality as an analytic device to trace historical changes in its meanings, which leave behind "genetic traces, as it were" (ibid.). If we do this, Halperin is confident that we'll see sexuality as an "eloquent" expression of "the historical accumulation of discontinuous no-

tions sheltered within [a] specious unity" (ibid.)—sexuality as a sedimentary formation that balances diverse elements in a "thinly coherent" fashion (Ghaziani and Baldassarri 2011).

3. REJECT DUALISMS. Power operates through the imposition of conceptual binaries such as gay *or* straight, male *or* female, masculine *or* feminine. According to cognitive sociologist Eviatar Zerubavel (1996), this process of "lumping and splitting" the world is inconsistent with an "essentially continuous" reality. As an example, Halperin (1993) shows that antiquity was populated by "molles" (soft or unmasculine men who depart from cultural norms of manliness by embracing femininity) and "tribades" (masculine women who are eager to have sex with other women). When historian George Chauncey (1994) used the archives to visit early twentieth-century New York City, he uncovered a world filled with "trade," "husbands," "wolves," "fairies," "third-sexers," and "punks." Sociologist Peter Hennen (2008) notes that the "wedding date" of effeminacy and homosexuality was written into the popular imagination in the eighteenth century, while Halberstam (1998) asserts that masculinity exists apart from the male body and its effects. By extending the study of gender and sexuality across geographical and temporal domains, we can act on the queer impulse to distinguish Western and non-Western epistemologies as well (Babayan and Najmabadi 2008). All these studies show that queer worldmaking and livability require us to embrace multiplicity and pluralism, not binaries and dualisms. Because existing categories imperfectly map onto many of our lived experiences, queer methods reject a close-fit assumption across categories, identities, attraction, arousal, and sexual behavior. Multiple categories, new categories, and continua are among a number of innovative possibilities that emerge from queer methods.

4. REJECT INTEREST GROUP POLITICS. According to the final hallmark, lobbying and other forms of electoral, single-issue identity politics are not the most effective ways to create change. Queer theorists initially examined street-level forms of provocation, parody, and coalitional politics that had cultural revisionism, or what we define as normal and natural, as their goal (Berlant and Freeman 1993). Scholars have continued to expose the risks

of identity politics by tracing how power is unevenly distributed through, not just against, categories of minority genders and sexualities. These efforts include critiques of homonormativity (Duggan 2003), homonationalism (Puar 2007), and legal inclusion (Spade 2011). British-Australian feminist writer and independent scholar Sara Ahmed's call for an "affinity of hammers" (2016a) similarly rejects identity in favor of a model of trans/feminist politicality that draws on the lived experiences of different people who share the feeling of being hammered by oppressive systems (see Cohen 2001 for another example). Ahmed's work suggests that we can use how identity *feels* as a way to study the isolating perils of identity politics. In a recent blog post, political scientist Paisley Currah proposes another approach that uses a model of gender asymmetry rather than gender neutrality or even plurality that is typically associated with newer transgender analysis. He writes, "Any conceptual framework, from the sex/gender binary to the transgender-cisgender dichotomy, risks ossification, risks turning what had been a provisional and generative idea into a methodological imperative that over time obscures more than it reveals. But I do think that, in particular moments and circumstances, we need a transgender feminist approach that is not gender-neutral— that dares to identify *asymmetry* when it sees it" (2016). A turn to queer methods can navigate such complex returns—to politics, identities, isolation, asymmetries, worldmaking, and livability.

Existing research methods only partially capture the "mess of social worlds" (Browne and Nash 2010a, 13). That's because "parts of our world are caught in our ethnographies, our histories, and our statistics. But other parts are not" (Law 2004, 2). As we outlined in our first provocation, queer theory sees a world that is "vague, diffuse or unspecific, slippery, emotional, ephemeral, elusive, or indistinct, changes like a kaleidoscope, or doesn't really have much of a pattern at all" (ibid.). The methodological directive that follows from a mandate to *embrace the mess* is to devise new modes of inquiry and analysis. British sociology professor John Law elaborates, "If we want to think about the messes of reality at all then we're going to have to teach ourselves to think, to practice, to relate, and to know in new ways. We will need to teach ourselves to know some of the realities of the world using methods unusual to or unknown" to us (2004, 2). Following a trail of breadcrumbs left behind by queer theory, we have shown that queer methods can guide our data collection techniques around the "playful possibilities of unstable and indeterminate subjectivities and for transgressive practices that challenge binaries" (Browne and Nash 2010a, 5). Queer methods can access hidden histories by negation (Muñoz 1996), by emphasizing instability and the disruptive (Krahulik 2006), and by using deconstructive practices.

The Second Provocation: Queering Methods

"Queer methods" is a noun. It connotes a new set of protocols and procedures. "Queering methods" functions as a verb, and it inspires a different question: How can we use queer insights to adjust established protocols in the humanities and social sciences? Our second provocation is a revisionist effort that begins by identifying the limitations of extant models, metrics, or empirical approaches and then innovates based on the signature strengths of queer studies. Let's assume that our methodological toolkits are robust in general but ill-suited for responding to the distinctiveness of sexuality.

Plummer (2005, 366–67) coins the term "subversive ethnographies" to describe "relatively straightforward ethnographies of specific sexual worlds that challenge [heteronormative] assumptions." Laud Humphreys's (1970) study of tearoom trade is a classic example in the social sciences, and Jason Orne's (2017) research on "sexy communities" in Chicago gay bars provides a contemporary illustration from sociology that foregrounds the role of sex in queer communities. Gender studies scholar Marlon Bailey's (2013) first-person performance ethnography of ballroom culture in Detroit offers an organic method for examining queer cultural formations that resist normative genders, sex, and kinship.

Plummer also raises the notion of "scavenger methods" (2005, 367), and cites Halberstam's (1998) work as an example. He shows how humanists can "raid" literary textual methods, film theory, field research, historical surveys, archival records, and taxonomies to produce unique arguments about "female masculinity." More recently, Peter Hennen

(2008) chronicles how three groups of gay men (faeries, bears, and leathermen) respond to the historical association of effeminacy with male homosexuality. Inspired by Halberstam and echoing Plummer, Hennen calls his approach a "scavenger method" as well because he uses existing techniques to "produce information on subjects who have been deliberately or accidentally excluded from traditional studies of human behavior." He mixes "methods that are often cast as being at odds with each other," such as participant and nonparticipant observation, interviews, historical data, and archival data, and "refuses the academic compulsion toward disciplinary coherence" (Halberstam 1998, 13, qtd. in Hennen 2008, 23).

Studies like these assume that "queerness is often transmitted covertly" (Muñoz 1996, 6). The Cuban American academic José Esteban Muñoz explains the consequences of this assumption for research practice: "Leaving too much of a trace has often meant that the queer subject has left herself open for attack." This alters the nature of evidence. "Instead of being clearly available as visible evidence, queerness has instead existed as innuendo, gossip, fleeting moments, and performances that are meant to be interacted with by those within its epistemological sphere—while evaporating at the touch of those who would eliminate queer possibility" (ibid.). The covertness of queerness compels Muñoz to propose "ephemera as evidence," as he titles his essay. Ephemera include all those things that remain after a performance, a "residue" (11) that provides "evidence of what has transpired" (10). The ephemeral provides a type of proof that traditional methods would miss, especially "structures of feeling" (10) that drive queer "worldmaking capabilities" (11).

Methods are *queered* when we use the tenets of queer theory to tweak or explode what is possible with our existing procedures. The most common pursuits include making strange the otherwise commonplace or familiar; interrogating alternate possibilities for worldmaking and livability; negotiating differences; resisting categorization or adopting an anticategorical stance altogether; disrupting ideals of stability, rationality, objectivity, and coherence; rethinking the meaning of empiricism and our assumptions about data; critiquing heteronormative practices and recentering the lens on queer lives; and "deconstructing rather than reifying social constructs" (McDonald 2017, 134–35) like gender and

sexuality, as we would expect, but also disability (McRuer 2006), failure (Halberstam 2011), intelligibility (Martinez 2013), loss (Love 2007),
migration (Manalansan 2003), racism (Holland 2012), shame (Halperin
and Traub 2009), and time (Halberstam 2005). Unlike the first provocation, the goal in this second one is not to establish a "discrete or stable
queer methods," communications scholar James McDonald hastens to
add, since "queering is an ongoing process" that requires "an attitude of
unceasing disruptiveness" (2017, 8). The ambition, at least for sociologists like Kristen Schilt, Tey Meadow, and D'Lane Compton (2018), is "to
find ways to gather empirical data about the experiences of people who
are politically and socially marginalized without reproducing such marginalization through practices of research and theorizing that conflate
objectification with 'good science.'"

The Third Provocation: Queering Methodology

Our discussion thus far has focused on methods. The word denotes
"what is 'done,' that is, techniques of collecting data (interviews, ques-
tionnaires, focus groups, photographs, videos, observation, *inter alia*)"
(Browne and Nash 2010a, 10). Having considered some possibilities for
a distinct queer methods as well as queering established methods, we
turn now to concerns of *methodology*, which entail "sets of rules and
procedures that guide the design of research to investigate phenomenon
or situations; part of which is a decision about what methods will be
used and why" (ibid.). To speak of methodology means to articulate the
logic that links our theoretical frameworks with the choices we make
about how to study the expressions of those theories in texts, ephemera,
performances, conversations, discourses, memories, corporeality, interactions, and behaviors. How can queering our rules, procedures, and
practices illuminate the epistemologies and ontologies that we deploy
when we try to understand gender and sexuality? Three themes strike
us as especially urgent: knowability and queer reflexivity, zombie categories, and quantification of the subject.

By connecting queer theory with protocols for data collection and
analysis, both humanists and social scientists challenge basic precepts of
the research process, including the "knowability of the social" (Browne
and Nash 2010a, 13). Some scholars go further and declare that the social

is dead. They favor alternatives like "assemblages" (Puar 2007) that reject "the idea of the social as coherent" or else shift focus to "objects, animals, environments, [and] materials" (Browne and Nash 2010a, 13). Rather than tumbling into methodological nihilism, this exercise can free how researchers think about concepts like "methodology" and "empirical research" (McDonald 2017, 134) along with the "knowledge-power relations" (Di Feliciantonio, Gadelha, and DasGupta 2017, 405) between us and what or whom we study. Questions of knowledge-power frequently implicate related concerns of whether we should adopt a stance of "emotional neutrality" (Burkhart 1996, 34). Doing so is often costly for LGBTQ field researchers. Hennen responds to the "positive science emphasis on distance and objectivity" by advocating a "sensitivity to borders" (2008, 26). He says that we should "identify freely" with our study participants, since doing so creates "an enormous amount of good will" (27) and builds rapport in interviews. Deconstructing accepted understandings about the practice of research, as Hennen does, requires that we adopt a skeptical stance toward "traditional claims to objectivity" (McDonald 2017, 135). Those who travel down this road encourage us to be reflexive; hence, "queer reflexivity," which McDonald defines as "a form of reflexivity that entails reflecting on the performativity and closeting of identities over the course of the research process, with particular attention to the ways in which heteronormativity is enacted and resisted in the field" (2017, 135).

Queering methodologies also draws attention to what the German sociologist Ulrich Beck (2003) calls "zombie categories." These are categories that "once had life and meaning but for many now mean very little" (Plummer 2005, 358). So why do we keep using them? Plummer muses, "We probably go on using them because at present we have no better words to put in their place. Yet dead they are." As a testament to the growing chasm between undifferentiated categories like "gay" and the complexities of worldmaking and livability, we only have to consider the proliferation of terms like queer, of course, but also bisexual, same-gender loving, and MSM (men who have sex with men). In avoiding a conventional identity-based category, the goal of epidemiologists who coined MSM was to find a way of counting "non-gay-identified MSM" without automatically assuming that they are closeted gay men (Carrillo and Hoffman 2016). The category "unscrambles sexual behavior from sexual identity" (Ghaziani 2017, 151) and prevents researchers from conflating these two dimensions of sexuality. MSM didn't stick beyond certain academic and medical circles; other terms like "heteroflexible," "mostly straight," and "bicurious" have become more popular. As one of us argues elsewhere, "These neologisms expand the definition of heterosexual . . . by incorporating same-sex desires and practices into the sex cultures of straights" (Ghaziani 2017, 151). For our purposes here, the terms also stress the need to address zombie categories by creating newer ones that better resonate with the diverse aspects of queer lives. Cultural and linguistic anthropologist David Valentine's (2007) ethnography of "transgender" as a category is a creative example of this tradition and its sensitivity to language.

Perhaps the biggest area of contention between humanist and social scientific investments in queer theory pertains to counting. Sociologists of sexualities often feel cornered in this conversation. On the one hand, they struggle with the acutely normative pressures induced by hypothetico-deductivism. We constantly confront "positivist gatekeepers who evaluate the significance of research in terms of p-values and generalists who prioritize broad 'so what' claims" (Schilt, Meadow, and Compton 2018) that are best handled by flaunting large sample sizes. On the flip side, social scientists are also burdened by anxieties that they are "'not yet queer enough' in the eyes of our humanistic colleagues" (ibid.). Humanists are clearer on the matter of quantifying the subject. Muñoz asserts that "the inability to count as proper proof" is a "profoundly queer" position (1996, 6). As an alternative to quantification, queer theorists like him propose a "worldmaking project" that promotes "queerness as a possibility" over counting bodies (or "same-sex partner households," to invoke a zombie category that demographers use; see Spring 2013). He emphasizes "a sense of self-knowing, a mode of sociality and relationality" (6) over quantification. Allergic reactions to counting among humanists don't surprise social scientists who are versed in queer theory. They recognize that it may be "illogical to count subjects once one has argued that a countable subject does not exist" (Schilt, Meadow, and Compton 2018). Until recently, this created an impasse because of binary thinking about methodology: you either count or you don't. In our volume, we will showcase the surprising compatibilities between quantification and queerness.

The Final Provocation: Queer Pedagogy

A book about interdisciplinary approaches to queer methods must acknowledge our intellectual forebearers, especially the black lesbian feminist collective who co-edited the anthology *All the Women Are White, All the Blacks Are Men, But Some of Us Are Brave: Black Women's Studies* (Hull, Bell-Scott, and Smith 2015). Of that founding document's many contributions, its innovations in pedagogy continue to resonate and inspire, and we organize our final provocation around this theme. What are the implications of a queer methods collection for classrooms and for relations of teaching and learning?

As editors, we believe that an inclusive set of essays from across academic fields will make for a better text, but we became more committed to exploring the relationship between queer methods and pedagogies when we realized that our contributors have teaching experiences across a broad spectrum of institutions in higher education. When conversations about queer methods are collected as we have done here, cross-class perspectives necessarily emerge. This makes our effort an expansive pedagogical project, potentially indicating a new way to figure the field of queer studies in relation to socioeconomic class and institutional status.

Our authors teach at commuter schools, elite private liberal arts colleges, sprawling public urban university systems, and Research 1 flagship campuses. Some are graduate students who have recently returned to the academy; others hold endowed chairs at prestigious sites of knowledge production; still others are artists. They write from the United Kingdom and Canada, and in the United States they are based at institutions that are situated in the South, the Northeast, the Midwest, and the West. The scholars in this volume teach students who are earning their associate, bachelor's, master's, and doctoral degrees. They work in places that span from prisons to the Ivy League and in certificate programs, night schools, graduate programs, and community centers. They teach students who are homeless, from the working poor, middle class, upper class, and the one percent. They teach and train people of color, Dreamers, and in our contributor Zandria Robinson's words, "first-gen-of-all-races scrappers" (2015), as well as students who receive the special accommodation of legacy admission at highly selective schools. As they write *about* and crucially *with* people at all levels of socioeconomic status, they speak as scholars who come *from* disparate socioeconomic statuses.

It makes sense that the scholars who are thinking today about queer methods are also engaged in debates about the class-inflected inequalities that structure queer worldmaking and the conditions that make our lives livable. It shouldn't be a surprise that the question of how to teach queer methods frequently forms in tandem with inquiries about institutional access and status. Yet queerness and class have historically been difficult vectors to hold in tension, despite calls to do so by thinkers such as Elizabeth Lapovsky Kennedy and Madeline D. Davis (1993) and Allan Bérubé (2011). This has been particularly true in the context of the dominant narrative of class mobility in higher education. Class has always been a moving target for queer studies, and for all its gorgeous and generative introspection, queer studies has not fully engaged with its own class-based institutional life. The essays that we have gathered here coalesce around the potential of queer methods to intervene in these concerns and to democratize intellectual work in the academy and beyond, a project made urgent by the fact that institutions of higher education in the United States have over the past forty years become symbols of the expansion of opportunity *and* the explosion of class stratification. What should we make of the coincidence that the rise and relative success of queer studies has been contemporaneous with the academy's massive redistribution of resources and people according to class and socioeconomic status? The collection that you hold in your hands offers leverage in the struggle not simply to reverse this course but also to creatively and concretely redirect it.

The less recognizable but perhaps more exciting pedagogical possibilities that this volume puts into play extend across disciplines, across institutions, and across class backgrounds. The need for such structural crossings-over among scholar-teachers working at different types of colleges and universities is imperative, English professor and higher education innovator Cathy Davidson (2017) argues. Now more than ever, higher education reflects and reproduces shocking degrees of class stratification. Socioeconomic inequality has become the defining feature of higher education as institutions ruthlessly sort students by class background (with the attendant racial implications of that class sorting as well). From this perspective, the academy couldn't be more in lock-step with the "real world" against which it is so frequently pitted. What does queer studies have to say about class dynamics in the academy? How do we contribute to the processes of stratification that divides the field of queer studies from itself along the lines of class and institutional status? How might queer collaborations across peer and nonpeer institutions offer a model for the redistribution of intellectual and material resources? And how might a fresh volume on queer methods, rather than another on queer theory, galvanize the kinds of interclass, cross-institutional queer formations that don't rely on the aspirational model of progress that our administrators adore? Eve Sedgwick once said, "You can write your way out of anywhere." But what if "out" means not just up but also down, sideways, and around? What if "anywhere" mapped not just the institutional locations we want to leave but the universe of other destinations toward which we wish to direct ourselves? Where can queer methods take us?

If pedagogy is a relation of teaching and learning, we propose that *queer pedagogies* are central to interdisciplinary articulations of queer studies and the integration of queer-class worksites across the academy. In other words, we see queer methods as capable of recoding operations of institutional differentiation (rank, cost, and reputation) as operations of institutional integration by envisioning class as a queer connective tissue rather than a divisive barrier in higher education. Queer pedagogies facilitate queer-class linkages because students can see how scholars do queer studies differently when they're faced with different institutional resources, student demographics, regional locations, and career goals. A program of queer methods can help us recognize and communicate across those differences. Seeing queer methods invented and adapted in relation to institutional status—which itself closely relates with socioeconomic class in today's educational landscape—can teach our students about their own intellectual investments, including what they prioritize in research and how they connect research to their own often-unarticulated class locations. Paula Krebs, the dean of the College of Humanities and Social Sciences at Bridgewater State University, suggests in the *Chronicle of Higher Education* (2016) that pedagogical programs such as the one we are promoting here can help graduate students prepare for academic careers in and beyond the R1 universities for which they are almost exclusively trained. Queer pedagogies can orient us, even in the midst of the powerfully disorienting forces of the neoliberal academic marketplace, by allowing us to think critically and expansively about what kind of teacher-scholars we want to be—with whom, for whom, and where.

Perhaps the best reason for depressurizing queer theory at this moment is because of its longstanding association with elite sites of knowledge production and institutional privilege. While queer theory has "traveled," to borrow from Katie King's (1995) framing of feminist theory—and while it has even traveled methodologically—we believe that a focus on methods can offer a more public form for the transportation of queer ideas at a time when privatization, class and racial exclusions, and institutional status overdetermine how the academy works and, at times, how queer studies works within the academy. This is not a critique of high theory but rather of the structural embeddedness of queer studies in a class-stratified university system. The essays gathered here suggest, often individually but collectively for certain, that queer methods can act as a "relay" (Henderson 2013) across queer-class divides in higher education. We understand this work not as primarily compensatory (à la shiny diversity initiatives) but integral, not assured but possible. Queer methods can offer critical and pedagogical *ways*.

A Renaissance in the Making

Queer studies is in the midst of a renaissance. The incitement to explore queer methods and methodologies that we present in this volume offers an opportunity to reevaluate a number of practical, philosophical, and pedagogical issues about the craft of our disciplines, along with academia's attachments to class, privilege, and status. As you travel through these pages, you will notice that some problems persist and endure, plaguing the scholars here just as they did those who came before us. But there are also issues on which we have made much progress, including our capacity to think in nuanced ways about sexuality and its complementarities with methods.

We have organized our volume with a goal of dramatizing the possibilities of, and for, queer methods. That impulse is reflected in the title of our book, which positions the boundless and protean queer imagination alongside more disciplinary and deliberate methods. The book's structure includes innovations that playfully upend genre conventions, such as offering two introductory chapters (ours and another written by Heather Love) that speak to the novice and the expert. And just as the introductory "Methods/Mess" section emphasizes multiple entry points into the volume, each of the four parts that follow evoke plenitude and possibilities in doing queer research. We actively resist intellectual silos; none of our sections is populated solely by essays in the humanities or social sciences. We wish instead to enable unexpected combinations, configurations, and conversations. We debated whether to use a "slash" or "and" in our section headings. We settled on the slash, as you can see, because it declares that a relationship exists without confining its nature, leaving you the reader with a sense of unease that we believe is generative as you embark upon using these ideas in your own work and life. Part I: "Subjecting/Objecting" urges you to maintain an inventive tension between performativity and positivism, to be both intimately present and precise. After that, in "Narrating/Measuring," our contributors show that while quantification might seem incompatible with interpretive methods, the two are not always easy to disentangle, let alone distinguish. The third part, "Listening/Creating," rejects the passive/active duality as our contributors incorporate the voices of others into their visions for the shared queer work ahead of us all. The final section, "Historicizing/Resisting," will propel you beyond this volume with a set of essays that reflect the urgency of imagining new methods for queer intellectual and pedagogical engagements.

Before our ink dries, we offer a call to action to ensure that the fountain ever flows: drawing on your own desires, disciplinary protocols, assumptions, horizon of expectations, and hopes, identify the patterns that leap out from the essays in this collection and use them to build a productive, plentiful, powerful, and pleasurable queer worldmaking and livability project of your own. Onward—bravely turn the page.

NOTES

1 *Queer Method.* 2013. Blog. www.queermethod.tumblr.com/.

2 "Tourists in an Unknown Town: Remapping the Social Sciences," *University of Chicago Magazine* 93 (2) (December 2000). https://magazine.uchicago.edu/.

3 Quoted in "Homosexuality: Born or Bred?" *Newsweek*, February 24, 1992, 46, 48.

WORKS CITED

Abbott, Andrew. 2001. *Chaos of Disciplines*. Chicago: University of Chicago Press.

Ahmed, Sara. 2016a. "An Affinity of Hammers." *Transgender Studies Quarterly* 3 (1–2): 22–34.

Ahmed, Sara. 2016b. "Interview with Judith Butler." *Sexualities* 19 (4): 482–92.

Babayan, Kathryn, and Afsaneh Najmabadi, eds. 2008. *Islamicate Sexualities: Translations across Temporal Geographies of Desire*. Cambridge, MA: Harvard University Press.

Bailey, Marlon. 2013. *Butch Queens up in Pumps: Gender, Performance, and Ballroom Culture in Detroit*. Ann Arbor: University of Michigan Press.

Beck, Ulrich. 2003. *Individualization*. London: Sage.

Berlant, Lauren, and Elizabeth Freeman. 1993. "Queer Nationality." In *Fear of a Queer Planet*, edited by Michael Warner, 193–229. Minneapolis: University of Minnesota Press.

Bérubé, Allan. 2011. *My Desire for History: Essays in Gay, Community, and Labor History*. Chapel Hill: University of North Carolina Press.

Brim, Matt, and Amin Ghaziani. 2016. "Introduction: Queer Methods." *WSQ: Women's Studies Quarterly* 44 (3–4): 14–27.

Browne, Kath, and Catherine J. Nash. 2010a. "Queer Methods and Methodologies: An Introduction." In *Queer Methods and Methodologies: Intersecting Queer Theories and Social Science Research*, edited by Kath Browne and Catherine J. Nash, 1–23. Farnham, UK: Ashgate.

Browne, Kath, and Catherine J. Nash, eds. 2010b. *Queer Methods and Methodologies*. Farnham, UK: Ashgate.

Burkhart, Geoffrey. 1996. "Not Given to Personal Disclosure." In *Out in the Field: Reflections of Lesbian and Gay Anthropologists*, edited by Ellen Lewin and William L. Leap, 31–48. Urbana: University of Illinois Press.

Carrillo, Héctor, and Amanda Hoffman. 2016. "From MSM to Heteroflexibilities: Non-Exclusive Straight Male Identities and Their Implications for HIV Prevention and Health Promotion." *Global Public Health* 11 (7–8): 923–36.

Chauncey, George. 1994. *Gay New York: Gender, Urban Culture, and the Making of the Gay Male World, 1890–1940*. New York: Basic Books.

Clarke, Kevin A., and David M. Primo. 2012. "Overcoming 'Physics Envy.'" *New York Times*, March 30.

Cohen, Cathy J. 2001. "Punks, Bulldaggers, and Welfare Queens: The Radical Potential of Queer Politics?" In *Sexual Identities, Queer Politics*, edited by Mark Blasius, 200–228. Princeton, NJ: Princeton University Press.

Compton, D'Lane, Tey Meadow, and Kristen Schilt, eds. 2018. *Other, Please Specify: Queer Methods in Sociology*. Berkeley: University of California Press.

Coviello, Peter. 2013. *Tomorrow's Parties: Sex and the Untimely in Nineteenth-Century America*. New York: NYU Press.

Currah, Paisley. 2016. "Feminism, Gender Pluralism, and Gender Neutrality: Maybe It's Time to Bring Back the Binary." *Paisley Currah*. Blog. https://paisleycurrah.com/tag/legislation/.

Davidson, Cathy N. 2017. *The New Education*. New York: Basic Books.

Di Feliciantonio, Cesare, Kaciano B. Gadelha, and Debanuj DasGupta. 2017. "Queer(y) ing Methodologies: Doing Fieldwork and Becoming Queer." *Gender, Place, and Culture* 24 (3): 403–12.

Duggan, Lisa. 2003. *The Twilight of Equality? Neoliberalism, Cultural Politics, and the Attack on Democracy*. Boston: Beacon Press.

Foucault, Michel. 1978. 1978. *The History of Sexuality*, Volume 1: *An Introduction*. Translated by Robert Hurley. New York: Random House.

Freeman, Elizabeth. 2010. *Time Binds: Queer Temporalities, Queer Histories*. Durham, NC: Duke University Press.

Ghaziani, Amin. 2017. *Sex Cultures*. Boston: Polity Press.

Ghaziani, Amin, and Delia Baldassarri. 2011. "Cultural Anchors and the Organiza- tion of Differences: A Multi-Method Analysis of LGBT Marches on Washington." *American Sociological Review* 76 (2): 179–206.

Halberstam, Jack. 2011. *The Queer Art of Failure*. Durham, NC: Duke University Press.

Halberstam, Jack. 1998. *Female Masculinity*. Durham, NC: Duke University Press.

Halberstam, Jack. 2005. *In a Queer Time and Place: Transgender Bodies, Subcultural Lives*. New York: NYU Press.

Halperin, David M. 1993. "Is There a History of Sexuality?" In *The Lesbian and Gay Studies Reader*, edited by Henry Abelove, Michele Aina Barale, and David M. Hal- perin, 416–31. New York: Routledge.

Halperin, David M. 2000. "How to Do the History of Male Homosexuality." *GLQ: A Journal of Lesbian and Gay Studies* 6 (1): 87–124.

Halperin, David M. 2002. *How to Do the History of Homosexuality*. Chicago: University of Chicago Press.

Halperin, David M., and Valerie Traub, eds. 2009. *Gay Shame*. Chicago: University of Chicago Press.

Harper, Phillip Brian. 2005. "The Evidence of Felt Intuition: Minority Experience, Ev- eryday Life, and Critical Speculative Knowledge." In *Black Queer Studies: A Critical Anthology*, edited by E. Patrick Johnson and Mae G. Henderson, 106–23. Durham, NC: Duke University Press.

Henderson, Lisa. 2013. *Love and Money: Queers, Class, and Cultural Production*. New York: NYU Press.

Hennen, Peter. 2008. *Faeries, Bears, and Leathermen: Men in the Community Queering the Masculine*. Chicago: University of Chicago Press.

Holland, Sharon Patricia. 2012. *The Erotic Life of Racism*. Durham, NC: Duke Univer- sity Press.

Hull, Akasha [Gloria T.], Patricia Bell Scott, and Barbara Smith, eds. 2015. *All the Women Are White, All the Blacks Are Men, but Some of Us Are Brave: Black Women's Studies*. New York: Feminist Press.

Humphreys, Laud. 1970. *Tearoom Trade: Impersonal Sex in Public Places*. New York: Aldine de Gruyter.

Katz, Jonathan Ned. 1990. "The Invention of Heterosexuality." *Socialist Review* 20 (1): 7–33.

Kennedy, Elizabeth Lapovsky, and Madeline D. Davis. 1993. *Boots of Leather, Slippers of Gold: The History of a Lesbian Community*. New York: Routledge.

King, Katie. 1995. *Theory in Its Feminist Travels: Conversations in U.S. Feminist Movements*. Bloomington: Indiana University Press.

Krahulik, Karen Christel. 2006. "Cape Queer? A Case Study of Provincetown, Massachusetts." *Journal of Homosexuality* 52 (1–2): 185–212.

Krebs, Paula. 2016. "Applying to a Public Regional University?" *On Chronicle Vitae*, January 26. https://chroniclevitae.com/.

Law, John. 2004. *After Method: Mess in Social Science Research*. New York: Routledge.

Love, Heather. 2007. *Feeling Backward: Loss and the Politics of Queer History*. Cambridge, MA: Harvard University Press.

Love, Heather. 2013. "Close Reading and Thin Description." *Public Culture* 25 (3): 401–34.

Love, Heather. 2016. "Queer Messes." *WSQ: Women's Studies Quarterly* 44 (3–4): 345–49.

Love, Heather, Christina Crosby, Lisa Duggan, Roderick Ferguson, Kevin Floyd, Miranda Joseph, Robert McRuer, Fred Moten, Tavia Nyong'o, Lisa Rofel, Jordana Rosenberg, Gayle Salamon, Dean Spade, and Amy Villarejo. 2012. "Queer Studies, Materialism, and Crisis: A Roundtable Discussion." *GLQ: A Journal of Lesbian and Gay Studies* 18 (1): 127–47.

Manalansan, Martin IV. 2003. *Global Divas: Filipino Gay Men in the Diaspora*. Durham, NC: Duke University Press.

Martinez, Ernesto Javier. 2013. *On Making Sense: Queer Race Narratives of Intelligibility*. Stanford, CA: Stanford University Press.

McDonald, James. 2017. "Queering Methodologies and Organizational Research: Disrupting, Critiquing, and Exploring." *Qualitative Research in Organizations and Management: An International Journal* 12 (2): 130–48.

McIntosh, Mary. 1968. "The Homosexual Role." *Social Problems* 16 (2): 182–92.

McRuer, Robert. 2006. *Crip Theory: Cultural Signs of Queerness and Disability*. New York: NYU Press.

Mills, C. Wright. 1959. *The Sociological Imagination*. New York: Oxford University Press.

Mohr, John W., and Amin Ghaziani. 2014. "Problems and Prospects of Measurement in the Study of Culture." *Theory and Society* 43 (3–4): 225–46.

Morgensen, Scott. 2015. "A Politics Not Yet Known: Imagining Relationality within Solidarity." *American Quarterly* 67 (2): 309–15.

Muñoz, José Esteban. 1996. "Ephemera as Evidence: Introductory Notes to Queer Acts." *Women & Performance: A Journal of Feminist Theory* 8 (2): 5–16.

Orne, Jason. 2017. *Boystown: Sex and Community in Chicago*. Chicago: University of Chicago Press.

Plummer, Ken. 2005. "Critical Humanism and Queer Theory." In *The Sage Handbook of Qualitative Research*, edited by Norman K. Denzin and Yvonna S. Lincoln, 357–73. Thousand Oaks, CA: Sage.

Puar, Jasbir. 2007. *Terrorist Assemblages: Homonationalism in Queer Times*. Durham, NC: Duke University Press.

Robinson, Zandria. 2015. "Zeezus Does the Firing 'Round Hurr," *New South Negress*. http://newsouthnegress.com/.

Schilt, Kristen, Tey Meadow, and D'Lane Compton. 2018. "Introduction: Queer Work in a Straight Discipline." In *Other, Please Specify: Queer Methods in Sociology*, edited by D'Lane Compton, Tey Meadow, and Kristen Schilt. 1–36. Berkeley: University of California Press.

Sedgwick, Eve Kosofsky. 1990. *Epistemology of the Closet*. Berkeley: University of California Press.

Spade, Dean. 2011. *Normal Life: Administrative Violence, Critical Trans Politics, and the Limits of Law*. Brooklyn, NY: South End Press.

Spring, Amy L. 2013. "Declining Segregation of Same-Sex Partners: Evidence from Census 2000 and 2010." *Population Research and Policy Review* 32 (5): 687–716.

Stein, Arlene, and Ken Plummer. 1994. "'I Can't Even Think Straight': 'Queer' Theory and the Missing Sexual Revolution in Sociology." *Sociological Theory* 12 (2): 178–87.

Stevens, S. S. 1959. "Measurement, Psychophysics, and Utility." In *Measurement: Definitions and Theories*, edited by C. West Churchman and Philburn Ratoosh, 18–63. New York: Wiley.

Stevens, S. S. 1975. *Psychophysics*. New York: Transaction.

Valentine, David. 2007. *Imagining Transgender: An Ethnography of a Category*. Durham, NC: Duke University Press.

Ward, Jane. 2016. "Dyke Methods: A Meditation on Queer Studies and the Gay Men Who Hate It." *WSQ: Women's Studies Quarterly* 44 (3–4): 68–85.

Warner, Michael. 1992. "From Queer to Eternity: An Army of Theorists Cannot Fail." *Literary Supplement* 106: 18–26.

Zerubavel, Eviatar. 1996. "Lumping and Splitting: Notes on Social Classification." *Sociological Forum* 11 (3): 421–33.

"How the Other Half Thinks"

An Introduction to the Volume

HEATHER LOVE

"The facts alone will not save us."
—Ruha Benjamin (2016)

In *After Method: Mess in Social Science Research*, John Law comments on the inadequacy of traditional methods to describe things that are "complex, diffuse, and messy" (2004, 2). He argues that, in approaching the world as a set of determinate processes, scholars strip it of contingency, ephemerality, and indistinctness. Rather than creating the world in the image of the knowledge we produce about it, Law suggests that social scientists develop new methods that aim not to stabilize the world but rather to allow for its vagueness, its ineradicable messiness. Law's account of the paradoxes and challenges of defining what eludes capture resonates with the experience of queer scholars. Not only has queer scholarship dealt centrally with untidy issues like desire, sexual practice, affect, sensation, and the body, it has also struggled continually to resist what Michael Warner has called "normal business in the academy." In an early statement, Warner wrote, "For academics, being interested in queer theory is a way to mess up the desexualized spaces of the academy, exude some rut, reimagine the publics from which and for which academic intellectuals write, dress, and perform" (1993, xxvi). When it comes to being messy, *we are*.

From the start, queer scholars have acknowledged, or often celebrated, the messiness of their subject matter, and have invented new modes of research, writing, and performance to deal with it. If they have been slow to identify these new modes as *methods*, it is both because the term as it is generally understood is ill suited to address the vagaries of embodied life.[1] In their introduction to this volume, Matt Brim and Amin Ghaziani remark on the "apparent incommensurability" of the phrase queer methods (5). The phrase evokes a classic odd couple, uptight *methods* attempting to impose order on the slovenly *queer*. As Jane Ward writes in this volume, "to pair the terms 'queer' and 'methodology'—the former defined by its celebrated failure to adhere to stable classificatory systems or be contained by disciplinary boundaries, and the later typically defined by orderly, discipline-specific, and easily reproducible techniques—produces something of an exciting contradiction, a productive oxymoron" (262).

Today, queer method, if not quite a recognizable subfield, is more than an oxymoron. Over the past several years, queer scholars across fields have turned to the question of method. The publication of Kath Browne and Catherine J. Nash's edited volume *Queer Methods and Methodologies: Intersecting Queer Theories and Social Science Research* (2010) was crucial in articulating this shift. In the introduction, Browne and Nash argue that "[q]ueer researchers are in good company with other scholars drawing on poststructuralist and postmodernist approaches such as some feminist, anti-racist, and postcolonial scholars, in consciously seeking to articulate their ontologies and epistemologies but who are seemingly less inclined to consider the implications of these approaches to methodologies and methods (1)." Browne and Nash see the critique of traditional method as central to queer studies, and situate this aspect of the field in relation to other fields that regularly struggle with the problem of impossible or ephemeral evidence. But they argue that the field has failed to develop beyond the moment of critique to develop full self-consciousness about its epistemology and its relation to disciplinary, institutional, and material structures.

My engagement with questions of queer method began several years back when I ventured beyond my discipline (literary studies) and undertook a series of research projects in the history of the social sciences. In 2012, I taught a PhD class called "Queer Method" to which I invited several scholars in gender and sexuality studies. When I asked them to talk about their method and their training, they responded by saying, "I have no method." For a scholar in queer studies to avow a method is to undermine, as Brim and Ghaziani put it, "queer theory's constitutional claims to inter/anti-disciplinarity" (2016, 15)—as well as its self-understanding as an outsider to the university. By capitulating to academic norms, we may seem to compromise both our critical stance and the minoritarian ethics developed in the field. Of course, queer critics do draw on traditional methods, as they both rely on and resist their disciplinary training. Scholars in the field have also developed methods, often quite widely influential ones. Nonetheless, these methods tend to get framed in other terms. Regarding Eve Kosofsky Sedgwick's viral account of "reparative" reading, for instance, Warner observes, "It is not so much a method as (principled?) avoidance of method" (2004, 18).

As someone trained in literary studies (as well as poststructuralist theory and psychoanalysis), I harbor resistance to traditional method and to the constraints of professional scholarship. But over the last several years I have to come to see this unwillingness rather differently. I see the failure to acknowledge that queer scholars, too, have methods as a disavowal of forms of institutional belonging, attachment, and affiliation (see Wiegman 2012). This refusal to locate ourselves or to identify our methods has resulted in a failure to grapple with queer studies as positive knowledge project. But queer studies is a field as much in need of the self-reflexivity that Browne and Nash describe as any other. To see one's practices as beyond method and utterly undisciplined is a failure to reckon with queer scholars' position in the university; it fails to recognize the violence of *all* scholarly research—even its most insurgent and intimate forms.[2] It was out of a commitment to a more robust avowal of the disciplinary and institutional frameworks of queer studies, as well as a recognition of the field's ongoing innovations in method, that a group of us planned the conference "Queer Method" at the University of Pennsylvania in 2013.[3] Over the past several years, queer scholars have engaged questions of method by addressing institutionalization, the history of the disciplines, and pedagogy; examining the conditions of academic work through attention to archives, funding structures, and labor; engaging fields of inquiry that had been sidelined in the field such as philology, biology, and sexology; and taking up outré tools such as taxonomy and quantification. The superb essays in this volume, which represent a wide range of disciplines and approaches, offer both further articulation of the paradoxes of queer method and proof of concept.

What has driven the turn toward queer method? The institutionalization of queer studies, incomplete as it is, has made the field's antidisciplinary stance harder to countenance. But the shift also reflects a return of the social sciences into the conceptual center of the field. Queer theory developed largely in the humanities in the early 1990s, a heady mix of activist energies and poststructuralist theory. Kadji Amin discusses this history and its consequences at length in this volume, suggesting that this combination of abstraction and urgency resulted in the definition of queer as "an almost infinitely mobile and mutable theoretical term" (279). Queer emerged, Amin argues, as a term that "seemed *to carry within it* the loaded transgression and charged sense of struggle around sex and sexual cultures" that defined the moment of its birth. This origin has given the term incredible traction, staying power, and range, but it has also led to the odd framing of queer studies as an academic field "paradoxically defined by its lack of a defined object of study" (283). This framing of queer was, as Amin suggests, not inevitable, but rather a contingency of this moment. Early scholarship in the field drew on but also displaced the contributions of black feminism, lesbian-feminist and gay male theory, radical sex cultures, transsexual activism, social history, Marxist sociology, and ethnic studies. In recent writing, I have argued that legacy of deviance studies was absorbed and disavowed by the field, and have traced how this movement led a field stance against method (Love 2015).

Queer studies has never been exclusively situated in the humanities, and social scientists working in the field have never accepted its definition as a theoretical and interpretive rather than an empirical and grounded field. But many have noticed the imbalance, and have bemoaned its material and intellectual consequences.[4] In a 1995 *GLQ* essay, Lisa Duggan noted the "progressive impoverishment of the empirical, historical grounding for textual analyses" in sexuality studies research: the ascendancy of queer theory had given rise to an "impressive expansion of increasingly sophisticated analyses . . . balanced precariously atop a stunted archive," she wrote (181). In 2005, E. Patrick Johnson and Mae G. Henderson echoed this point in their introduction to the collection *Black Queer Studies*, citing Roderick Ferguson's account of the antagonism toward "African American culture and nonnormative sexualities" in canonical sociology. As a result, they argued, "much of the interventionist work in the areas of race and sexuality has come out of the humanities and not the social sciences

(2)." Over twenty years later, in their contribution to this volume, Zandria F. Robinson and Marcus Anthony Hunter cite Johnson and Henderson's claim, and suggest the situation has not changed: "Black queer and black feminist work has certainly increased and advanced in the social sciences since the publication of *Black Queer Studies*; however, the continued marginalization of black feminist and black queer perspectives in the epistemology of queer social scientific work has rendered interventionist, liberatory work all the more difficult in the social sciences" (172).

In each of these articulations, scholars describe a situation of (at least) double marginalization: traditional social scientific fields dismiss the interventions of queer and black queer (and feminist) scholars, seen as too partial and particular to matter to the discipline as a whole; in the face of such resistance, misrecognition, and lack of support, queer scholars deepen their antipathy toward disciplinary methods. This antipathy is real, and is based on sound argument, and yet one senses a widespread chagrin about the impoverishing effects of the split. The frustration of queer social science scholars confronting this division over the years is palpable, and has hardly been assuaged by humanities scholars' frequent claims about the interdisciplinary nature of their scholarship.[5] As much as disciplinary boundaries are crossed and recrossed in queer studies, focusing on the question of method—turning from "what" to "how"—tends to make visible more fundamental differences in epistemology and practice. If scholars in the social sciences have never forgotten (have never been able to forget) the existence of such differences, some humanities scholars have begun to notice them, and to express some curiosity about how the other half thinks. Conflict is an inevitable but perhaps not a regrettable effect of this rapprochement. Avowing her commitment to "confronting frictions, disciplinary and otherwise," Valerie Traub (2016) writes, "An emphasis on method, I suggest, helps us appreciate that protocols that would lubricate interactions are still in the process of being worked out. Not only does such as practice entail valuing the thorny issue, the dilemma, the impasse, but it also enjoins a willingness to unpack incommensurate idioms and resist the impulse to either assume sameness in the room or strive for premature unity. Rather, the naïve question, which denaturalizes what is taken for granted within disciplinary knowledge, can provide a key tactic for managing collaborations—whether with one's own interdisciplinary self or one's disciplinary others" (337).[6]

One notable difference in responses to "queer method" by scholars in the humanities and social sciences is where they locate the difficulty with the phrase. For those trained in traditional empirical methods, adding the volatile *queer* to *method* introduces the scandal of theory, aesthetics, and cultural studies: jargon; small sample sizes, and in some cases of a single (fictional) text; unclear standards of evidence; lack of attention to representativeness; and disconnection from real people, places, and things. For those trained in the humanities, the scandal is just the opposite: the anchoring of *queer* to *method* threatens to drain its political potential by submitting to regimes of statistical reduction, the reification of identity, the overvaluing of visible behavior, and the foreclosure of the speculative, the counterfactual, and the "not yet here" José Esteban Muñoz designated as queer utopia (2009, 1). As is clear from this brief discussion, epistemological questions cannot be separated from pressing and unsolvable questions of ethics and politics—questions that can barely be stabilized because of the divergent perspectives from which they are asked. Grounded or empirical research appears exemplary because of its orientation toward social and materiality reality and its engagement with the experience of individuals and communities. But in its truck with practices of quantification and reduction, "grounded" research practice can seem strangely immune to the real people and situations it describes. Humanities scholarship has no such immunity, dedicated as it is to complexity, affective witness, and the art of narrative. Queer research in a humanities framework is not guilty of reduction, but is characterized by attentiveness to what Lauren Berlant, in an analysis of the case study as genre, refers to as "tender singularities" (2007, 669). Yet the fear is that such scholarship brings its considerable methodological resources to bear on merely fictional, idiosyncratic, or hypothetical instances, far removed from the exigencies of anyone's life.[7]

One of the great pleasures of working in interpretive disciplines is the intellectual (as well as aesthetic and emotional) freedom that it affords. Depending on your perspective, this ability to tarry with uncertainty is either the greatest gift of the humanities or its greatest curse.[8] In a recent essay arguing for the utility of speculative methods for African American studies, Ruha Benjamin (2016) writes,

In this moment of social crisis, where even the most basic assertion that black lives matter is contested, we are drowning in "the facts" of inequality and injustice. . . . In this context, novel fictions that reimagine and rework all that is taken for granted about the current structure of the social world—alternatives to capitalism, racism, and patriarchy—are urgently needed. Fictions, in this sense, are not falsehoods but refashionings through which analysts experiment with different scenarios, trajectories, and reversals, elaborating new values and testing different possibilities for creating more just and equitable societies. Such fictions are not meant to convince others of *what is*, but to expand our own visions of what is *possible*. (2)

Benjamin shares her conviction that the "facts are not enough" with many scholars of African American life.[9] In this remarkable essay, she puts this conviction into practice, drawing on her training in social studies of science to write a story about racial violence and biotechnology ("Ferguson Is the Future") set in 2064.

Sarah Schulman reflects in this volume on the significance of fiction in doing lesbian history. In the case of this insistently minor field, complexity, indeterminacy, and the refusal of self-nomination can create a situation of scholarly discretion that shades into indifference. Silence about same-sex intimacy does not always indicate absence, and even in the case of absence, there is more to say.[10] By contrast, and drawing on her work as a novelist, Schulman argues for robust imagination of the many facets—some sexual, some not—of women's relations with each other:

I propose that we look into the emotional, psychological, economic, political, intellectual, artistic, sexual, daily, and lifelong experiences of women who allowed or refused the embrace. The conversations that did happen and did not. The words permitted, and those uttered without permission. The invitations refused and accepted. The fears. The imaginations, erotic and projected. The walks in the woods, the fucking, the pleasure of the company acknowledged and refused. The meals, the conversations, how and what conversations provoked, the actions, the artworks, the articles, books, tears, orgasms realized/failed/imagined/remembered, caresses, tendernesses, the refusals of tenderness, kisses that were and should have been, and how this moved the earth, the culture, the society, or even just one or two people's small lives. (297)

Calling for more and more fine-grained and detailed accounts of "the things we did and didn't do," Schulman suggests how empiricism and fictionality—apparently opposed—might be understood as complementary.[11]

Despite the extreme diversity of perspectives represented in this volume, there is widespread agreement about what constitutes ethics in research, and how to mitigate the violence of traditional methods. The fact of queer studies as a shared context partly explains this congruence. When scholars attend to complexity, refuse to equate behavior with identity, address stigmatized activities without judgment, or "hustle" between disciplines and academic and vernacular frames of reference, they bear witness to core queer values (and furthermore suggest the extent to which queer studies has developed recognizable methods).[12] Other areas of congruence are less clearly identified with queer studies, but instead reflect the consensus of scholars in the humanities and in the qualitative social sciences over the past few decades. Across these essays, scholars attest to the importance of practices including careful listening; inviting the participation of their research subjects; attending to these subjects' acts of resistance, including their resistance to the research process itself; sharing, insofar as it is possible, the risk and vulnerability involved in such encounters; and cultivating reflexivity, openness, and the willingness to be surprised. These are qualities about which there is very little disagreement. But scholars disagree about how much these good intentions matter, how to put them into effect, and to what extent they mitigate (if at all) the inequality that structures the field of knowledge production.

At its best, queer studies can exemplify the intimacy, uncertainty, erotics, boundary-crossing, and activist energies that gave rise to it, while engaging critically and productively with the resources of traditional disciplinary knowledge. Several scholars in the collection argue that queer method can serve as a bridge between the social sciences and the humanities. For instance, Amin Ghaziani argues that "queer methods create space for the coherent and the chaotic," the former typically identified with conventional social science and the latter associated with queer theory (116). As is so often the case in these essays, theory is united with practice: Ghaziani backs up this vision of queer method with a granular and step-by-step account of specific research problems and advice for how to solve them. However, in contrast to such methodological optimism, and to the desire for queer to bring out the best in the humanities and the social sciences, the volume also includes the perspective of methodological pessimists. In place of the both/and, they look at method more in terms of neither/nor. They suggest that idealizing queer method does not fully come to terms with "knowledge production as the scene of political struggle" (Wiegman, cited by Fields, (69), and the violence—some might say, the inevitable violence—of relations in the field.[13]

Jessica Fields is alert to this danger in her account of the "racialized erotics" of field research, and for this reason refuses to close her account on complicity and incitement by imagining "a shiny new method" (79). With stunning vividness and granularity, Fields attends to the visceral entanglements between researchers and the subjects they study; recalling her own work with women in prison, Fields recounts how showing how, despite her best intentions, she was drawn into a nexus of "violence, pleasure, affirmation, and exploitation" (75). Because of structures of race and class inequality, and their imbrication in desire and sexual practice, it is impossible to steer clear of this nexus; one can simply navigate it with awareness. Rather than seeing such dynamics as "spoiling" the research or counseling her readers on how to avoid them, Fields suggests that they constitute a resource. She writes, "Anxious situations—failures, flirtations, and misreadings—are not obstacles to empiricism; rather, I see them as visceral experiences of social difference and affinity in which researchers, participants, and collaborators assert their personhood" (70). Several other contributors join Fields in taking on this intersection of violence, incitement, pleasure, and knowledge. There is widespread agreement in the volume about the value of minoritarian experience and of perspectives "from below." In his analysis of John Keene's *Counternarratives*, Brim points to the narrator Burunbana's claim "that some who have been condemned to the most foul contumely do reside, nevertheless, in Truth, and so this missive proceeds from that strange and splendid position" (Keene, cited in Brim, 157). This account of the intimate relation between contumely and surplus knowledge echoes W. E. B. Du Bois's account of the origins of double-consciousness, a state of being inaugurated by the question: "How does it feel to be a problem?" ([1903] 1996, 5). Though often "unasked," this question lingers in the atmosphere surrounding minoritarian research.

There is a temptation, in the face of the difficulties posed by method, to give it all up, to throw, as Zandria F. Robinson and Marcus Anthony Hunter write, "measurement away altogether" (165). Several authors in this volume contemplate this possibility, citing Audre Lorde's dictum that "*The master's tools will never dismantle the master's house*" (Lorde 1984). However, despite much grappling with these "hard lines," no one in this volume actually suggests a full retreat.[14] Collectively, the contributors attest to the gains—intellectual, pragmatic, and personal—to be won via an engagement with method. The utility of such methods is not in doubt in Petra Doan's essay, which perhaps best exemplifies the pragmatic orientation of the volume as a whole. Despite the question implied by her essay's title ("To Count or Not to Count"), Doan insists that epistemological and ethical qualms about statistical methods should not keep scholars from doing crucial work. She writes, "If compulsory heterosexuality 'others' queer populations, then counting them may undermine this 'otherness' by demonstrating the legitimate needs of the LGBTQ+ population. For the transgender population, the urgent need for access to safe bathrooms and social services, including medical care, more than justifies the act of counting" (121). With such necessities clearly in view, Doan unambiguously identifies the aim of her research—to count "as broadly as possible" (124)—as a form of advocacy. This articulation conjoins one of the most traditional (and, within the humanities, reviled) methods—counting—with the activist and strategic aims of queer studies. It is for this reason that Doan reckons counting a "queerly radical act" (138).

Doan's essay demonstrates how queer method, despite its paradoxes, can be put to work; it also recalls a broader history of politicized uses of method. According to Robinson and Hunter, blanket dismissals of social science and quantitative methods ignore "how marginalized people have harnessed measurement to liberate themselves from enslavement, challenge and upend the status quo, and rewrite history" (165). Du Bois's 1901 study *The Philadelphia Negro* constitutes a crucial example of this deployment of statistics. Although Du Bois's multigeneric, narrative, and rhetorical works make him a model for scholarship that is anti- or at least counterdisciplinary, his marshaling of statistics to refute charges of black morbidity suggest the strategic utility, the urgency, of counting (see Hunter 2015; also Katz and Sugrue 1998). The pragmatic orientation and real-world impact of research are clearest in an essay like Doan's with explicit links to policy. Yet the evidence of an orientation toward action and demonstrable stakes is clear across the collection, even in pieces by scholars in literary and cultural studies, which tend to be grounded in the material practices of pedagogy and curation—or, as Brim describes it, "put[ting] books in each other's hands" (160).

Reading these essays together, the creativity and resourcefulness of these scholars in dealing with the problems of queer method is striking. But even more striking, and affecting, is their moral courage in facing these problems. In the face of the most daunting and unsolvable ethical dilemmas, they forge ahead, suggesting either explicitly or by example that retreat is both intellectually misguided and ethically questionable. Schulman suggests that through robust imagining of lesbian history we should give no one any more excuses than they already have for "hesitant obscuration." E. Patrick Johnson puts the case most forcefully. In discussing the ethics of undertaking his oral history project with African American queer women from the American South as a black gay man, he writes:

> I believe that the benefits of the research far outweigh the potential pitfalls, for to not conduct this research based *simply* on the fact that I am a man would be to fall prey to what the late performance ethnographer Dwight Conquergood called the "skeptic's cop-out," a pitfall of ethnographic research that retreats to quietism, paralysis, and cynicism based on "difference." According to Conquergood, this position is the most morally reprehensible on his moral map of performative stances toward the other . . . because the "skeptic's cop-out" forecloses dialogue altogether. (55)

Johnson reiterates Conquergood's views that to allow ethical qualms to get in the way of actually doing the research is morally bankrupt. In the case of the occluded, marginal, and disregarded narratives that these scholars hope to represent, the stakes are simply too high.

Lorde's judgment on "the master's tools" is not merely a critique of the design or implementation of a particular research method. Instead, she offers a more sweeping critique, pointing out the limits of academic scholarship as a whole. "*Survival is not an academic skill*" (1984, 14; emphasis in original), she writes. Not only will the master's tools not dismantle the master's house, but they are also being employed for ends they were never meant to serve. The facts won't save us, not only because they are bad facts, but also because facts are indifferent to survival and salvation both. Lorde indicts the insularity of the university, and the tendency of feminist scholarship to drift away from the experience of those "who stand outside of this society's definition of acceptable women" (14). As we commit or recommit to the oxymoron of queer method, we should recall Lorde's words, which not only challenge our thinking but also shift the ground beneath our feet. The tension between *queer* and *method* is not merely ideological—it is material, and it is here to stay. Queer studies developed as an activist field, and it has always maintained skepticism and even hostility toward the business of academic life. From the perspective of a radical queer tradition, the turn to method can seem like the surrender, the final capitulation to academic business as usual. But avowing our place as academics may be necessary to recognizing what in the world is *not academic*: the ongoing struggles for survival that exceed our methods, our countermethods, and our antimethods.

NOTES

1 The bibliography of work on mess and messiness in queer studies is extensive; recently it includes more work that considers intersections between mess and method, which has emerged primarily out of new work on archives. For work on mess and messiness within queer studies, see Martin F. Manalansan IV's recent work on immigration, everyday practice, and informal archives (2014; 2015); José Esteban Muñoz's indictment of the ideology of rigor (1996); Ann Cvetkovich (2003); and Rebecka Taves Sheffield (2014).

2 See, for instance, Judith Stacey (1988) on the inevitability of betrayal in the field.

3 Many of the ideas for the conference were generated in the 2012 seminar, named above. For a list of all those involved in planning and organizing, as well as conference aims and speakers, see www.queermethod.tumblr.com/.

4 Scholars who contributed to this critique include Gayle S. Rubin, John D'Emilio, Jeffrey Escoffier, Arlene Stein, Jeffrey Weeks, Ken Plummer, John Gagnon, William Simon, Kath Weston, Steven Epstein, Peter M. Nardi, and Beth E. Schneider. To take one example, typical in its tone of frustration, see Jeffrey Weeks's 1998

reflection on the legacy of Mary McIntosh's 1968 essay "The Homosexual Role." Weeks writes, "It is frustrating for those of us who have been toiling in this particular vineyard since the turn of the 1960s and 1970s to have our early efforts in understanding sexuality in general, and homosexuality in particular, refracted back to us through post-Foucauldian abstractions . . . and then taken up as if the ideas are freshly minted" (1998, 132). A great deal of bridging work has been undertaken by queer scholars trained in the social sciences or working between disciplines, for instance Roderick Ferguson, Lisa Duggan, Nayan Shah, Jafari Allen, Margot Weiss, Anjali Arondekar, and others.

5 I have described Stephen Greenblatt's engagement with Clifford Geertz's concept of "thick description" as one such example of a claim to interdisciplinary practice by a humanities scholar that does not grapple with more fundamental epistemological differences between the disciplines. See Love (2013), especially 402–4, 410–11. In the rest of this essay, I explore other grounds on which it might be possible to link textual reading with observational practices in the field more robustly. Several contributors also take up this question. See, for instance, Rivera and Nadal's discussion of close reading as a qualitative and observational practice (204). See also Brim on the pragmatic and conceptual work of reading in the classroom, and Brim and Ghaziani on the overlap between reading and counting (6–7).

6 Traub is responding to a set of short essays about her book *Thinking Sex with the Early Moderns* (2015) published in the "Queer Methods" special issue of *WSQ*. She is a humanities scholar with ties to the social sciences, through her use of historical methods in her own work and her chairing of a multidisciplinary Women's Studies Department at the University of Michigan.

7 In a related analysis, Margot Weiss considers the ambivalence of empiricism in queer theory. Contrasting the "conceptual simplicity of our theoretical categories" (2011, 650) with the complexity of community knowledge turned up by the core disciplinary methods of ethnography and participant observation, she also resists the call for "more data" to enrich the field. Instead, she argues that theory and data are forever entangled, and suggests that we see the (impossible) longing for grounded theory as a spur to pay "more attention to the production of all knowledge" (662).

8 Robinson and Hunter express acute frustration with this aspect of humanities scholarship, tying the abstraction and ambiguity of poststructuralist theory to a failure to address the realities of racism and poverty. They write that queer theory and intersectionality "gained traction in academic discourse just as 'people,' 'bodies,' and 'oppression' were being replaced by the poststructural language of 'identities,' 'signifiers,' and 'difference.' . . . While sociology can claim some immunity from this largely humanities-based turn, it was not unaffected by its tendency to obscure. This language and its accompanying methodological shadowboxing distances us further and further from the roots of organizing for liberation of all dispossessed persons" (170).

9 On the limits of fact in the context of contemporary racial violence, see Browne, *Dark Matters* (2015).

10 Cf. Benjamin Kahan (2013) on celibacy, or the absence of sex, as a disposition and set of practices worth attending to. Kahan, like Schulman, uses the occasion of celibacy to engage a broad rethinking across disciplines and genres of the "epistemology of the closet."

11 This account, as I have hinted, suggests a queer reading of the Magnetic Fields song "The Things We Did and Didn't Do." Smith (in this volume) proposes "redaction-as-revelation" as a method for rereading queer women's communication. Redaction-as-revelation "functions via paradox: by 'blacking out' text, its aim is *not* to hide or delete (with all the word's ominous overtones in a context of oppression) but to rejoice in the transformative powers of the substance, or body of blackness, and its encounter with the white page" (216–17).

12 Thrasher (in this volume) proposes "hustling" as method to account for his movement between scholarship and journalism. The concept recalls some canonical methods in cultural studies, for instance bricolage (Michel de Certeau), and also recalls Marcus Anthony Hunter's concept of "the nightly round" as an informal practice of knowledge gathering and building social capital. See Hunter 2010.

13 On the inevitability of violence, Patrick Grzanka argues that "all methods, both quantitative and qualitative, conceal a capacity for violence," epistemic and otherwise (89), but points out that capacity is not the same thing as perpetration.

14 The phrase is from Carolyn Steedman's work of critical memoir, *Landscape for a Good Woman* (1986, 2), itself a profound meditation on feminist method and the ethics of research. Kay's [Steedman's] mother says this to her after being dressed down by a home health visitor.

WORKS CITED

Benjamin, Ruha. 2016. "Racial Fictions, Biological Facts: Expanding the Sociological Imagination through Speculative Methods." *Catalyst: Feminism, Theory, Technoscience* 2 (2). http://catalystjournal.org/.

Berlant, Lauren. 2007. "On the Case." *Critical Inquiry* 33 (4): 663–72.

Brim, Matt, and Amin Ghaziani. 2016. "Introduction: Queer Methods." *WSQ: Women's Studies Quarterly* 44 (3–4): 14–27.

Browne, Simone. 2015. *Dark Matters: On the Surveillance of Blackness*. Durham, NC: Duke University Press.

Browne, Kath, and Catherine J. Nash, eds. 2010. *Queer Methods and Methodologies: Intersecting Queer Theories and Social Science Research*. New York: Routledge.

Cvetkovich, Ann. 2003. *An Archive of Feelings: Trauma, Sexuality, and Lesbian Public Cultures*. Durham, NC: Duke University Press.

Du Bois, W.E.B. (1903) 1996. *The Souls of Black Folk*. New York: Penguin.

Duggan, Lisa. 1995. "The Discipline Problem: Queer Theory Meets Lesbian and Gay History." *GLQ: A Journal of Lesbian and Gay Studies* 2: 179–91.

Hunter, Marcus Anthony. 2010. "The Nightly Round: Space, Social Capital, and Urban Black Nightlife." *City & Community* 9 (2): 165–86.

Hunter, Marcus Anthony. 2015. *Black Citymakers: How "The Philadelphia Negro" Changed Urban America*. New York: Oxford University Press.

Kahan, Benjamin. 2013. *Celibacies: American Modernism and Sexual Life*. Durham, NC: Duke University Press.

Katz, Michael B., and Thomas J. Sugrue, eds. 1998. *W.E.B. Du Bois, Race, and the City: "The Philadelphia Negro" and Its Legacy*. Philadelphia: University of Pennsylvania Press.

Law, John. 2004. *After Method: Mess in Social Science Research*. London: Routledge.

Lorde, Audre. 1984. "The Master's Tools Will Never Dismantle the Master's House." In *Sister Outsider: Essays and Speeches*. Berkeley, CA: Crossing Press.

Love, Heather. 2013. "Close Reading and Thin Description." *Public Culture* 25 (3): 401–34.

Love, Heather. 2015. "Doing Being Deviant: Deviance Studies, Description, and the Queer Ordinary." *differences: A Journal of Feminist Cultural Studies* 26 (1): 74–95.

Manalansan, Martin F. IV. 2014. "The 'Stuff' of Archives: Mess, Migration, and Queer Lives." *Radical History Review* 120 (Fall): 94–107.

Manalansan, Martin F. IV. 2015. "Queer Worldings: The Messy Art of Being Global in Manila and New York." *Antipode* 47 (3): 566–79.

Muñoz, José Esteban. 1996. "Ephemera as Evidence: Introductory Notes to Queer Acts." *Women & Performance: A Journal of Feminist Theory* 8 (2): 5–16.

Muñoz, José Esteban. 2009. *Cruising Utopia: The Then and There of Queer Futurity*. New York: NYU Press.

Sheffield, Rebecka Taves. 2014. "The Bedside Table Archives: Archive Intervention and Lesbian Intimate Domestic Culture." *Radical History Review* 120 (Fall): 108–20.

Stacey, Judith. 1988. "Can There Be a Feminist Ethnography?" *Women's Studies International Forum* 11 (1): 21–27.

Steedman, Carolyn Kay. 1986. *Landscape for a Good Woman: A Story of Two Lives*. New Brunswick, NJ: Rutgers University Press.

Traub, Valerie. 2016. "A Response: Difficulty, Opacity, Disposition, Method." *WSQ: Women's Studies Quarterly* 44 (3–4): 336–42.

Warner, Michael. 1993. "Introduction." In *Fear of a Queer Planet: Queer Politics and Social Theory*, edited by Michael Warner, vii–xxxi. Minneapolis: University of Minneapolis Press.

Warner, Michael. 2004. "Uncritical Reading." In *Polemic: Critical or Uncritical*, edited by Jane Gallop, 13–38. New York: Routledge.

Weeks, Jeffrey. 1998. "The 'Homosexual Role' after 30 Years: An Appreciation of the Work of Mary McIntosh." *Sexualities* 1 (2): 131–52.

Weiss, Margot. 2011. "The Epistemology of Ethnography: Method in Queer Anthropology." *GLQ: A Journal of Lesbian and Gay Studies* 17 (4): 649–64.

Wiegman, Robyn. 2012. *Object Lessons*. Durham, NC: Duke University Press.

PART I

Subjecting/Objecting

1

Put a Little Honey in My Sweet Tea

Oral History as Quare Performance

E. PATRICK JOHNSON

In her 2008 essay "Who Is the Subject? Queer Theory Meets Oral History," a historian of queer San Francisco, Nan Alamilla Boyd, raises important questions about the challenges that queer theory poses for gay and lesbian history. Boyd, in her survey of key texts in what she names as a "fledgling" subfield of U.S. history, rightly questions whether oral history as a method can ultimately escape the trappings of subjectivity "because it is through coherent and intelligible subject positions that we learn to speak, even nonverbally, about desire," which sometimes reifies notions of sexual identity rather than sexual desire (2008, 189). She summarizes John D'Emilio's *Sexual Politics, Sexual Communities* (1983), Allan Bérubé's *Coming Out under Fire* (1990), Elizabeth Kennedy and Madeline Davis's *Boots of Leather, Slippers of Gold* (1993), Esther Newton's *Cherry Grove, Fire Island* (1993), George Chauncey's *Gay New York* (1994), and John Howard's *Men Like That* (1999), and finds that only Howard's text represents a truly queer example of how historians might chronicle same-sex desire by moving "beyond the limits of intelligible speech, that is, racially coded articulations of desire, in order to produce a more complex accounting of the history of sexuality and sexual communities" (2008, 186). While I agree with Boyd's assessment, I believe the "challenges" to oral history posed by queer theory are less about oral history as a method per se, and more about the disciplinary protocols of history as a field. In other words, history as a field trains researchers, including oral historians, to capture a narrative that provides insight about a particular time and place—training that Boyd notes sometimes gets in the way of tracking a libidinal economy of desire outside of identity politics.

Coincidentally, my book *Sweet Tea: Black Gay Men of the South—An Oral History*, appeared in the same year as Boyd's essay. In the introduction I, too, laud Howard's intervention in queer historiography, while also marking the difference between my approach to oral history as a performance theorist as opposed to a historian's. Unlike historians who, according to historian of the U.S. South Nell Irvin Painter, are invested in creating "historical narrative" (2005, iv), I am committed to attending to the storytelling act itself by "co-performatively bearing witness" (Conquergood 2002, 149) to the story. Oral history *in conjunction* with performance, then, calls attention to the fictive nature of oral history, but not necessarily as a methodological "problem," as it were. Rather, it situates oral history as an index of the meaning-making process of history itself, what cultural anthropologist Allen Feldman calls "historicity" (1991, 2). In other words, the narration is a recollection of historical events and facts in relation to an "authentic" self or "identity"; and it is at the same time a phenomenological experience—the moment of storytelling itself is an epistemological and embodied experience of the self as same, the self as other, and the intersubjectivity between teller and listener. The performance frame exposes not only the erotics in/ of narration, but also the erotic tension between the researcher and the teller, which has enormous implications for queer history. Rather than a "transhistorical and cross-cultural interpretation of history that conflates same-sex behavior with the ipso facto existence of sexual identities" (Boyd 2008, 179), the performance approach to oral history resists linear, progressive, or stable renderings of any one "history" by what Della Pollock calls "making history go" (1998, 1).

Since I have responded in my earlier work to some of the anxieties about queer historiography that Boyd expresses, in this essay I wish to engage a different set of methodological conundrums based on my current research. My book *Black. Queer. Southern. Women.—An Oral History* (*BQSW*) focuses on the oral histories of African American women who express same-sex desire who were born, reared, and continue to reside in the American South. It is meant as a companion text to *Sweet Tea*. As with *Sweet Tea*, my desire in *BQSW* is that the oral histories collected account not only for the way the narrators embody and relay historical material about race, region, class, sexuality, and gender, but also for how storytelling as a mode of communication is simultaneously a quotidian form of self-fashioning and theorizing. Although they do not always overcome the challenges of being black quare Southern women,[1] their oral narratives stand as testaments to the power of voicehood, self-determination, and tenacity in how one simultaneously navigates and mediates the conflicting, complicated, and confounding ideologies of the South while at the same time indexing a quare history of same-sex desire.

Because I am a cisgender, black gay man conducting research on mostly cisgender, black quare women, the performative frame of oral history I employed in *Sweet Tea* became even more prescient in *BQSW*. Issues of power, difference, and self-disclosure all came to the fore. In what follows, I recount how I navigated these methodological hurdles in collaboration with the narrators. Specifically, I situate my approach as decidedly quare *and* feminist, while also highlighting how framing oral history as performance elides some of the challenges to queer historiography.[2]

Quare Beginnings

I started collecting oral histories of these women because I wanted to learn more about the interior lives of Southern black lesbians and their journey toward selfhood in the South. As a child, the concept of "lesbian" was not in my consciousness, nor necessarily in the lexicon of my western North Carolina black community. The typical slang of "funny," "that way," and "sissy" were certainly common but were mostly used in reference to men who were thought to be gay. I sometimes heard at the barbershop the oblique reference to a woman as a "bulldagger" but had no idea the meaning of that term, only that it was negative. In hindsight, I realize that I actually grew up with quite a few black lesbians, one of whom is Anita, whose narrative I include in my book. In fact, it was not until I was much older that I realized just how many women in my community were "sweet" on other women. Thus, I was curious to hear the stories about same-sex desire from these women's early childhoods to see if there were overlaps with the black Southern gay men with whom I have spoken, and my own story, or if there are significant differences based on gender. For example, a few of the young girls with whom I was friends growing up were what many would refer to as "tomboys," girls who were more interested in climbing trees, building hot rods, and playing basketball than they were in caring for dolls, playing house, or making mud pies, as I so loved to do. I don't recall them being teased about being tomboys, however. I, on the other hand, was often called "sissy" because of my soft, soprano voice, big butt, noticeable lisp, and interest in art and "girly" things. What explains this difference in treatment based on gender expression and play interests? Conducting these interviews gave me some insight and perspective on that question, as many of the women in *BQSW* revealed that they believe that tomboyish girls are generally tolerated—at least until they are a certain age and expected to become Southern "ladies."

And even after adulthood, some women—at least in my community growing up—were not bound by a narrow sexual "identity" when they engaged in nonnormative sexual behavior or expressed same-sex desire. Although folks may have whispered about them, their dalliances with the same gender did not necessarily make them "lesbian" as much as it made them just another eccentric whose membership in and contributions to the community outweighed their sexual behavior.

One humorous story in this regard involves my now deceased uncle, Johnny "Shaw Man" McHaney. For all intents and purposes, Uncle Johnny would have been considered a "dirty old man." He never seemed to discriminate in his attraction to the other sex, but he definitely had a quare sensibility about him—both in his attraction to nonnormative women (i.e., women who did not fit within or even aspire to traditional standards of beauty within white or black communities) and his linguistic play with gender (e.g., he often called me "Baby Doll").

Uncle Johnny was always taking pictures at family gatherings and holidays with his Polaroid camera. Unsurprisingly, many of the photos were of women guests at our family events or of women whom he had met at his favorite barbershop where he hung out every day after work and on the weekends. Several years ago my mother asked him to bring some of his pictures over to our house so that she could look through them and find ones that she could use as part of a photo collage for an upcoming family reunion. Mixed in with the photos from past family reunions were pictures of various women—some in compromising positions, scantily clad, or nude. Aunt Marylee stumbled across a picture of Sylvia, a woman who I remembered lived up the road from us when I was a child and who was the mother of two daughters close to my age.

Trying to needle Uncle Johnny, Aunt Marylee asked in a shrill voice, "Johnny, ain't this a picture of Sylvia?" Uncle Johnny slipped the picture out of Aunt Marylee's hand and studied it as if lost in an erotic reverie: "Yeah, that's Syl. You know she's half and half," he replied. "Well, if she half and half, what *YOU* doin' wit' 'er then?" Aunt Marylee responded incredulously. "I was with the half I could be wit'," Uncle Johnny quipped without missing a beat. Although totally scandalized and clutching her pearls,[3] even my mother joined the rest of the family in the room in the uproar of laughter.

It was my memory of Aunt Marylee and Uncle Johnny's repartee and description of Sylvia as "half and half," meaning that she had sex with both men and women, that brought into clarity the ways in which black Southern women's sexual desire, sexual practice, and sexual identity are not always one and the same. As a scholar of gender and sexuality, of course I know intellectually that this is not the case, but I had not thought about it *experientially* in the context of my own upbringing and family history until now. "Half and half" in this context signifies quare sexual desire rather than "bisexual" or "lesbian" *identity* per se, for the phrase exemplifies the verbal play of black folk vernacular that eschews fixed meanings. Aunt Marylee already knew that Uncle Johnny did not discriminate when it came to women. Thus, she already assumed what he was "doing" with Sylvia, especially given some of the other photos of women sprawled across my mother's kitchen table (e.g., a picture of Uncle Johnny and a woman with one breast and another of a naked woman with a very large behind standing in front of Uncle Johnny's television). And Uncle Johnny's coy response about being with only one "half" of Sylvia also cannot be read literally in terms of his denying a "lesbian" side of Sylvia in order to be with a "straight" side. More likely, the "half" to which Uncle Johnny, given his proclivities for kink, refers is nonnormative sex. The point here is that Sylvia did not refer to herself as a lesbian and the community did not project that identity onto her; they only knew that she engaged in quare sex without the encumbrance of a label or identity to accompany this behavior or desire. This was common among many of the women that I interviewed. While the same phenomenon was true for some of the men I interviewed for *Sweet Tea*, it certainly was not the dominant narrative, as many of the men typically did identify under some label or category. This phenomenon made me

think differently about the particularly vexing problem of how to conduct research on sexuality beyond identity "in order to produce a more
complex accounting of the history of sexuality and sexual communities"
(Boyd 2008, 178). Ultimately, this is why "lesbian" does not appear in the
title of the book.[4]

"Outsider Within": On Quaring Positionality

Unlike my experience with the men in *Sweet Tea*, I was never asked to
"do" anything during my visits with quare women, such as help cook
dinner or run errands. This may have been due to the gendered ways
in which women in the South are socialized to "serve" men, particularly with some of the older women I interviewed who treated me like
one of their own children or nephews. Nonetheless, a few of the women
prepared dinner in anticipation of my visit. One of the last women I
interviewed, Lenore Stackhouse, unfortunately passed away unexpect-
edly just three months later. She prepared a lovely "Sunday dinner"
for me of potato salad, collard greens, baked chicken, rolls, and—of
course—sweetened iced tea.

In general, my interactions with these women—most of whom I was
meeting for the first time—were familial and familiar, not in the sense
that I *knew* them but in the sense that we were kin based on our Southern roots, our queerness, and, I believe, my "soft" masculinity. In fact,
during some of the exchanges a few women would refer to me as "girl"
or "honey," when responding to a question, and then become embarrassed by the slip of tongue. I was heartened by these easy interactions,
given the warnings from friends and colleagues that I might not be able
to find women to talk to me for the book and, if I did, they would not be
forthcoming about the intimate details of their lives because I am a man.
I did have a few women cancel at the last minute or stand me up altogether, but this only happened in Tallahassee, Florida. I have no explanation for this, for it was the only city where this occurred. A total of four
women failed to follow through with the interview there after agreeing
to be a part of the book. They have yet to respond to my follow-up calls
to find out what happened or to reschedule.

Before embarking on this research, I understood that the stakes were
different because of the gender difference between the researcher and

the subjects. Rather than view this as an obstacle, however, I viewed it as an opportunity to engage questions of gender, sexuality, and region across the gender divide. Moreover, I grew up in a single-parent home with a mother who instilled in her children Southern manners, grace, and respect for others. And, it was lesbian-of-color feminism that brought me into my consciousness around my own sexuality. So, it was not a matter of my not knowing how to *act* around these women. It was more about me understanding how my male privilege—despite my upbringing and personal politics—might influence not only how I collected these oral histories, but also how my gender might reinscribe some of the very structures and institutions that these women critique in their narratives. Thus, I want to take some time here to walk through my process of collecting these narratives as a way of engaging what performance and communication studies scholar Bryant Keith Alexander calls "critical reflexivity," which he defines as "both a demonstration and a call for a greater sense of implicating and complicating how we are always already complicit in the scholarly productions of our labor, and the effects of our positions and positionalities with the diverse communities in which we circulate" (2006, xviii–xix).

In this respect I am an "outsider/within," to borrow black feminist theorist Patricia Hill Collins's phrase (1991, 11), since my interlocutors and I share many of the same identity markers (e.g., queerness, Southernness) and not others (e.g., gender, class position). This experience of conducting research within a community to which I belong, albeit across gender boundaries, was not new to me, as I conducted an oral history of my grandmother's life as a live-in domestic worker for my doctoral dissertation research. The power dynamic between the two of us shifted variously as I negotiated being "scholar-in-charge" and "deferential grandson" and she negotiated being "subject-of-study" and "grandmother-in-charge." These power dynamics are inescapable within the context of oral history and ethnographic research. It is a matter of the researcher's being aware of such dynamics, approaching and working through them with a sense of ethics and moral responsibility. Alexander perhaps sums it up best when he writes: "These are the moral issues of avoiding egoism and promoting cultural knowledge as a mechanism for generating critical reflexive processes in/for audiences. And the moral issues of dealing with voice as cultures of thought"

(2006, xix). Thus, my methodology for collecting these oral histories was guided by a sense of ethics and a moral obligation to render these women's lives in a way that acknowledges my male privilege—not just in the interview setting but also in the world. This latter point, however, is again one of the reasons why I chose to do this work in the first place: as an act of male feminist praxis.

Indeed, much of my work as a scholar has been about the celebration and promotion of women's lives—from the research on my grandmother's life as a domestic worker to drawing on her black folk feminism to critique the field of queer studies (see Johnson 2005), to providing a platform for black women solo artists to showcase their work, to collaborating with black feminist colleagues to team-teach courses on feminism and queer studies.[5] My scholarly and political praxis, therefore, is decidedly feminist, but not in the sense that black feminist political scientist Joy James critiques when she uses the term "opportunistic feminism" for "profeminists," (straight) male scholars of color who are seemingly (in James's estimation) down with the female cause but who nonetheless "see most women as supporting helpmates or damsels to be succored" (2002, 157). James's suspiciousness about the motivations of male academics that identify as feminist is well warranted based on the usurpation of black women scholars' control over their own work by their male colleagues. And while all of James's examples of such poaching are by self-identified heterosexual men, I know, too, that gay men also engage in sexist and misogynist behavior—even those who presume to be in solidarity with their lesbian sisters. In fact, I remember a gay male couple, both friends of mine, sharing a story about socializing on another friend's sailboat, in which a lesbian guest got into a discussion with them about the AIDS epidemic. She suggested that if the disease had infected and affected lesbians more disproportionately than gay men, that gay men would have "stepped over women's diseased bodies to get to the club instead of helping them." My friends thought her comment was appalling and an exaggeration, but I don't know that she was too far off the mark, for the gay male community benefits from patriarchy and doesn't always work to dismantle it—even in solidarity with those with whom they share a common sexual identity or affinity and despite the fact that patriarchy and misogyny undergird homophobia. Nonetheless, this does not mean that all men—straight, gay, or queer—are beyond doing ethical, self-reflexive, antisexist work. I can never totally "undo" my male privilege—a privilege, I might add, that is never absolute, as it is contingent in various contexts in relation to my race, class, and sexuality. But what I can do is the work that my soul was called to do, and that is to work to destroy oppressive institutions of power, including patriarchy.

Within the context of the oral history interviews for *BQSW*, my disavowal of patriarchy consisted of my taking a feminist approach. An example of this was eschewing what Kristina Minister calls the "standard oral history frame," which "denies women the communication form that supports the topics women value" (1991, 35). Although Minister recommends that only women should conduct interviews of other women to truly honor women's communication patterns (a point that I think has an essentialist component), I believe that the ways in which I conducted the interviews with the women of *BQSW* allowed for more flexibility in terms of having a set of questions but not necessarily privileging getting through the questions as the most important aspect of the interview. There were many times when I got to ask a question only every fifteen or twenty minutes, such as when I interviewed Iris in Atlanta. I might have asked Iris a total of ten questions, despite the interview lasting five hours over two meetings! Further, Minister argues that male oral historians focus more on "activities and facts" than on "feelings and attitudes," which women value more. This was definitely not the case with this research. In fact, many of the questions asked the women to describe how they felt about a particular event in their lives or their beliefs about something. For example, one of the questions I asked was, "How do you *feel* about the life choices that you have made in light of being a black lesbian?" Another was, "Do you *feel* a sense of community among black lesbians here in your town?" These, among other questions that asked the women about their *thoughts*, actually privileged the women as feeling and thinking subjects rather than as objects from which "facts" and information are extracted and abstracted.

Moreover, I believe the fact that I express a soft, quiet masculinity that is sometimes read as effeminacy allowed me to connect with these women in ways that I would not have otherwise been able to do. I am soft-spoken, polite, and a good listener—all self-effacing attributes that helped to set a tone of openness and vulnerability. Paradoxically, my being a man with these attributes provided a space for some of the women to be even more open about their experiences. Lisa (a pseudonym) told me, when I shared with her that a few of my academic colleagues were skeptical about women opening up to me because of my gender, that the opposite was true for her. She revealed that she agreed to the interview *because* I am a man, for she felt that a woman interviewer would judge some of the decisions she had made in her life, like having an abortion or being sexually promiscuous with men. I also suspect that women shared certain things with me because they would assume that women would already know some of these experiences because they are women. This was one advantage to being an "outsider/ within."

Similar to performance scholar Della Pollock, who theorizes the power dynamic between researcher and researched in her work on birthing narratives, I entered each interview with a sense of humility and vulnerability. Pollock writes:

> I made myself . . . vulnerable to being moved. Listening and writing, I saw myself as the register of someone else's power. Against the grain of current obsessions with the power of the researcher to shape, tame, appropriate, and control the worlds he or she investigates . . . I more often than not felt unnerved and overwhelmed, "othered," interrogated, propelled into landscapes of knowing and not knowing I would not otherwise have dared enter. (1999, 23)

This vulnerability that Pollock describes was key to the empathetic connection I had with many of my interlocutors. Indeed, there were moments when I was so enraptured by a powerful story being told that time seemed to be suspended as I entered the lifeworld being created before my eyes. I can think of two instances in which I became so emotional due to the intensity of the story—both about sexual trauma—that the narrator actually began to comfort me: "It's all right, Baby. I'm okay. I done worked through this"—all the while rubbing my back and handing me a tissue. In another instance, the narrator and I just sat in silence for what seemed an eternity, while we both sobbed and comforted each other. These are examples of a feminist practice of oral history and ethnography in which the researcher emphasizes empathy, collaboration, intersubjectivity, and a sharing of the emotional labor to tell the story. As oral historians Karen Olson and Linda Shopes remind us, "The peculiar intimacy available to strangers who share an important experience seems to create in at least some interviews a social space where normal power relations perhaps get blunted" (1991, 195–96).

Feminist sociologist Judith Stacey questions, "Can there be a feminist ethnography?" Though she is dubious about a "fully" feminist ethnography, she concedes: "[T]here can be (indeed there are) ethnographies that are partially feminist, accounts of culture enhanced by the application of feminist perspectives. There also can and should be feminist research that is rigorously self-aware and therefore humble about the partiality of its ethnographic vision and its capacity to represent self and other" (1991, 117). Given my position as a male oral historian and ethnographer, and keeping in mind the critique of male scholars who do research on women as posed by Joy James (2002) and others, I, too, concede that *BQSW* is a "partially feminist" ethnography. Yet, despite its feminist partiality, I believe that the benefits of the research far outweigh the potential pitfalls, for to not conduct this research based *simply* on the fact that I am a man would be to fall prey to what the late performance ethnographer Dwight Conquergood called the "skeptic's cop-out," a pitfall of ethnographic research that retreats to quietism, paralysis, and cynicism based on "difference." According to Conquergood, this position is the most morally reprehensible on his moral map of performative stances toward the other—which also includes the "custodian's rip-off," "curator's exhibitionism," and "enthusiast's infatuation"—because the "skeptic's cop-out" forecloses dialogue altogether (2013, 71–75). On the contrary, I engaged this research and these women's narratives to initiate more than just a dialogue; I also wanted to create a living archive of black women's sexual desire in the South.

On Quare Methods

I wish now to pivot from my role as a male oral historian and ethnographer to a discussion of oral history and performance as key methods for collecting the oral history of black Southern women who love women.[6] I could have chosen from a number of methods to chronicle the history of black lesbians from and living in the southern part of the United States, including a more traditional archival project whereby I spent time poring over ephemera, newspaper articles, diaries, and other historical documents to piece together a historical narrative of Southern, black, same-sex-loving women. My desire to use oral history, however, was undergirded by my investment and training in performance studies, which privileges the body and regards it necessarily as archive (see, e.g., Taylor 2003). In the act of performing one's life history, the self is affirmed through the interaction with another who bears witness to the story being told. As performance ethnographer D. Soyini Madison suggests in her summary of Kristin Langellier and Eric Peterson's theorization of embodiment in oral history, "Narrative as *embodied* emphasizes the living presence of bodily contact. Bodies are within touch, not simply representing, displaying, or portraying a past moment" (2012, 37; emphasis in original). Indeed, African American novelist and folklorist Zora Neale Hurston's character Janie in the novel *Their Eyes Were Watching God* comes into voice through the telling of her story to her best friend, Phoeby. In her description of Janie and Phoeby on Janie's back porch, Hurston makes note of the two women's proximity—their closeness— that provides a safe space for Janie to share her tale: "They sat there in the fresh young darkness close together, Phoeby eager to feel and do through Janie, but hating to show her zest for fear it might be thought mere curiosity. Janie full of that oldest human longing—self revelation" (1990, 6). I played Phoeby to many of my interlocutors' Janie, as I bore witness to their affirmation of self, their trials, tribulations, and trivialities, their reveries, repulsions, and recollections. Through laughter, tears, and contemplation, I witnessed these women reveal themselves to me and to themselves—sometimes for the first time. For black women, this is an important feature of finding their own voice, because historically they have been silenced. Gwendolyn Etter-Lewis argues, "It is oral narrative that is ideally suited to revealing the 'multilayered texture of black women's lives'" (1991, 43). And if this is true for heterosexual black women, it is especially true for black women with same-sex desire. There exists a tradition of heterosexual black women's storytelling, but that has not been the case for black lesbians outside of fiction.[7]

I do not wish to overstate or romanticize oral history as a method for archiving Southern black lesbian history. I am keenly aware of the paradox of oral histories since their transmission occurs through text. As Claudia Salazar points out, "[O]nce discourse becomes text, its openness as dialogue, together with its evocative and performance elements, are lost: the punctuation and silences of speech are gone; the life events in the life of the narrator often follow a chronological pattern, partly induced by the questions the ethnographer imposes; it is edited, translated, and, finally, given a title" (1991, 98). But here again, I return to performance, which becomes a rejoinder, if you will, an antidote to the textuality of the printed page, as when I perform Michelle's narrative. What gets distilled and flattened in the transcription to the page is enlivened through the re-performance of the oral narrative in a way that adds yet another layer to the meaning-making process by not only making visible what print disavows, but also by indexing that multiple truths are always already in play: the storyteller's memory of her life, the researcher's "report" of what happened as shared through their body; and the audience's truth as the witness to that intersubjective dynamic.

I am also interested in the value of what the oral history performance does for the storyteller herself. This is not to say that I am not interested in the actual historical content of what the narrator shares. Nonetheless, I also am not invested in an uncontested "truth" so much as I am in the validation of the narrator's subjectivity. Madison suggests that:

> Oral history performances . . . do not function as factual reports or as objective evidence, nor are they pure fictions of history. Instead, they present to us one moment *of* history and how that moment *in* history is *remembered* through a *particular* subjectivity. . . . It is at the matrix of materiality, memory, subjectivity, performance, imagination, and experience that memory culminates in oral history performance, a culmination of layers that are all mutually formed by each other. (2012, 34–35; emphasis in original)

To exemplify what Madison describes above, I share below an excerpt from the narrative of one of my interlocutors, Michelle, who tells the story of how she comes full circle with her father, who molested her as a child, when he is the person to help her when she is about to succumb to drug addiction. It is important to note that I have performed Michelle's narrative on several occasions in the context of a lecture about this research where she has been a member of the audience. She narrates:

> On March the 7th, 2004, I was sitting in my backyard. [Begins to weep.] Excuse me, it's still real. I was ready to blow my brains out. I had three

options. I gave myself three options. Either I can go take another hit [of crack cocaine] and I can blow my heart up. I can go get that gun and I can blow my brains out because I'm on the cycle and I can't stop right now. Or I can try to get some help. The third one seemed so far-fetched. At that time, as I began to stand up to go and get that gun, because I needed it to end, because I couldn't end it myself, I heard this voice speaking just as clear as I'm speaking right now. And it said, "Not yet, my child, I'm not finished with you, I'm not through with you yet." And I know today that that voice was none other than the voice of God speaking to me. And I took a shower, got in my car . . . I called Dad. I said, "I . . . I can't breathe and . . . and I need some help. Can you meet me?" That one that violated me, the one that talked bad about me, called me names, all kinds of stuff, was the one that met me. So they checked me in. When I finally got up to the psych unit it was March the 8th. So, my clean date is March 8, 2004. And by God's grace and mercy I'm eight years clean.

Although Michelle had been sober for eight years at the time of the telling, the memory of the pain is visceral as she's overcome with emotion, interrupting the narration to apologize to me for her tears, when she says, "Excuse me, it's still real." Despite the "realness" of the events, however, it is Michelle's desire to have someone bear witness to the telling that makes the pain of the rememory bearable. As literary scholar Jennifer L. Griffiths argues, "Testimony . . . depends on a relationship and a process between the survivor and the witness, as memory emerges and reunites a body and a voice severed in trauma. These fractured pieces of the survivor's self come together in the reflection of the listener, and memory comes into meaning through this bodily transaction, rather than simply creating a narrative in language" (2009, 2). In the act of performing one's life history, the self is affirmed through the interaction with another who bears witness to the story being told. The healing, then, is in the survivor's desire to tell and the willingness of the listener to bear witness. It is the communion of teller and listener, the affective corporeal dynamic between two people being suspended in the liminal space of memory—of co-performative witnessing. Performance, then, functions on a number of registers, theoretically, methodologically, epistemologically, and affectively to render the life histories of these black queer southern women.

As historians and anthropologists of queer culture have demonstrated for decades, no method of documenting queer desire is without its challenges. My research on black quare women of the South is no different. Repeatedly, however, I have called on my own interdisciplinary home of performance studies to bring a different perspective to traditional disciplinary approaches to queer culture-making and history. While performance is certainly not without its own theoretical and methodological quagmires—for it, like history writ large, cannot escape the politics of representation—it does in the instance of oral history carefully traverse several minefields through its capacity to view history as processual. It thereby holds in tension the discursive and the material, while exposing the trappings of teleological approaches to everyday life, which cannot always be rendered through the gaze of "objectivity." Ultimately, no matter the method(s) of documentation, it is important that the lives of queers and the stories we tell—about ourselves and about others—remain a priority for scholars in various fields who are invested in queering (and quaring) the archival record.

NOTES

1 I use the term "quare" as opposed to "queer" to register the specific black vernacular reference to nonnormative sexuality. See Johnson 2005.

2 My use of "performance" in this essay operates at the level of theory, method, and practice. To employ performance as a theory is to analyze human communication and social interactions as performance events. An example would be framing pedagogy as a type of performance whereby the person in charge of imparting knowledge is performing the role of "teacher" or "professor" and the person(s) receiving the knowledge is performing the role of "student(s)." Performance as method can range from what in anthropological terms is referred to as "participant observation" to someone adapting a literary or nonfiction text to the stage to explore its meaning. Performance as practice entails actually embodying a text or an other. While I argue that performance is one way to reconcile some of the cleavages between history and queer theory, I also want to note that performance as theory, method, and practice emerges from disciplinary training in performance studies and might not be the most productive approach for scholars who do not acquire such training or deeply engage in the theories in performance. Indeed, in the instance of performance as method and practice, scholars who are not trained can do more harm than good by attempting to perform the stories of their research subjects.

3 "Clutching pearls" in black gay vernacular means expressing surprise.

4 Throughout this essay, I use various terms to indicate same-sex desire, including "same-sex-loving," "queer," "quare," "gay," and "lesbian" because the women I
interviewed identify variously among these or disavow labels altogether.

5 See Johnson 1996 and Johnson and Rivera-Servera 2013. I codeveloped and team-
taught a course with Sandra Richards on black feminism and black queer theory
for eight years, a course I now teach by myself.

6 I conducted seventy-nine interviews between May 2012 and September 2014.
The women ranged in age from eighteen to seventy-four and hailed from Texas,
Louisiana, Arkansas, Alabama, Mississippi, Tennessee, Georgia, South Carolina,
Florida, North Carolina, Virginia, Kentucky, Washington, DC, and Maryland.
They ranged in occupation from factory workers, local government administrators, entrepreneurs, counselors, professors, librarians, schoolteachers, musicians,
writers, community organizers, DJs, truck drivers, and housewives to unemployed. Educational background also differed, but the majority of the women
had completed high school, many had had some college education, and a few had
postgraduate and professional degrees. The criteria for being interviewed required
that the woman be born in a Southern state (meaning a state below the Mason-
Dixon Line or a state that had previously been a slave-holding state, such as
Missouri and Oklahoma), be primarily reared in the South for a significant portion of her life, and be currently living in the South. I made a few exceptions to
these criteria if a woman had not been born in the South as I have defined it, but
had been reared there as an infant to toddler onward. I also made one exception
about what constitutes the South and expanded the boundaries of "blackness" by
including the narrative of a woman born in Puerto Rico who identifies as black.

7 For more on black (heterosexual) women's storytelling traditions, see Brown and
Fauk 2010; Dance 1998; Hill 1991; and Vaz 1997.

WORKS CITED

Alexander, Bryant Keith. 2006. *Performing Black Masculinity: Race, Culture, and Queer Identity*. New York: AltaMira Press.

Bérubé, Allan. 1990. *Coming Out under Fire: The History of Gay Men and Women in World War Two*. New York: Free Press.

Boyd, Nan Alamilla. 2008. "Who Is the Subject? Queer Theory Meets Oral History." *Journal of the History of Sexuality* 17 (2): 177–89.

Brown, Leslie, and Anne Fauk. 2010. *Living with Jim Crow: African American Women and Memories of the Segregated South*. New York: Palgrave.

Chauncey, George. 1994. *Gay New York: Gender, Urban Culture, and the Making of the Gay Male Underworld, 1890–1940*. New York: Basic Books.

Christian, Barbara. 1988. "The Race for Theory." *Feminist Studies* 14 (1): 67–79.

Collins, Patricia Hill. 1991. *Black Feminist Thought: Knowledge, Consciousness, and the Politics of Empowerment*. New York: Routledge.

Conquergood, Dwight. 2002. "Performance Studies: Interventions and Radical Research." *TDR* 46 (2): 145–56.

Conquergood, Dwight. 2013. "Performing as a Moral Act: Ethical Dimensions of the Ethnography of Performance." In *Cultural Struggles: Performance, Ethnography, Praxis*, edited by E. Patrick Johnson, 65–80. Ann Arbor: University of Michigan Press.

Dance, Daryl Cumber. 1998. *Honey Hush! An Anthology of Black Women's Humor*. New York: W. W. Norton.

D'Emilio, John. 1983. *Sexual Politics, Sexual Communities: The Making of a Homosexual Minority in the United States, 1940–1970*. Chicago: University of Chicago Press.

Etter-Lewis, Gwendolyn. 1991. "Black Women's Life Stories: Reclaiming Self in Narrative Texts." In *Women's Word: The Feminist Practice of Oral History*, edited by Sherna Berger Gluck and Daphne Patai, 43–58. New York: Routledge.

Feldman, Allen. 1991. *Formations of Violence: The Narrative of the Body and Political Terror in Northern Ireland*. Chicago: University of Chicago Press.

Griffiths, Jennifer. 2009. *Traumatic Possessions: The Body and Memory in African American Women's Writing and Performance*. Charlottesville: University of Virginia Press.

Hill, Ruth Edmonds, ed. 1991. *The Black Women's Oral History Project*. 10 vols. Munich: K. G. Saur.

Howard, John. 1999. *Men Like That: A Southern Queer History*. Chicago: University of Chicago Press.

Hurston, Zora Neale. 1990. *Their Eyes Were Watching God*. New York: Harper & Row.

James, Joy. 2002. *Shadow Boxing: Representations of Black Feminist Politics*. New York: Palgrave.

Johnson, E. Patrick. 2018. *Black. Queer. Southern. Women.—An Oral History*. Chapel Hill: University of North Carolina Press.

Johnson, E. Patrick. 1996. "Never Had uh Cross Word: Feminist Practice in the Oral History of Black Domestic Workers." PhD diss., Louisiana State University.

Johnson, E. Patrick. 2005. "'Quare' Studies or (Almost) Everything I Know about Queer Studies I Learned from My Grandmother." In *Black Queer Studies: A Critical Anthology*, edited by E. Patrick Johnson and Mae G. Henderson, 124–57. Durham, NC: Duke University Press.

Johnson, E. Patrick. 2008. *Sweet Tea: Black Gay Men of the South—An Oral History*. Chapel Hill: University of North Carolina Press.

Johnson, E. Patrick, and Ramón Rivera-Servera, eds. 2013. *solo/black/woman: scripts, essays, and interviews*. Evanston, IL: Northwestern University Press.

Kennedy, Elizabeth, and Madeline Davis. 1993. *Boots of Leather, Slippers of Gold: The History of a Lesbian Community*. New York: Routledge.

Madison, D. Soyini. 2012. *Critical Ethnography: Method, Ethics, and Performance*. 2nd ed. Thousand Oaks, CA: Sage.

Minister, Kristina. 1991. "A Feminist Frame for Interviews." In *Women's Word: The Feminist Practice of Oral History*, edited by Sherna Berger Gluck and Daphne Patai, 27–42. New York: Routledge.

Newton, Esther. 1993. *Cherry Grove, Fire Island: Sixty Years in America's First Gay and Lesbian Town*. Boston: Beacon Press.

Olson, Karen, and Linda Shopes. 1991. "Crossing Boundaries, Building Bridges: Doing Oral History among Working-Class Women and Men." In *Women's Word: The Feminist Practice of Oral History*, edited by Sherna Berger Gluck and Daphne Patai, 189–204. New York: Routledge.

Painter, Nell Irvin. 2005. *Creating Black Americans: African-American History and Its Meanings, 1619 to the Present*. New York: Oxford University Press.

Pollock, Della. 1998. "Introduction: Making History Go." In *Exceptional Spaces: Essays in Performance and History*, edited by Della Pollock, 1–45. Chapel Hill: University of North Carolina Press.

Pollock, Della. 1999. *Telling Bodies Performing Birth: Everyday Narratives of Childbirth*. New York: Columbia University Press.

Salazar, Claudia. 1991. "A Third World Woman's Text: Between the Politics of Criticism and Cultural Politics." In *Women's Word: The Feminist Practice of Oral History*, edited by Shema Berger Gluck and Daphne Patai, 93–106. New York: Routledge.

Stacey, Judith. 1991. "Can There Be a Feminist Ethnography?" In *Women's Word: The Feminist Practice of Oral History*, edited by Shema Berger Gluck and Daphne Patai, 111–20. New York: Routledge.

Taylor, Diana. 2003. *The Archive and the Repertoire: Performing Cultural Memory in the Americas*. Durham, NC: Duke University Press.

Vaz, Kim Marie. 1997. *Oral Narrative Research with Black Women: Collecting Treasures*. Thousand Oaks, CA: Sage.

2

The Racialized Erotics of Participatory Research

A Queer Feminist Understanding

JESSICA FIELDS

To study sexuality with women who are incarcerated in U.S. jails is to enter a world of stark and embodied injustices and inequalities. Incarcerated women are typically young, poor, unemployed, and undereducated people of color without affordable and safe housing (see Conly 1998; Covington and Bloom 2007). Many are addicted to drugs or abusing them (Kantor 2003). Before entering jail or prison, many women endure gendered violence and discrimination such as physical, sexual, and emotional abuse; vilification of their sexual desires; and denial of their capacity to mother (Richie 1996; 2002). Violence and discrimination often continue during their incarceration at the hands of prison staff and others (Human Rights Watch 1996).

While bleak patterns and statistics help to establish the urgency of women's experiences of mass incarceration, they do not promise a meaningful understanding of vulnerability and risk in incarcerated women's lives (Fine and Torre 2006). My focus in this essay is on a participatory action research (PAR) study of the felt experiences of intimacy, HIV/ AIDS risk and infection, and systemic violence and regulation (Fields et al. 2008). With funding from the California HIV Research Program and the U.S. Conference of Mayors, Isela Ford and I secured the assistance of student researchers and launched workshops in which incarcerated women would participate in research design and inquiry, rather than serve purely as objects of research. So too would jail-based educators and students who might otherwise only support faculty researchers' aims.

Isela and I adopted PAR as a methodological framework that prioritizes learning *for* and *with*, not only *about*, people who might otherwise be only the objects of study (K. Lewin 1946). In PAR, students, teachers, study participants, and researchers work together as co-researchers, participating in research design and inquiry that supports their making meaningful social change in their lives. Isela and I were especially interested in PAR's capacity to counter the conditions of incarceration, in which prisoners are systematically "robbed of any right to complex personhood and robbed of any capacity to change" (Gordon 2004, 43). Allowing for complex personhood would resist pathologizing hierarchies and lay bare that "all people . . . remember and forget, are beset by contradiction, and recognize and misrecognize themselves and others" (Gordon 1997, 4). Our inquiry came to be marked by the embodied experiences of researchers, collaborators, and participants, including those which are racialized, gendered, sexualized, and classed; participatory and exclusionary; enervating and exhausting. Shifting relationships created a new terrain on which we could meet and exchange ideas. When we met on this new terrain, the differences among us proved troubling, exciting, and inseparable from any insights we might gain from our work.

PAR serves as a call for community members to enter the process of knowledge production and for researchers to participate in embodied curiosities. Working at the intersections of PAR, queer theory, and women-of-color feminism, I explore the place of "the erotic," which I understand as an entanglement of visceral sensations (Allen 2012; Lorde 1978), in these calls. I focus on my own erotic experiences: met and unmet, palpable, straining, and enlivening desires—what Sharon Patricia Holland describes as the racialized and sexualized "feeling that escapes or releases when bodies collide in pleasure and in pain" (2012, 6). Methodological attention to those feelings can help queer, feminist, and PAR researchers remain cognizant of the stark vulnerabilities that characterize our participants' lives and the snarl of social interactions that threaten and promise to undo our sense of who we are in queer feminist PAR, in social research, and in the world.

PAR across Differences

I first met Isela, an experienced jail-based HIV educator and counselor with a graduate degree in public administration, in a summer course I co-facilitated for sexuality educators on questions of social inequality and justice. I accepted a general invitation to visit the jail that Isela issued to the class, and we talked more over a long lunch. Isela shared with me her commitment to working with marginalized Latinas and to ensuring women of color were among San Francisco's priorities in HIV treatment and prevention strategies. I shared my history as a gender and sociology instructor in men's and women's state prisons, as the daughter of a corrections officer and eventual warden, and as a teenager who, after trouble at home and in school, had been sentenced to a year in a drug and behavioral treatment facility.

The study began on grounds marked by these divergent and shared biographies and commitments. Some critics assert that disparities in power and privilege make collaborative and egalitarian relationships impossible despite PAR researchers' intentions and practices (Williams et al. 2005). Indeed, equality was elusive in our work, even if collaboration was possible. Participants included researchers from San Francisco State University (student assistants and me), HIV educators from the San Francisco Department of Public Health (Isela and colleagues), and women incarcerated in San Francisco County Jail. We were women of color and white women; researchers, educators, and students; in our twenties, thirties, and forties. We were lesbian, queer, and straight; mothers and women not parenting. Some had spent time in jail, prison, and treatment centers, and others had never been arrested or locked up. Some held high school, college, and postgraduate degrees, and others had not completed high school. We were members of the middle class and people living in poverty.

Categorical disparities fostered additional disparities in collaborators' experiences of the study. Isela, the student assistants, and I had reliable access to project resources, including funding and supplies. Incarcerated researchers' access was contingent on our returning to the jail, admitting them to the workshop, and welcoming them into the practices of inquiry. Isela also encountered limits: though a lead investigator, she did not spend her days at the university and could not incorporate the collaboration as neatly into her workday. At the jail, however, Isela enjoyed inestimable credibility, and the balance of power shifted. Her endorsement allowed the team access to the jail, and her ongoing counsel helped us navigate unfamiliar and intimidating bureaucracies and interactions. Isela's direction was sometimes difficult to follow. For example, she urged us not to share our personal lives with prisoners. As an out lesbian, I found the direction to keep my sexuality private discomfiting, but I heeded Isela's advice.

The incarcerated women faced the greatest obstacles to collaboration. The militarism and restriction inherent in jails and prisons make PAR with incarcerated populations particularly challenging (Fine et al. 2003; Fine and Torre 2006). Prisoners have little control over their time, and correctional staff can place a unit or facility into lockdown, allowing no movement or visitors. Unlike state and federal prisons, jails are city and county facilities in which prisoners usually serve shorter terms, typically seventy-two hours to five months. The higher turnover means greater uncertainty and volatility and greater opportunity to provide short-term education, health care, and other services to which women may not otherwise have access (Clarke et al. 2006). We could not expect women inside the jail to be long-term collaborators. However, we could expect to involve many women and to work with some of them outside the jail after their release.

To maximize access to the project inside the jail, the workshops allowed incarcerated women to join at many points and, whenever they entered, to help shape data collection, analysis, and dissemination. This gesture built on established PAR practices of offering training in study design, implementation, and analysis, and ensuring collaborators have the skills necessary for meaningful participation (Minkler et al. 2003). Each cycle consisted of four two-hour training and research workshops. Figure 2.1 depicts workshop aims and activities. Isela and the student researchers with training as HIV educators opened the first workshop with a discussion of health-promotion strategies. The workshop concluded with a collective effort to identify obstacles to adopting these strategies. This discussion informed an interview guide that participants constructed cooperatively. In the second workshop, student researchers and I trained women to implement the guide. Incarcerated researchers then interviewed one another in pairs, audio recording their conversations. Over the next week, student assistants, Isela, and I identified one to three recordings to transcribe. We then supported the incarcerated researchers in the third workshop as they examined the selected transcripts for themes and patterns. This coding generated new questions and observations for discussion in the fourth

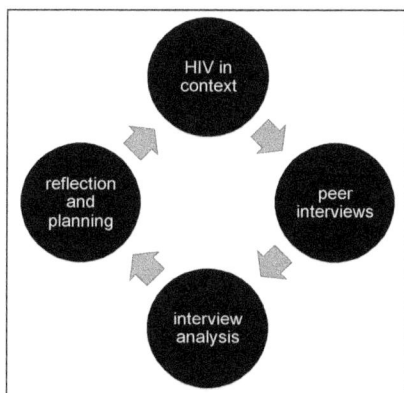

Figure 2.1. Participatory workshop cycle.

workshop. The outcomes of that discussion guided the structure and content of the next cycle. For example, when interviews about discussing safer sex with partners revealed that women stay in relationships they consider bad for them, the next workshop series focused on women's decisions to stay in unhealthy relationships and obstacles to their leaving. Analysis workshops never focused on the erotic experiences I examine here; this theme emerged after the workshops concluded.

Workshops began in January 2007 and continued through June 2007 in a housing unit dedicated to drug treatment. The meeting room was small, allowing eighteen women to sit comfortably. Deputies could look through a wall of windows at the workshops, but they could not hear the discussions. The limited space and the popularity of the workshops meant we turned people away each week and added names to a waiting list. In order that the project could benefit from participants' growing research expertise, women who had previously attended a workshop had priority. Because we wanted to understand HIV in the context of racial, gender, and sexual inequalities, women of color were the next priority. To make room for newcomers, women left the cycle after four workshops. We offered refreshments and twenty dollars in exchange for participation (up to eighty dollars for four workshops). Isela's and my work on the project was folded into our salaried positions. We paid student assistants an hourly wage using grant funds.

Seventy-four women participated in at least one workshop, with an average attendance of three workshops. Incarcerated participants were an average of thirty-six years old, with ages ranging from nineteen to sixty-three. In a typical workshop, nine women were African American, three women were Latina, one was Asian/Pacific Islander, and one was American Indian or Alaskan. Three quarters of the women were mothers, with an average of three children. Workshop participants reported an average of five male sex partners, less than one female sex partner, and no transgender partners in the last year. Almost four in ten women reported having had sex for money, food, or drugs in the last year, and approximately two in ten said they had injected drugs. Three reported HIV-positive status in an anonymous demographic survey.

Of the seventy-four women who attended a workshop, thirty-seven completed four workshops; we recognized these women as "graduates" with certificates and applause at the end of their fourth workshop. Those who wanted to continue working with the project joined a "graduates group" of five to eight women. These graduates designed projects of their own, including focus groups on women's health concerns and a report on violations of women's privacy in jail-based health care. The graduates successfully used that report to advocate for better jail medical treatment, including increased safeguards for prisoners' privacy. Graduates also conducted an evaluation of the workshops and presented the results to the housing unit. I conducted in-depth, open-ended interviews with four graduates in part to better understand the differences between interview data collected in peer interviews and in more conventional researcher-researched interviews. I wrote this second interview guide with Isela and the student and formerly incarcerated research assistants, and the questions focused on vulnerability and intimacy in the women's lives inside and outside jail. I conducted interviews in private meeting rooms inside the housing unit in late 2007. Women received twenty dollars for their participation.

Since the workshops, graduates have been active participants in the team's work, including feedback sessions held inside and outside the jail over a two-year period in which we shared emerging analyses of the interview transcripts and field notes. Two graduates joined the team as paid research assistants upon release from jail. They and other team members have presented project findings at professional conferences and on university campuses. Other collaborations have built on the project, including a digital storytelling project Isela facilitated with Margaret Rhee, Kate Monico Klein, and Allyse Gray (Rhee et al. 2013).

Queer Feminist PAR Methodology

For some social science and public health researchers, community-based participatory methods represent an opportunity to produce more reliable and valid research findings (cf. Minkler and Wallerstein 2008). PAR promises to support vulnerable communities in a move from being studied (objects of inquiry) to doing the studying (subjects directing inquiry). Scientific discoveries and subsequent changes in practice and policy should thus reflect community needs.

I bring to PAR an additional commitment to the contested cross-disciplinary project of articulating an empiricism that is rooted in feminist and postpositivist social research and queer thought (Browne and Nash 2010; Ferguson 2007; Love 2015). My PAR reflects a feminist understanding of "knowledge production as the scene of political struggle" (Wiegman 2012, 71), and a queer commitment to that struggle's generative possibilities. I pursue queer feminist PAR as a response, not a solution, to what geographers Kath Browne and Catherine J. Nash, who write about queer methods, describe as "the messiness of social life and the place of the research/researcher in (re)creating it" (2010, 14). Even when committed to methodological integrity, insights emerge not with answers to questions or the settling of uncertainties but from collaborators' struggles to know and be known in our complex personhood.

Queer feminist PAR refuses to seek refuge in methodology from the ethical, affective, and intellectual challenges raised in inquiry. Instead, it lingers in the demands of systematic, empirical inquiry and lays bare and learns from moments of difficulty. Maintaining a sense of social life as "contingent, multiple, and unstable" (Browne and Nash 2010, 4) and finding insight even in failure (Halberstam 2011) requires what sociologist Avery Gordon, writing about radical thought in action, describes as "a different way of seeing, one that is less mechanical, more willing to be surprised, to link imagination and critique" (1997, 24). Research is enlivened by turning away from methodological conventions that "drain anxiety from situations in which we feel complicitous with structures of power, or helpless to release another from suffering, or at a loss as to whether to act or to observe" (Behar 1996, 6). Anxious situations—failures, flirtations, and misreadings—are not obstacles to empiricism; rather, I see them as visceral experiences of social difference and affinity in which researchers, participants, and collaborators assert their personhood. Such moments facilitate queer feminist empirical inquiry.

Even in its most conventional forms, PAR draws attention to relationships between researchers and the people we study. Although PAR may cast those relationships as paths to democratic inquiry, queer feminist PAR approaches participation and inquiry as deeply felt encounters rife with possibility and disappointment. Collaboration incites not only a process of knowledge production but also (and of particular interest in my essay and in this volume) the erotics of racialized, gendered, and sexualized power—erotics that can span differences to bring collaborators together even as they also threaten to disrupt the promise of shared effort and insight. Indeed, as the celebrated Black, feminist, lesbian, and activist poet Audre Lorde argues, the erotic offers a "basis for understanding much of what *is not* shared" (1978, 56; emphasis mine), allowing for the possibility of connection between those who differ. At the intersections of PAR, queer method, and women-of-color feminism, erotic exchanges serve as "a bridge" (56), sometimes solid, other times swaying, still other times foreclosing crossings, and always reaching between and across particular locations and forging relationships between researchers' own situated selves and those of the people they seek to understand. A new relational terrain becomes apparent, a terrain pitted with power, difference, affinity, and desire and marked by the vulnerability of recognition and misrecognition.

In other words, this is not an erotic simply of pleasure. Building on Lorde, anthropologist Jafari Allen argues the erotic is central to "deepening and enlivening" people's experiences of themselves and one another as it traces and bears traces of the ways people's bodies, desires, and relationships are inhabited by the worlds in which they live (2012, 327). The erotic is found in "practices of desire" that are "not only realized by confrontations with extrinsic power or structure but also, more pointedly, are made through and form one part of a complex process constituted by embodied experiences, which include gender, race, color, and nationality" (326). Such a definition of the erotic is decidedly queer, reflecting "a praxis of resistance . . . marking disruption to the normative order" (Tinsley 2008, 199) and grounded in queer of color critique that begins with "explicit formulations of racialized sexuality and sexualized race" (205). A queer feminist PAR engaged with the erotic thus points to want *and* to wanting, that is, to the ways race, gender, sexuality, and other social differences and inequalities inflect desires, their satisfaction, and their denial.

In queer feminist empiricism, the erotic becomes something to document and analyze, part of a faithful recounting of researchers' time in the field. In the methodological considerations I offer here, I look for explicit accounts of desire in field notes and transcripts. Recognizing implicit injunctions against erotic attachments in the field, I also read for traces of the erotic in research. These moments are among the many in which researchers help constitute the realities they study, coconstruct knowledge with other participants, and establish the racialized, gendered, and sexual stakes of the worlds they seek to understand (González-López 2011; E. Lewin and Leap 1996). I present extended accounts of data collection and excerpts from field notes and transcripts in order to suggest what was said and left unsaid. I offer the data and my interpretation and then leave room for "disagreement and alternate readings" (Frankenberg 1993, 30). Throughout, I ask: How does methodological attention to the erotic expose fault lines between the promise and limits of democratic inquiry and thus open PAR to the surprise and demands of participation?

Tracing Desire in Field Notes

Our assigned room and workshop budget accommodated fourteen women per workshop (and four researchers), and every Monday the demand for seats exceeded the available space. As lead researcher, I took on the task of welcoming women and turning others away. I was the classic gatekeeper: gesturing toward a door behind which food, cash, and attention awaited, but allowing only some women access to those resources. Though our project's limited resources frustrated me, I was pleased by the popularity of the workshops. My authority to adjudicate the difficult scene embarrassed me.

One Monday morning, agitated and tired after admitting fourteen women, I took my seat in the crowded circle of gray plastic chairs.

Bianca—a young African American woman attending her second workshop—took a seat across the circle and then, spotting me, quickly stood. As I wrote in my field notes in 2007:

> Bianca grins at me and says she wanted to "come over and sit next to Jessica," the person in the room who is "in charge." Her comment is flirty, and I laugh as she walks toward me. Shana [another incarcerated woman] tells me Bianca has just talked on the telephone to "one of her baby daddies" and is feeling good. I ask Bianca if this was true, and she nods at me with a smile on her face. I laugh again as I take in how absolutely gushy Bianca seems. Bianca seems turned on, feeling good about herself, and wanting to stay in the moment a bit longer. (Unpublished data)

The laughter suggests I was rattled; I recall also feeling flattered and hoping to appear good-natured. I enjoyed being pulled into Shana's and Bianca's confidence and the feeling of Bianca having chosen to sit near me. With my laughter, I hoped to appear friendly and to defuse an erotically charged moment. I did the same with my field notes, describing Bianca as "turned on, feeling good about herself, and wanting to stay in the moment a bit longer" and not claiming those feelings for myself. I was turned on; I felt good about myself; and later, as I composed an extended field note account, I lingered in the moment a bit longer. I defended myself against these uncomfortable feelings of desire and pleasure by projecting them onto Bianca's body. My field notes continue:

> Bianca turns toward me. With something of a pout, she says, "You didn't even notice my braids." I look at the tiny cornrowed braids weaving across her scalp and say that I like them. I ask if she did it herself. She shakes her head "no" and turns so I can see the back of her head, where there is a larger braid making its way up the center of her scalp. This one she did. I hadn't seen that one, I say, but now that I have I can see how good it looks. I tell her I remember her hair from last week: it was straight and swept around her head, and I'd liked it. (Unpublished data)

I remember looking closely at the hair wending its way up Bianca's scalp, the smell of her hair and skin, and the sight of pores and freckles on her scalp. I remember sensing that, though undisclosed as Isela had encouraged, my lesbian sexuality was not necessarily undetected. Regardless, occupying as I did the role of "person in charge," I was available to offer Bianca the attention her absent lover might have offered. Finally, I remember finding in this exchange with Bianca momentary relief from constraining ideas of authority and difference.

Having not reflected on these feelings in my field notes, I can now only recall my experience of occupying the authority, aesthetics, and demeanor of a white woman professor as the workshop began. I describe in my field notes Bianca's body, behaviors, and (observed) feelings, but the field notes offer no details about *my* body and behaviors and little account of the relief and other emotions *I* felt. Obscuring my embodied erotic experiences and speaking with confidence about those of Bianca, the ostensible object of inquiry, I elide questions raised by imagining myself as an object of desire in a setting marked by stark inequalities. For example, how do race and gender help constitute the terrain of PAR? How does the researcher navigate that terrain and its erotics? How might a concerted and collaborative investigation of erotic desire— including researchers' desires—have allowed me to interrogate the ethical and methodological implications of being a free woman wanting to learn more about a woman in jail, a white woman imagining herself the object of a Black woman's desires, and a researcher finding pleasure in a flirtatious moment with a participant?

Finding the Erotic in Transcription

While the erotic's traces are sometimes faint in field notes, the convention of recording researchers' and respondents' contributions in interview transcripts renders my participation in erotic exchanges more transparent. My experiences and behaviors become discernible and thus available for analysis and critique in ways field notes may hinder.

Undone by the Erotic

Jaye was a leader among her peers: other women cheered when she spoke with a preacher's cadence at a Black History Month celebration and sought her friendship inside the jail. She was among the first to hug team members at the close of workshops; she frequently declared that she considered the workshops "a blessing." Jaye completed the workshop cycle and participated in the graduates group; she encouraged other women to attend workshops and vouched for our trustworthiness.

The interview guide included questions about vulnerability and agency in women's sexual lives. When I asked Jaye about a time she got what she wanted from a sexual partner, she described smoking crack and then "pay[ing] a lady" four or five times in a single night. I did not understand and asked her to elaborate. Jaye explained:

> When I get so high, I go looking. Just like an old man, a pervert would do. And I mean, not saying taking advantage of them because I don't do it. Now if you weren't out there and I felt that if you weren't out there, and you're looking for something and you ask, I say, "Well, maybe you can accommodate me and I can accommodate you." (Interview with the author, November 20, 2007)

Still unsure, I asked Jaye again to elaborate:

> JESSICA: Okay. Let me, I just want to make sure I understand a couple things.
> JAYE: [*Laughter*] I know. Jessica, are you okay?
> JESSICA: I'm totally okay.
>   (Interview with the author, November 20, 2007)

I was okay, though not totally. I was confused by Jaye's account, and I recall feeling simultaneously grateful for Jaye's solicitousness and anxious about losing control of the interview. To regain my footing, I asked some clarifying questions: What drug was Jaye using? (Crack.) Did "accommodating" mean she and the woman she approached would trade sex for drugs? (Sometimes.) What did "sex" mean in this context? (Sex began with a flirtation as Jaye assessed how far women would go and how safe she felt with them.) Where did Jaye go to meet women? (Several neighborhoods.) Jaye then took a breath and described these interactions:

> I would have her to, uh, just sit there and kinda admire her own body. You know, like kinda play with herself or whatever and I'll look or you'd

like to dance or whatever. Whatever's going to turn me on that night and whatever I like. Something that's going to make me climax. Sometimes I won't even climax. Sometime I just admire them, sometime I help them to get them off the street. Then I tell them, I say, "Well, check this out 'cause I don't play games. . . . If you want a hit of crack I will give you a hit of crack, but if you're not sure then don't come on. . . . 'Cause if you freak out I'm going to freak out 'cause I'm high too." (Interview with the author, November 20, 2007)

Jaye described herself high on crack, admiring a woman she met on the street, exchanging drugs for the promise of sexual pleasure, watching a woman dance, masturbating to orgasm (or not). The account was filled with risk—drugs, exchange sex, the possibility of freaking out. While I recognized those risks, I also recognized the pleasures—a woman's body, intoxication, and a fragile agreement to articulate one's desires and remain true to the exchange.

In a moment reminiscent of the care she offered to women she met on the street, Jaye asked again if I was okay. I was, but the exchange had become, for me, more than a research interview. Jaye's story not only helped me understand what it meant for her to make a sexual life in the midst of vulnerability but also compromised any claim I might make to a dispassionate stance. Though the transcript includes no description of my visceral experience of the moment, it does document some of my efforts to regain control in response to Jaye's evocative description— for example, asking clarifying questions, asserting that I was okay, and remaining in the interviewer's role. I remember appreciating why one would pursue the promised pleasures of sex, drugs, danger, and excitement despite the risks; I also sensed the pleasures available to objects of Jaye's attentions. I felt Jaye treat me much as she described treating women from the street—asking, "Jessica, are you okay?" and seeking reassurance I would not "freak out" and exit.

Jaye's story allowed me to glimpse the impossibility of disentangling pleasure and vulnerability on the streets, in interviews, or in participatory research. I encountered both of our personhoods through the intermingling of violence, pleasure, affirmation, and exploitation. Method offered me no refuge from the realizations that I could easily imagine the pursuit of risky pleasures and that Jaye's desires were not so distinct from mine. I could seek clarity and maintain a facade of composure, but I could not escape the demands of erotic connection—a connection through which Jaye resisted the pathologizing of her behaviors, forged a link with me, and called on me to recognize her humanity and rethink normative responses to risk.

Made in the Erotic

Caia—a charismatic African American woman in her early thirties—had an enviable sense of humor, a history of crack use, and a longer history of sexual abuse perpetrated by men in her family and on the streets. Like Jaye, she completed four workshops and entered the room each week enthusiastically. Caia chatted and laughed easily with us; her gently teasing jokes often came quietly at our expense.

The interview guide included the question, "You identified as [racial identity] on the fact sheet; can you tell me what that has meant for you in your life?" When I asked Caia, she explained being Black had meant

> a lot of hard times . . . like, growing up, "Nigga this, Nigga that." But, it adds trauma to you. It really don't bother me. I don't, the ignorance doesn't bother me. . . . Me and my girlfriend, we be like, "Bitch, come here." It's a habit, and it's no disrespect. I look at that like: people say things, and it ain't even meant like that. It's just—it doesn't bother me because I'm cute, so it doesn't bother me. (Interview with the author, November 29, 2007)

I wanted to learn more about Caia's resilience, so I asked, "What do you mean, 'because you're cute'?" She replied:

> Everybody that gets high, and stuff, that's Black, the majority of them, they teeth are missing, they all fucked up. I got all my teeth, they cocaine white [laughs]. So, I still got action in this game, you know. . . . [B]ecause when I go on a john, I got action, you know? I still got back [laugh]. You know? I could still get married, find me a good man. He say, "My baby got all her teeth." That's right, baby. (Interview with the author, November 29, 2007)

With that, Caia laughed, opened her mouth, and asked me to look at her teeth. Startled, I leaned forward, peered inside, and agreed. "It's true," I said. "You look like all your teeth are right in there."

The moment was intimate and horrible. Looking inside Caia's mouth, I felt myself pulled into a reenactment of images of Southern white slave traders and owners inspecting slaves' teeth for signs of disease and inferior market value. As much as I wanted to pull away from the interaction and the history that haunted it, I felt obligated to remain. To retreat would be to deny Caia the affirmation she sought. To stay was to participate in persistent degradation and violence.

I turned away from Caia toward the interview guide. However, when I tried to wrest myself out of the moment, Caia insisted I remain—a source of routine trauma even as I tried desperately not to be:

JESSICA: And, so, um. Does it matter if it's uh—like who says "bitch" or who says . . .

CAIA: Nigga.

JESSICA: Yeah. Does it matter? You know what I mean, like?

CAIA: Say it: nigga, nigga.

JESSICA: You want me to say it? Why do you want me to say it?

CAIA: Yeah. 'Cause, you actin' like you scared to say it.

JESSICA: I'm not scared; I just try not to say it.

CAIA: It doesn't bother me. To me, I don't know. It might bother other people, but, it's like, I don't pay attention to a lot of shit that other people say, right. I always blank people out.

    (Interview with the author, November 29, 2007)

With that, Caia relinquished her call for me to utter a racist epithet. Her point was made. Without my even saying the ugly term, it loomed—an everyday traumatizing utterance that could not be reclaimed, that scared me, and that Caia could taunt, ignore, and ultimately survive.

I could not affirm Caia's desirability and strength—inspecting her teeth, witnessing her resilience—without also enacting white racism. The collaborative spirit of PAR, the queerness of my questions about incarceration and sexuality, and my refusal to "say it" do not allow me to escape that legacy—they instead suggest my desires to escape. Caia, on the other hand, was unwilling to articulate or satisfy any desires I might pretend lay outside the racist structures defining our collaborative exchange. As Sharon Patricia Holland notes in *The Erotic Life of Racism*, "[D]esire and subjugation, belonging and obligation, are linked in theory and practice" (2012, 14). Researchers may try to fashion a space beyond this link, seeking refuge in conventional empiricism and method; lingering in the erotic, queer feminist PAR remains accountable to the link's demands.

Sustaining Methodological Tensions

Workshops and interviews in this project took place at discomforting intersections of sexuality, racism, and incarceration in women's lives. The insistently alive personhood of incarcerated women, queer feminist scholars, and those committed to democratic knowledge production became clear once we no longer leaned on "the whole panoply of rational argumentation and knowledge" about not only jail and prison but also sexuality, vulnerability, and research (Gordon 2004, 65). As personhood became apparent, so too did an embodied history of U.S. racism that infused my careful looks at their sexualities and that haunted even the democratizing efforts of PAR.

Perhaps I should have extricated myself from these moments with Bianca, Jaye, and Caia once I noticed their erotic character. Readers might worry that allowing for the erotic compromises researchers' ethics, invites coercion, and undermines absolutely the possibility of democratic knowledge production. But exiting would have denied the ways Bianca, Jaye, and Caia spoke back to incarceration, research, and racism—institutions prone to casting them and other incarcerated women as victims. In exiting, I would have lost an opportunity to note that my collaborators and I came together as not only researcher and researched but also free and imprisoned, criminalized and legitimized, Black and white. The erotic laid the grounds for connection, empathy, recognition, and betrayal in institutions and interactions marked by persistent yearnings, vulnerabilities, and victimizations.

PAR is one moment in a long feminist and queer history of scrutinizing the terms of knowledge production. How can we interrogate inequalities and hardships without reproducing them in our research?

Though well-intentioned, these interrogations also reflect a "progress narrative" (Wiegman 2012) central to feminist scholarship: the pursuit of a conceptual apparatus that will ensure the strength of our analysis. The progress narrative compels many discussions of PAR methods and social research, raising certain questions about the account I offer here. How frank should ethnographers be in their accounts and analyses of erotic experiences? How can researchers best respond to flirtation from participants? How might researchers better anticipate erotic exchanges in the field?

I want to resist these questions. We cannot count on a "better method" to bring us closer to inclusiveness, accuracy, or ease. Instead, the pursuit and critique of that elusive possibility signal our membership in a queer feminist community (Fields 2013). Rather than pursue a method that calms the tensions inherent to queer feminist research, I ask: How can researchers keep those tensions alive as signs of the promise of reimagining the possibilities in queer research? Research practices central to participatory models hold the potential to disrupt disenfranchising practices of learning even as they require us to navigate risk, betrayal, desire, and violence—all our erotic longings. I thus conclude with some tentative responses heeding the advice proposed by queer, feminist, and critical race theorist Robyn Wiegman. Even as I offer these provocations, I want to resist the urge to turn an attention to the erotic in research into a shiny new method that could tame the unruliness and unpredictability the erotic introduces.

The erotic is a relation made in the research encounter, and it leaves its trace across the data. Empirical researchers—and perhaps PAR scholars in particular—have a responsibility to read the field notes, interview transcripts, and analytic memos we produce for insight into participants' lives *and* the collaborative exchanges in which we come to these insights. A queer feminist PAR recognizes that any effort to democratize inquiry carries the traces of the racialized, gendered, sexualized desires brought to and generated in the encounter. So too do the understandings our inquiries yield.

The erotic demands the attention of PAR and of queer feminist researchers. Collaboration, knowledge production, and the making and unmaking of relations are visceral experiences, wrought through desires for connections, alternatives, and understandings. PAR incites participation in all of the structural and ideological conditions that collaborators and researchers inhabit: democratizing, oppressive, bridging, and severing. The erotic demands that we feel and understand those conditions through our PAR and queer feminist research methods.

The erotic lurks in the "silences" (Brim and Ghaziani 2016, 17) lingering in our research accounts. The traces of the erotic will not always be immediately apparent, even to queer feminist researchers with a commitment to exploring the erotic. Researchers' accounts may slide past these moments, focusing instead on interactions more easily discerned and described. Our reading practices will have to vary according to the conventions of documentation: Are we relying on transcription? Recalled accounts? Queer feminist researchers, PAR and otherwise, will read data archives as products of social interaction, warranting the same interrogation we commit to the other products of our settings.

Finally, the erotic surprises, disrupts, and generates possibilities both welcome and terrible. Silences in data are not problems to be solved with more accurate field notes or transcripts. PAR calls collaborators into a dynamic and generative process of inquiry in which understandings and selves are made and unmade, desires are met and unmet. The task for queer, feminist, participatory research is to greet the arrival of the erotic with curiosity and openness, so that we might become better readers of the worlds and lives we study and inhabit. Noticing how the erotic made its way through my encounters with collaborators pointed my analysis toward the imprint that social inequalities left on desires for connection, insight, affirmation, and relief. Even as our wants feel singular, an analysis of our erotic entanglements in the research setting sends us out in the world of grim statistics and diminished life chances for evidence of how those brute realities come to affect, however contingently, what we want for ourselves and others. The erotic bridges what may seem like disparate worlds, allowing moments of shared desires; but those desires, and so research, are marked by the intersecting personal and social histories of love, loss, discrimination, violence, and intimacy. PAR highlights the promise and limits of democratic inquiry and the surprise and demands of participation. The queer feminist turn in PAR—indeed in empiricism broadly—would see these erotic entanglements as simultaneously the grounds of teaching and learning, a path to understanding, and their potential undoing.

Acknowledgments

My deepest thanks go to the incarcerated women-of-color co-researchers and the many team members who contributed to this project, including Isela Ford, Elena Flores, Allyse Gray, Kathleen Hentz Beach, Margaret Rhee, Catherine White, Lanice Avery, Valerie Francisco, Kate Monico Klein, L. Lemercier, and Christina Monroe. I benefited from presenting earlier versions of this article at the 2014 meeting of the American Sociological Association, University of Minnesota Sociology Department Workshop Series, and York University Qualitative Research and Resource Centre. I thank Darius Bost, Jen Gilbert, Amy Gottlieb, Didi Khayatt, Jonathan Silin, Judith Taylor, Anna Wilson, anonymous *WSQ* reviewers, and editors Amin Ghaziani and Matt Brim for incisive suggestions and critique. Thanks also to Tina Fetner and Sarah Sobieraj for their writing support and inspiration.

WORKS CITED

Allen, Jafari. 2012. "One Way or Another: Erotic Subjectivity in Cuba." *American Ethnologist* 39 (2): 325–38.

Behar, Ruth. 1996. *The Vulnerable Observer: Anthropology That Breaks Your Heart.* Boston: Beacon Press.

Brim, Matt, and Amin Ghaziani. 2016. "Introduction: Queer Methods." *WSQ: Women's Studies Quarterly* 44 (3–4): 14–27.

Browne, Kath, and Catherine J. Nash, eds. 2010. *Queer Methods and Methodologies: Intersecting Queer Theories and Social Science Research.* Farnham, UK: Ashgate.

Clarke, Jennifer G., Megan R. Herbert, Cynthia Rosengard, Jennifer S. Rose, Kristen M. DaSilva, and Michael D. Stein. 2006. "Reproductive Health Care and Family Planning Needs among Incarcerated Women." *American Journal of Public Health* 96 (5): 834–39.

Conly, Catherine. 1998. *The Women's Prison Association: Supporting Women Offenders and Their Families.* Washington, DC: National Institute of Justice.

Covington, Stephanie S., and Barbara E. Bloom. 2007. "Gender Responsive Treatment and Services in Correctional Settings." *Women & Therapy* 29 (3–4): 9–33.

Ferguson, Roderick. 2007. "The Relevance of Race for the Study of Sexuality." In *A Companion to LGBT/Q Studies,* edited by Molly McGarry and George Haggerty, 109–23. Hoboken, NJ: Blackwell Publishers.

Fields, Jessica. 2013. "Feminist Ethnography: A Practice of Ambivalent Observance." *Journal of Contemporary Ethnography* 42 (4): 492–500.

Fields, Jessica, Isela González, Kathleen Hentz, Margaret Rhee, and Catherine White. 2008. "Learning from and with Incarcerated Women: Emerging Lessons from a

Participatory Action Study of Sexuality Education." *Sexuality Research and Social Policy* 5 (2): 71–84.

Fine, Michelle, Kathy Boudin, Iris Bowen, Judith Clark, Donna Hylton, Migdalia Martinez, Missy, Rosemarie A. Roberts, Pamela Smart, María Elena Torre, and Debora Upegui. 2003. "Participatory Action Research: From Within and Beyond Prison Bars." In *Qualitative Research in Psychology: Expanding Perspectives in Methodology and Design*, edited by Paul M. Camic, Jean E. Rhodes, and Lucy Yardley, 173–98. Washington, DC: American Psychological Association.

Fine, Michelle, and Maria E. Torre. 2006. "Intimate Details: Participatory Action Research in Prison." *Action Research* 4: 253–69.

Frankenberg, Ruth. 1993. *White Women, Race Matters: The Social Construction of Whiteness*. Minneapolis: University of Minnesota Press.

González-López, Gloria. 2011. "Mindful Ethics: Comments on Informant-Centered Practices in Sociological Research." *Qualitative Sociology* 34 (3): 447–61.

Gordon, Avery F. 1997. *Ghostly Matters: Haunting and the Sociological Imagination*. 2nd ed. Minneapolis: University of Minnesota Press.

Gordon, Avery F. 2004. *Keeping Good Time: Reflections on Knowledge, Power, and People*. Boulder, CO: Paradigm Publishers.

Halberstam, Jack. 2011. *The Queer Art of Failure*. Durham, NC: Duke University Press.

Holland, Sharon Patricia. 2012. *The Erotic Life of Racism*. Durham, NC: Duke University Press.

Human Rights Watch. 1996. *All Too Familiar: Sexual Abuse of Women in U.S. State Prisons*. New York: Human Rights Watch.

Kantor, Elizabeth. 2003. *HIV Transmission and Prevention in Prisons*. Berkeley: University of California Press.

Lewin, Ellen, and William L. Leap, eds. 1996. *Out in the Field: Reflections of Lesbian and Gay Anthropologists*. Urbana: University of Illinois Press.

Lewin, Kurt. 1946. "Action Research and Minority Problems." *Journal of Social Issues* 2 (4): 34–46.

Lorde, Audre. 1978. "Uses of the Erotic." In *Sister Outsider: Essays and Speeches*, 53–59. Trumansburg, NY: Crossing Press.

Love, Heather. 2015. "Doing Being Deviant: Deviance Studies, Description, and the Queer Ordinary." *differences* 26 (1): 74–95.

Minkler, Meredith, Angela G. Blackwell, Mildred Thompson, and Heather Tamir. 2003. "Community-Based Participatory Research: Implications for Public Health Funding." *American Journal of Public Health* 93 (8): 1210–13.

Minkler, Meredith, and Nina Wallerstein, eds. 2008. *Community-Based Participatory Research for Health: From Process to Outcomes*. New York: Wiley.

Rhee, Margaret, Kate Monico Klein, Isela González, and Allyse Gray. 2013. "'It's Your Story Too': Reconsidering Feminism, HIV/AIDS, and the Digital Divide." *FemBot Collective*. Blog. January 11. http://fembotcollective.org/blog/.

Richie, Beth E. 1996. *Compelled to Crime: The Gender Entrapment of Battered Black Women*. New York: Routledge.

Richie, Beth E. 2002. "The Social Impact of Mass Incarceration on Women." In *Invisible Punishment: The Collateral Consequences of Mass Imprisonment*, edited by Marc Mauer and Meda Chesney-Lind, 136–49. New York: New Press.

Tinsley, Omise'eke Natasha. 2008. "Black Atlantic, Queer Atlantic: Queer Imaginings of the Middle Passage." *GLQ: A Journal of Lesbian and Gay Studies* 14 (2–3): 191–215.

Wiegman, Robyn. 2012. *Object Lessons*. Durham, NC: Duke University Press.

Williams, Allison, Ronald Labonte, James E. Randall, and Nazeem Muhajarine. 2005. "Establishing and Sustaining Community-University Partnerships: A Case Study of Quality of Life Research." *Critical Public Health* 15 (3): 291–302.

3

Queer Survey Research and the Ontological Dimensions of Heterosexism

PATRICK R. GRZANKA

"Subjugated" standpoints are preferred because they seem to promise more adequate, sustained, objective, transforming accounts of the world. But how to see from below is a problem requiring at least as much skill with bodies and language, with the mediations of vision, as the "highest" technoscientific visualizations.
—Donna Haraway, "Situated Knowledges: The Science Question in Feminism and the Privilege of Partial Perspective" (1988)

I want to be clear about what I am *not* going to do here. First, I am not offering a defense of quantitative social inquiry. This has been done to varying degrees of success by many people who are more sophisticated statisticians than I (e.g., Cokley and Awad 2013; Jayaratne 1983; Westerman 2014). Rather, on the occasion of editors Amin Ghaziani and Matt Brim's field-defining provocation "to make space" for a more expansive methodological vision (Brim and Ghaziani 2016, 18), I am attempting to engage with one dominant, longstanding line of reasoning among critical social scientists and humanists suggesting that mathematical reduction is fundamentally problematic (Krenz and Sax 1986; Michell 2003; Pugh 1990). In this frame, essentially all attempts at quantitative measurement are necessarily inaccurate, misrepresentative, and potentially violent, particularly those contemporary approaches that we might identify with the rise of post-positivism (Eagly and Riger 2014). To the post-positivist, the myth of objective reality is apparently abandoned but actually reconstituted in the search for a close-enough approximation of the empirical universe, which is still presumed to exist somewhere "out

84

there." The "post" in post-positivism comes to serve as a political gesture more than as an epistemic reorientation: we probably won't find the truth, but we might as well keep trying. Some of the staunchest advocates of post-positivism in the social sciences are social psychologists, who are rightfully critiqued for having carved up the social universe via survey instruments, implicit association tests, and externally invalid experimental designs, which purport to tell us copious details about a world that looks very white, very masculine, and very American while claiming to be none of these things (Gergen 1973; Guthrie 2003). Central to many feminist, antiracist, Marxist, and queer critiques of social science is a rejection of quantitative reductionism that is perceived as immanent to post-positivism. By way of French philosopher and eminent historian of the human sciences Michel Foucault (1970), I suggest that this line of reasoning mistakes the *effects* of oppressive research practices for the *causes* of these reductionist paradigms.

What follows is also not a rubric of best practices for queer theory–informed statistical inquiry, partially because I have no idea what such a rubric would look like, and also partially because I think that a sustained interrogation of a queer method should actually start at the level of *methodology*—which feminist philosopher of science Sandra Harding (1987) famously distinguished as theories of research practices and the work they can do in the world, as opposed to the tools (i.e., methods) we use to conduct specific research practices (see also DeVault and Gross 2012). Accordingly, from the perspective of critical psychology, I am going to offer one example of a survey instrument that was developed with and through queer theoretical frames and that reflects a commitment both to statistical rigor and feminist objectivity (Haraway 1988). This particular instrument, the Sexual Orientation Beliefs Scale (SOBS) (Arseneau et al. 2013), may help us to examine complex relationships between heterosexist attitudes and ontologies of sexuality—in other words, beliefs about what sexual orientation actually is. I argue that the unique analytic potential of the SOBS is to reveal relationships between attitudes and beliefs that are otherwise obscured by hegemonic discourses about biological essentialism, or what sociologist of sexuality Jane Ward referred to as "the nearly obsessive focus on whether individual people are born gay or straight" (2015, 34). Biological essentialism is also integral to the neoliberal rights discourse that queer theorist Lisa Duggan named "Equality, Inc." (2003, 43). Finally, I will briefly introduce the results of one study in which my colleagues and I took a "person-centered" analytic approach, as opposed to a "variable-centered" approach, and found evidence of the weakness of biological-determinist beliefs about sexual orientation to distinguish between individuals with high versus low levels of modern homonegativity. With queer theory-informed instrumentation, I suggest that this person-centered approach possesses a provisional capacity to function as what Amin Ghaziani and Matt Brim, in the title of this innovative volume, call a "queer method."

Part 1: The Retreat of the Mathesis

In *The Order of Things* (1970), the question of quantification is actually subordinate to Foucault's broader concerns about representational practices in the social sciences. His archaeology, at once a history of science and a philosophical critique, explores the transformations in the structure of Western knowledge that anticipate the constitution of modern(ist) social science—specifically sociology, psychology, and anthropology. In the analytic crescendo of the book, he outlines the epistemic event in the order of knowledge that he identifies as the constitution of "man" (Foucault's gendered language) as an object of scientific knowledge—wherein man is a thing that can and should be known by way of empirical inquiry. He uses this event to distinguish between the classical and modern epistemes and writes at some length about the concept of the "mathesis," a kind of proto-Cartesian theory of everything. The mathesis was essentially a general theory of representation in which mathematics would possess universal explanatory power: the über-theory. Foucault elaborates:

> In the Classical period, the field of knowledge, from the project of an analysis of representation to the theme of the mathesis universalis, was perfectly homogenous: all knowledge, of whatever kind, proceeded to the ordering of its material by the establishment of differences and defined those differences by the establishment of an order. . . . Questioned at this archaeological level, the field of the modern episteme is *not ordered in accordance with the ideal of a perfect mathematization*, nor does it unfold, on the basis of a purity, a long descending sequence

of knowledge progressively more burdened with empiricity. (1970, 346; emphasis mine)

In a move that we can see in the retrospective context of his oeuvre as quintessentially Foucauldian, he suggests that critical attention to the rise of mathematics that we today would associate with the development of positivism, structural functionalism, and behaviorism (Orr 2006) actually effaces the epistemic choreography that makes the positivist human sciences so violent. He continues:

> But it is *not* in its relation to mathematics that biology acquired its autonomy and defined its particular positivity. And the same was true for the human sciences: *it was the retreat of the mathesis, and not the advance of mathematics*, that made it possible for man to constitute himself as an object of knowledge. . . . But to imagine that the human sciences defined their most radical project and inaugurated their positive history when it was decided to apply the calculation of probabilities to the phenomena of political opinion, and to employ logarithms as a means of measuring the increase of intensity in sensations, that would be to take a superficial counter-effect for the fundamental event. (Foucault 1970, 350–51; emphasis mine)

The "fundamental event" was not caused by an explosion of mathematic inquiry or technological advances that enabled the manipulation of increasingly immense datasets, according to Foucault. Conversely, he asserts that the advance of mathematics was the *consequence* of the retreat of the mathesis and the contemporaneous introduction of the empirically knowable object of "man"—not its cause. This is of special importance to an interrogation of queer methods, I think, insomuch as Foucault's archeology of the human sciences suggests that all social scientific optics of knowing—both quantitative and qualitative—possess the capacity for subjugation and unjust reductionism, which postcolonial feminist philosopher Gayatri Spivak calls "epistemic violence" (1988, 271) and Black feminist philosopher Kristie Dotson refers to as "repetitive, reliable" practices of silencing (2011, 241). The colonial ethnographer and the cybernetician are equivalent villains in Foucault's critique not because of their methods per se but because of their location in the modern episteme. In other words, the Likert scale is not a priori more oppressive than grounded theory—and in fact a fixation on the problematics of quantitative survey research actually diverts attention from the broader and pervasive practices of precarious knowledge production that are endemic to the social sciences.

For Foucault, the argument against statistics is the conceptual kin of the repressive hypothesis he later dismantles in *The History of Sexuality*, Volume 1 (1978). Foucault suggests that the commonsense argument that the rise of modernity corresponded with the repression of sexuality is not merely inaccurate. Rather, he argues that our investment in the concept of repression is actually symptomatic of, not in opposition to, a larger discourse on sexuality that is deeply oppressive. While prohibition has been commonly deployed as a form of sexual control, Foucault asserts that modernity is defined by a multiplication of discourses on sexuality, as opposed to a pervasive cultural silence around sex. Accordingly, in our pursuit of understanding and challenging discursive regimes of sexuality, he posits, "Perhaps the point to consider is not the level of indulgence or the quantity of repression but the form of power that was exercised" (1978, 41). Similarly, in the context of the fetishization of the quantitative among the social sciences, Foucault neither argues that statistics are inconsequential nor that quantitative inquiry is a rarely used form of representation. His point is not that statistical reductionism does not occur but that we are missing the point if we understand it to be the source of the social sciences' epistemic situation, which he describes as both "perilous and in peril" (1970, 379).

In the same way that *History* offers a glimmer of resistance to biopolitical regimes through the study of bodies and how they have come to matter, *The Order of Things* likewise alludes to opportunities for critical social inquiry. In "The Discourse on Language," Foucault (1972) explicates two modes of his own work—genealogy and critique—that enable him, first, to trace knowledge-power relations and, second, to challenge discursive, institutional structures organized by the "will to truth" that are seemingly impervious and unassailable. The "will to truth" produces the illusion that disciplinary technologies of knowing, from ethnography (Abu-Lughod 1990) to MRI (Joyce 2008), will reveal what sociologist Emile Durkheim ([1897] 2007) argued was positivism's promise: stable, impersonal knowledge. Marking, naming, and tracing the ritualistic practices of disciplinarity facilitates the destabilization of what appear as permanent, inflexible rules of disciplinary knowledge production. But what is less obvious from Foucault's writing is how we might actually go about the business of the social sciences without reproducing the will to truth. One can read his work, then, as an invitation to abandon the myth of achieving a position of exteriority to knowledge production practices—what feminist philosopher of science Donna Haraway (1988) would later call the "god trick"—and to consider how all methods, both quantitative and qualitative, conceal a capacity for violence. Capacity is not, however, equivalent to inevitability. And so Foucault evades the question of method, but he also creates an opening.

Part 2: Quantifying Ontologies

Much of my work, situated at the intersection of sociology, psychology, and science and technology studies, engages psychology's particular capacity for reiterating harm and promoting forms of social transformation and resistance (e.g., Grzanka 2016; Grzanka and Mann 2014). The SOBS was born out of an interdisciplinary queer research team at the University of Maryland, College Park, during a time when psychological discourse on the immutability of sexual orientation became a political maxim amid attempts to resist and prohibit sexual orientation conversion "therapies" (Brian and Grzanka 2014; Waidzunas 2015). As sexual minority graduate students immersed in critical feminist and queer theoretical perspectives, we were suspicious of the wholesale embrace of biologically inflected strategic essentialism as the tactic by which rights would be secured, including freedom from dangerous so-called therapies and freedom to marry and serve in the U.S. armed forces (Duggan 1994). The SOBS, which began as counseling psychologist Julie Arseneau's (2008) dissertation project, developed into an attempt to better understand what queer people actually believed about the nature of sexual orientation and then grew into an investigation of how LGBT-identified and straight people's beliefs about sexual orientation may differ (Arseneau et al. 2013). Ultimately, we hoped that the SOBS might help to illuminate how people understand sexual orientation categories and evaluate members of those categories.

Though the project began well before Lady Gaga turned "born this way" into a catchphrase, her zeitgeist suggested that we were on to something. In developing the instrument, we aimed to address several weaknesses in the extant psychological literature and took steps to infuse queer and feminist theories into our work. First, we started generating items for the SOBS via qualitative work, that is, conversations with queer people about their own sexual orientation beliefs and what they thought others believed. These conversations were formal and informal brainstorming sessions among academics, item generation in non-academic settings, and casual conversations with friends and colleagues. Furthermore, the entire first half of the initial validation study was conducted with queer people, in a marked departure from the existing literature on psychological essentialism, most of which focuses on majority group beliefs about minorities (e.g., Haslam and Levy 2006; Hegarty and Pratto 2001). In collecting and analyzing reactions from queer subjects about items developed by queer subjects about sexuality, we entered into the precarious position of representing and interrogating the beliefs of the variously marginalized. While we suspected that our queer respondents might have more sophisticated and critical understandings of sexual orientation than heterosexual respondents, whose straight privilege insulated them from having to think much at all about sexual orientation, we were committed to including a range of beliefs into the SOBS, not just those that reflected our political sensibilities.

Accordingly, we built three primary belief domains into the SOBS that would extend those already covered in the literature: essentialist, social constructionist, and constructivist beliefs. Social constructionist ideas about the historical and cultural contingency of sexual orientation categories had previously been elided in the research, and notions of sexual orientation agency and choice, which psychologists refer to as constructivist beliefs, had become somewhat taboo in contemporary sexual politics. For example, when actress Cynthia Nixon said that being gay is a choice for her, she received tremendous criticism from the gay left. She said, "A certain section of our community is very concerned that it not be seen as a choice, because if it's a choice, then we could opt out" (qtd. in Witchel 2012). The backlash against Nixon stood in stark contrast to the radical queer politics of the prior century, including well-known agentic arguments, such as the following from Gloria Anzaldúa:

"*I made the choice to be queer* (for some it is genetically inherent)" (1987, 41; emphasis in original). Rather than avoid constructivist themes or foreclose them as symptomatic of internalized homonegativity, we included several items that emphasized agency and choice in the constitution of sexual orientation. Although we developed ninety-one items that reflected a wide range of beliefs, we excluded those that were explicitly heterosexist so as to avoid developing an instrument that could be easily used to reinforce negative ideas about sexual minorities. Finally, we concentrated on the multidimensionality of sexual orientation beliefs, rather than the traditional psychometric priorities of parsimony and mutual exclusivity, so as to develop an instrument in which individuals could endorse multiple beliefs simultaneously, even if those beliefs might appear to contradict one another.

In our LGBT-identified sample of over six hundred online survey respondents, we found four groupings of sexual orientation beliefs that are conceptually distinct but correlated and together compose the thirty-five-item instrument. The first group of items (i.e., subscale), "Naturalness," describes four basic beliefs: sexual orientation is innate and biologically based, immutable, stable across cultures, and characterized by early life fixity. A sample item is, "Biology is the main basis of an individual's sexual orientation." The second subscale, "Discreteness," describes the belief that sexual orientation is organized with clear boundaries between category groupings and that an individual may claim membership in only one category grouping. A sample item from this subscale is, "Sexual orientation is a category with distinct boundaries: A person is either gay/lesbian or heterosexual." The third subscale, which included items such as "Knowing a person's sexual orientation tells you a lot about them," we called "Entitativity," which is a social psychology word for "group-ness." These items capture two essentialist beliefs: the informativeness of sexual orientation categories, and the interconnectedness and uniformity among sexual orientation group members. The final subscale, "Social and Personal Importance," is composed of items that emphasize the relative importance of sexual orientation either intrapsychically or interpersonally, such as "Using terms like 'lesbian,' 'gay,' 'bisexual,' and 'heterosexual' only reinforces stereotypes."

Next, we turned to the question of "factorial invariance" to examine if this particular organization of items would be replicated in a sample composed of straight-identified college students. In this independent sample of almost four hundred undergraduates, we found that the subscales and distribution of items were slightly different, which led us to create a thirty-one-item Form Two of the SOBS for use with samples involving straight and sexual minority respondents. The "Discreteness" and "Naturalness" subscales were nearly identical, but two new subscales emerged in our analysis. The items on the new "Homogeneity" subscale emphasized similarity among sexual orientation group members. The new "Informativeness" subscale was a combination of five "Social and Personal Importance" items from Form One plus three items that previously loaded on the "Entitativity" subscale. In contrast to our findings in the LGBT-only sample, this subscale included no explicitly political items and instead stressed the knowledge and information gained from knowing or perceiving an individual's sexual orientation.

The initial validation study established the means through which to explore these beliefs and their connection to attitudes about sexual minorities, as well as sexual minorities' own self-evaluations (see Morandini et al.'s 2015 use of the SOBS). Although several items that were developed to reflect social constructionist and constructivist themes remained in the final instrument as reverse-scored items (i.e., items that reflect the "opposite" ideas of the other items on a subscale), each of the subscales generally reflect essentialist themes. Nevertheless, the incorporation of social constructionist and agentic items alongside more traditionally recognized essentialist beliefs resulted in a multidimensional scale that was rooted in queer theory and queer-identified respondents' perceptions of sexual orientation. By synergizing queer and feminist theories with the social scientific tools of factor analysis and structural equation modeling, we created a queer instrument—or in Haraway's terms, a semiotic technology for making meanings (1988)—through which to interrogate the nature-culture nexus that is psyche and society (1991). But a survey instrument is just a series of words with scoring instructions. We may have scripted the technology with queer meanings (Akrich 1992), but its radical and/or conservative capacities—what it can or cannot tell us about the social life of sexual orientation ontologies, as well as how these knowledges may be used or abused—remains to be seen.

Part 3: Queer(ing) Statistics?

Although these beliefs are certainly interesting in and of themselves, to me the SOBS is only useful insomuch as it may be able to expose social dynamics that are obfuscated by dominant discourses about sexual orientation. Though qualitative research is adept at uncovering silences and excavating hidden meanings in textual data, quantitative analysis can also be useful for circumventing normative, hegemonic logics and for illuminating implicit or unconscious attitudes. While the SOBS is not a test of implicit attitudes in the social psychological sense of the term (e.g., Fazio and Olson 2003), it does attempt to capture beliefs without conflating them with attitudes. This means that the SOBS might illustrate how people who have similar beliefs about sexuality may have significantly different attitudes toward sexual minorities, and vice versa. I would argue that the connections between heterogeneous attitudes and beliefs are especially difficult to detect in the context of contemporary homonormative discourse that suggests being born gay is the only way to be gay (Duggan 2003; Osmundson 2011).

One common way to go about this kind of statistical inquiry is to use what my colleague Katharine Zeiders and her collaborators in developmental psychology have called a "variable-centered approach" (2013). In this framework, relationships among dependent and independent variables are foregrounded and explored through correlations, analysis of variance, or regression models based on means or sums of scores on particular measurement tools (see figure 3.1).

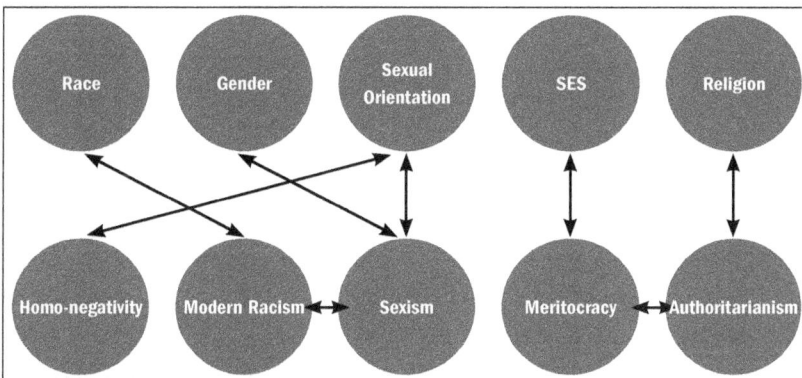

Figure 3.1. A variable-centered approach to statistical inquiry.

For example, we might examine how membership in a racial category (e.g., identifying as Black or white) might predict higher or lower
levels of "modern" or colorblind racism (Neville et al. 2013). We could
examine how gender identity might predict sexist attitudes and do the
same with sexual orientation, which might also correspond with psychometric constructs such as homonegativity (Morrison and Morrison
2002). Scholars have examined how socioeconomic status predicts beliefs in meritocracy (Horberg, Kraus, and Keltner 2013) and how religious affiliation and religiosity might correspond with authoritarianism
(Altemeyer and Hunsberger 1992). And we can also explore relationships between outcome or dependent variables, such as the correlations
between contemporary forms of aversive racism and ambivalent sexism, as well as the links between beliefs in meritocracy and right-wing
authoritarianism.

We know that relationships among constructs like those in figure 3.1
are actually more complex than bidirectional correlations or one-way
causal dynamics. There are often important qualifications to relationships between constructs, which means that we have to contend with
a moderating variable such that the relationship between X and Y depends upon Z. And what about when gender, race, sexual orientation,
and social class all affect homonegativity? We can conceptualize and test
four-way interactions and so forth, but statistical problems (e.g., power,
sampling error) aside, these models still prioritize variables over actual
respondents. In other words, variable-centered approaches are always
limited by their emphasis on variables themselves, such as how categorical variables (e.g., race) relate to continuous variables (e.g., a test of
racism). Although they can show correspondence and even causality,
variable-centered approaches often leave important practical questions
about the empirical world unanswered, including the following: How
frequently does a particular kind of response pattern occur on a given
instrument? What kinds of important factors might prevent X person
from responding like other X people, and Y person responding like
other Y people?

In contrast to a variable-centered approach, which focuses on a specific variable and links it to a specified outcome, Zeiders and colleagues
advocate a *person-centered* approach, which examines variables "ho-
listically and realistically" in order to garner a clearer perspective on

the cumulative and interactive relationships among multiple variables (2013, 604). A person-centered approach provides information about *patterns* of responses and how these patterns, as opposed to individual variables, relate to a specified outcome. This approach explains that a person-centered instrument can unpack qualitative and quantitative differences in response patterns. Though it may seem counterintuitive to a qualitative researcher, Zeiders and her colleagues suggest that person-centered statistics can qualify how relationships among variables may look different for different groups of people in the same sample—groups that might otherwise be invisible. In other words, a person-centered analysis illuminates qualitatively distinct patterns of responses to multiple variables and shows how commonly (i.e., quantitatively) these patterns occur in the data. In the context of the SOBS, a person-centered approach allows us to consider how endorsement of multiple beliefs measured by the SOBS (such as belief in discreteness and naturalness) may co-occur among a substantial number of respondents, even though these individual subscales are only weakly correlated with each other (Arseneau et al. 2013). Furthermore, such an approach helps us to identify what kinds of things may predict a particular constellation of beliefs, such as scoring high on all four SOBS subscales, or scoring low on one and high on the other three.

Latent Profile Analysis (LPA) is a person-centered approach that combines the best qualities of strategies like cluster analysis—which allows researchers to analyze response patterns—with elements of structural equation modeling, which necessitates comparisons across conceptual models to assess how well a variety of models may fit (or not fit) the data. LPA allows researchers to analyze variance in responses across multiple continuous variables, create groupings of response patterns, and investigate the probability of respondents falling into different "classes" based on their responses across multiple variables, such as the subscales of the SOBS. The "latent" part of Latent Profile Analysis is that it uncovers "groups" of respondents who feel or think similarly without respondents identifying explicitly as part of that respective group. Unlike variable-centered approaches, the analytic weight in LPA is placed on actual individuals' holistic responses to a battery of items, rather than on statistical relationships among variable scores divorced from the respondents who produced those scores.

Like arguably all forms of quantification, LPA involves commensuration, or what sociologists Wendy Nelson Espeland and Mitchell Stevens (1998) describe as the social process by which disparate things—in this case, beliefs—are organized into artificial groupings for the purposes of comparison. However, unlike variable-centered approaches that tacitly embrace commensuration as inevitable, LPA enables researchers to resist the arbitrary clustering of respondents and to consider nuanced, atypical, and even seemingly illogical response patterns that variable-centered approaches might dismiss or ignore.

Figure 3.2 visualizes the results of an LPA that my colleagues and I conducted in two independent samples of college students: one mixed-gender sample (N=379) and another sample of only women respondents (N=266) (Grzanka, Zeiders, and Miles 2016). We achieved similar results in both samples, so I have combined them here for conceptual clarity. We called the group with the squares "Naturalness-Only" (NO) (n=213). While these respondents were higher on "born this way"–type beliefs, they were lower on the other three belief domains, which are labeled on the y-axis. The group with high scores on all four subscales—the stars—we call "Multidimensional Essentialism" (ME) (n=166), because these respondents were relatively high (i.e., above the five-point scale's midpoint) on all four dimensions. We examined social class, gender, sexual orientation, and race to see if membership in particular identity groups would predict likelihood of falling in either class and found that only being heterosexual indicated a significantly lower probability of being in the "Naturalness-Only" group. Most importantly, the endorsement of "born this way" beliefs did not primarily distinguish these two groups. It was their relative endorsement of *other* sexual orientation beliefs that most significantly distinguished them. Conversely, it would be accurate to describe both groups as *sharing* a belief in the innateness and immutability of sexual orientation as measured by the SOBS.

In the second sample, we found two similar groups, both with shared endorsement of "born this way" beliefs but differing on the three other SOBS subscales—plus a new, third group. This relatively smaller group of only thirty-six respondents was high on "Discreteness," "Homogeneity," and "Informativeness," but lowest (though still above the midpoint with a mean score of 2.97 out of 5) on "Naturalness"; accordingly, we refer to them as "High-DHI." This time, sexual orientation did not cor-

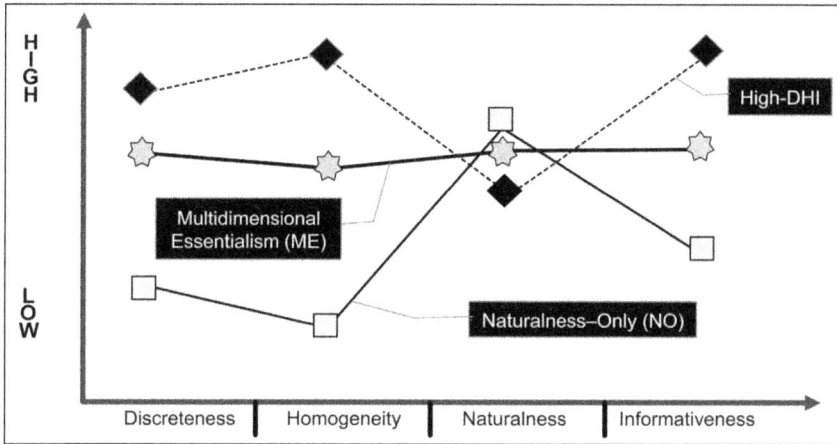

Figure 3.2. A person-centered approach to statistical inquiry. The *x*-axis represents the four subscales of the SOBS. The *y*-axis represents the respondents' scores on the subscales ranging from higher to lower. The Multidimensional Essentialism and Naturalness-Only profiles emerged in both samples (*N*=379 and *N*=266), whereas the High-DHI profile (*N*=36) was limited to the women-only sample.

respond with group membership, but we included attitudinal measures and found that lower scores on psychologists Melanie Morrison and Todd Morrison's (2002) test of modern homonegativity—basically, aversion as opposed to explicit hatred toward gay men—predicted membership in the "Naturalness-Only" group relative to the "Multidimensional Essentialism" and "High-DHI" classes. This means that multidimensional essentialists and those highest in discreteness, homogeneity, and informativeness were likely to also score high on homonegativity, *but* they scored similarly on "born this way" beliefs when compared to those with lower levels of homonegativity. So, here's what we're thinking: belief in the discreteness, homogeneity, and informativeness of sexual orientation categories *more significantly* distinguishes these groups of respondents than does belief in the naturalness of sexual orientation. Respondents high in all of these beliefs are more likely to be straight and homonegative. These beliefs are inevitably subject to transformation over time, and the SOBS cannot measure all possible beliefs about sexual orientation in the contemporary United States. The SOBS also does not tell us how people actually understand its individual items, only the degree to which they endorse them. Nonetheless, at least in terms of these samples derived from a college student population in the Southwest, our findings suggest that a lot of people believe in "born this way," but it's *what else* you believe about sexual orientation that really matters.

But that is not really my point. Rather, I would suggest that it is quite difficult to see these dynamics if we listen to mainstream LGBT left discourse, political moderates, or the conservative religious right, particularly as general support for the biological basis of sexual orientation continues to rise among Americans (Masci 2015). Feminist biomedicalization theory (Clarke et al. 2003) would suggest that biological and epigenetic accounts of sexual orientation's origins will persist—regardless of evidence to the contrary—as advanced biomedical technosciences continue to extend their reach into heretofore unseen dimensions of human experience (e.g., Waidzunas and Epstein 2015). If we examine biodeterminist beliefs in isolation—or only through exclusively qualitative, interpretivist means—we might not observe the meaningful differences in these beliefs that distinguish individuals who exhibit higher or lower levels of homonegative attitudes or fail to see how common (or uncommon) these beliefs actually are. This kind of statistical work, which emphasizes multidimensionality, embraces rather than shies away from complexity and social constructionism, and focuses on actual people's responses rather than aggregated and disambiguated variables, has the potential to realize the spirit of queer methods. Queer methods do not lead us outside or beyond the positivist origins of contemporary social science, but they do encourage reorientations toward the histories and potential futures of those methods. I suggest that queer statistics might reorient the methods by which we study sexuality in much the same way that queer of color critique and intersectionality theory have compelled interrogations and reorientations of queer theory itself (Ferguson 2004; 2012; Johnson 2001).

Statistical research is unquestionably rife with opportunities for error, including miscalculations, misinterpretations, and overgeneralizations. But uncoupling statistics from their epistemic anchor in post-positivist paradigms enables us to imagine quantification otherwise: to unmoor it from violent truth-making and to use numbers as *one* way of accounting, not the *only* or even *preferred* arithmetic for making sense of the social world. Person-centered approaches such as Latent Profile Analysis can be used complementarily, I contend, with critical, queer methodological orientations, and they can also be used to carve up the universe into reductionist slices that obscure relations of power and inequality. However, there are other ways to envision "slices" of the universe; Haraway (1997) calls them "diffractions." Diffractions are modest accounts of what you see that open up possibilities for other ways of knowing. The SOBS is a tool that, when put to use in queer ways to do some queer work in the world, can facilitate more adequate, sustained, radical interventions into our present and future, rather than simply reinforcing the strategic essentialism of Equality, Inc. (Duggan 1994; 2003).

WORKS CITED

Abu-Lughod, Lila. 1990. "Can There Be a Feminist Ethnography?" *Women & Performance: A Journal of Feminist Theory* 5 (1): 7–27.

Akrich, Madeleine. 1992. "The De-Scription of Technical Objects." In *Shaping Technology/Building Society: Studies in Sociotechnical Change*, edited by Wiebe E. Bijker and John Law, 205–24. Cambridge, MA: MIT Press.

Altemeyer, Bob, and Bruce Hunsberger. 1992. "Authoritarianism, Religious Fundamentalism, Quest, and Prejudice." *International Journal for the Psychology of Religion* 2 (2): 113–33.

Anzaldúa, Gloria. 1987. *Borderlands/La Frontera: The New Mestiza*. San Francisco: Aunt Lute Books.

Arseneau, Julie R. 2008. "'Born That Way' and Other Notions: Measuring Sexual Minority Individuals' Beliefs about Sexual Orientation." PhD diss., University of Maryland.

Arseneau, Julie R., Patrick R. Grzanka, Joseph R. Miles, and Ruth E. Fassinger. 2013. "Development and Initial Validation of the Sexual Orientation Beliefs Scale (SOBS)." *Journal of Counseling Psychology* 60 (3): 407–20.

Brian, Jenny Dyck, and Patrick R. Grzanka. 2014. "The Machine in the Garden of Desire." *American Journal of Bioethics: Neuroscience* 5 (1): 17–18.

Brim, Matt, and Amin Ghaziani. 2016. "Introduction: Queer Methods." *WSQ: Women's Studies Quarterly* 44 (3–4): 14–27.

Clarke, Adele E., Janet K. Shim, Laura Mamo, Jennifer Ruth Fosket, and Jennifer R. Fishman. 2003. "Biomedicalization: Technoscientific Transformations of Health, Illness, and U.S. Biomedicine." *American Sociological Review* 68: 161–94.

Cokley, Kevin, and Germine H. Awad. 2013. "In Defense on Quantitative Methods: Using the 'Master's Tools' to Promote Social Justice." *Journal of Social Action in Counseling and Psychology* 5 (2): 26–41.

DeVault, Marjorie L., and Glenda Gross. 2012. "Feminist Qualitative Interviewing: Experience, Talk, and Knowledge." In *Handbook of Feminist Research: Theory and Praxis*, edited by Sharlene Nagy Hesse-Biber, 206–37. Thousand Oaks, CA: Sage.

Dotson, Kristie. 2011. "Tracking Epistemic Violence, Tracking Practices of Silencing." *Hypatia* 26 (2): 236–57.
Duggan, Lisa. 1994. "Queering the State." *Social Text* 39: 1–14.
Duggan, Lisa. 2003. *The Twilight of Equality?: Neoliberalism, Cultural Politics, and the Attack on Democracy.* Boston: Beacon Press.
Durkheim, Emile. (1897) 2007. *On Suicide.* New York: Penguin.
Eagly, Alice H., and Stephanie Riger. 2014. "Feminism and Psychology: Critiques of Methods and Epistemology." *American Psychologist* 69 (7): 685–702.
Espeland, Wendy Nelson, and Mitchell L. Stevens. 1998. "Commensuration as a Social Process." *Annual Review of Sociology* 24: 313–43.
Fazio, Russell H., and Michael A. Olson. 2003. "Implicit Measures in Social Cognition Research: Their Meaning and Use." *Annual Review of Psychology* 54: 297–327.
Ferguson, Roderick A. 2004. *Aberrations in Black: Toward a Queer of Color Critique.* Minneapolis: University of Minnesota Press.
Ferguson, Roderick A. 2012. "Reading Intersectionality." *Trans-Scripts* 2: 91–99.
Foucault, Michel. 1970. *The Order of Things: An Archaeology of the Human Sciences.* New York: Vintage Books.
Foucault, Michel. 1972. *The Archaeology of Knowledge and the Discourse on Language.* Translated by A. M. Sheridan Smith. New York: Pantheon Books.
Foucault, Michel. 1978. *The History of Sexuality*, Volume 1: *An Introduction.* Translated by Robert Hurley. New York: Random House.
Gergen, Kenneth J. 1973. "Social Psychology as History." *Journal of Personality and Social Psychology* 26 (2): 309–20.
Grzanka, Patrick R. 2016. "Undoing the Psychology of Gender: Intersectional Feminism and Social Science Pedagogy." In *Intersectional Pedagogy: A Model for Complicating Identity and Social Justice*, edited by Kim A. Case, 61–79. New York: Routledge.
Grzanka, Patrick R., and Emily S. Mann. 2014. "Queer Youth Suicide and the Psycho-politics of 'It Gets Better.'" *Sexualities* 17 (4): 369–93.
Grzanka, Patrick R., Katharine H. Zeiders, and Joseph R. Miles. 2016. "Beyond 'Born This Way?': Reconsidering Sexual Orientation Beliefs and Attitudes." *Journal of Counseling Psychology* 63 (1): 63–75.
Guthrie, Robert V. 2003. *Even the Rat Was White: A Historical View of Psychology.* 2nd ed. Carbondale, IL: Pearson.
Haraway, Donna J. 1988. "Situated Knowledges: The Science Question in Feminism and the Privilege of Partial Perspective." *Feminist Studies* 14 (3): 575–99.
Haraway, Donna J. 1991. "A Cyborg Manifesto: Science, Technology, and Socialist-Feminism in the Late Twentieth Century." In *Simians, Cyborgs, and Women: The Reinvention of Nature*, 149–81. New York: Routledge.
Haraway, Donna J. 1997. *Modest_Witness@Second_Millenium.FemaleMan_Meets_OncoMouse: Feminism and Technoscience.* New York: Routledge.
Harding, Sandra. 1987. *Feminism and Methodology.* Bloomington: Indiana University Press.

Haslam, Nick, and Sheri R. Levy. 2006. "Essentialist Beliefs about Homosexuality: Structure and Implications for Prejudice." *Personality and Social Psychology Bulletin* 32 (4): 471–85.

Hegarty, Peter, and Felicia Pratto. 2001. "Sexual Orientation Beliefs: Their Relationships to Anti-Gay Attitudes and Biological Determinist Arguments." *Journal of Homosexuality* 41 (1): 121–35.

Horberg, E. J., Michael W. Kraus, and Dacher Keltner. 2013. "Pride Displays Communicate Self-Interest and Support for Meritocracy." *Journal of Personality and Social Psychology* 105 (1): 24–37.

Jayaratne, Toby. 1983. "The Value of Quantitative Methodology for Feminist Research." In *Theories of Women's Studies*, edited by Gloria Bowles and Renate Duelli Klein, 140–62. London: Routledge and Kegan Paul.

Johnson, E. Patrick. 2001. "'Quare' Studies, or (Almost) Everything I Know about Queer Studies I Learned from My Grandmother." *Text and Performance Quarterly* 21 (1): 1–25.

Joyce, Kelly A. 2008. *Magnetic Appeal: MRI and the Myth of Transparency*. Durham, NC: Duke University Press.

Krenz, Claudia, and Gilbert Sax. 1986. "What Quantitative Research Is and Why It Doesn't Work." *American Behavioral Scientist* 30 (1): 58–96.

Masci, David. 2015. "Americans Are Still Divided on Why People Are Gay." Pew Research Center, March 6. http://pewresearch.org/.

Michell, Joel. 2003. "The Quantitative Imperative: Positivism, Naïve Realism, and the Place of Qualitative Methods in Psychology." *Theory & Psychology* 13 (1): 5–31.

Morandini, James S., Alexander Blaszczynski, Michael W. Ross, Daniel S. Costa, and Ilan Dar-Nimrod. 2015. "Essentialist Beliefs, Sexual Identity Uncertainty, Internalized Homonegativity, and Psychological Wellbeing in Gay Men." *Journal of Counseling Psychology* 62 (3): 413–24.

Morrison, Melanie A., and Todd G. Morrison. 2002. "Development and Validation of a Scale Measuring Modern Prejudice toward Gay Men and Lesbian Women." *Journal of Homosexuality* 43 (1): 15–37.

Neville, Helen A., Germine H. Awad, James E. Brooks, Michelle P. Flores, and Jamie Bluemel. 2013. "Color-Blind Racial Ideology." *American Psychologist* 68 (6): 455–66.

Orr, Jackie. 2006. *Panic Diaries: A Genealogy of Panic Disorder*. Durham, NC: Duke University Press.

Osmundson, Joe. 2011. "'I Was Born This Way': Is Sexuality Innate, and Should It Matter?" *LGBTQ Policy Journal at the Harvard Kennedy School* 1: 15–25.www.hkslgbtq.com/.

Pugh, Ann. 1990. "My Statistics and Feminism—A True Story." In *Feminist Praxis*, edited by Liz Stanley, 103–13. London: Routledge.

Spivak, Gayatri C. 1988. "Can the Subaltern Speak?" In *Marxism and the Interpretation of Culture*, edited by Cary Nelson and Lawrence Grossberg, 271–313. Urbana: University of Illinois Press.

Waidzunas, Tom. 2015. *The Straight Line: How the Fringe Science of Ex-Gay Therapy Reoriented Sexuality*. Minneapolis: University of Minnesota Press.

Waidzunas, Tom, and Steven Epstein. 2015. "'For Men Arousal Is Orientation': Bodily Truthing, Technosexual Scripts, and the Materialization of Sexualities through the Phallometric Test." *Social Studies of Science* 45 (2): 187–213.

Ward, Jane. 2015. *Not Gay: Sex between Straight White Men*. New York: NYU Press.

Westerman, Michael A. 2014. "Examining Arguments against Quantitative Research: 'Case Studies' Illustrating the Challenge of Finding a Sound Philosophical Basis for a Human Sciences Approach to Psychology." *New Ideas in Psychology* 32: 42–58.

Witchel, Alex. 2012. "Life after 'Sex.'" *New York Times*, January 19. http://nytimes.com.

Zeiders, Katharine H., Mark W. Roosa, George P. Knight, and Nancy A. Gonzales. 2013. "Mexican American Adolescents' Profiles of Risk and Mental Health: A Person-Centered Longitudinal Approach." *Journal of Adolescence* 36: 603–12.

4

Methodological Problems and Possibilities in Gayborhood Studies

AMIN GHAZIANI

Consumer Affairs reported that the U.S. gay and lesbian population in 1990 clustered in coastal cities. By 2014, new hubs had emerged in Salt Lake City, Louisville, Norfolk, Indianapolis, and other places in conservative states, while traditional strongholds like Los Angeles, Atlanta, New York City, Miami, and Washington, DC, fell in the rankings of top residential locations.[1] As we make similar decisions about where to live (or where not to live), and as those patterns change over time, we redraw the cultural cartography of the city. Seattle provides a stark example. Between the 2000 and 2010 U.S. Census collections, the number of same-sex households increased in every single neighborhood—with one notable exception: the city's most visible gay district of Capitol Hill. There, the number of male and female same-sex households plummeted by 23 percent (Balk 2014). Zoom next onto the streets of San Francisco. A 2015 survey shows that 77 percent of people who have lived in the Castro for ten years or more self-identify as gay or lesbian. The percentage falls to 66 for those who have inhabited the area for five years or less, 61 percent for those who moved in during the last two years, and 55 percent for those who arrived in the past year (Staver 2015). Such migrations are inciting a "new turmoil" across the country, the *New Yorker* notes, as more straights select gay neighborhoods as their home while queer people fan out to other parts of the city and the suburbs, and into rural areas as well (Greenspan 2014).

What can we learn from the gayborhood? Rather than ask why they first formed or explain why they are changing in recent years, as I have done elsewhere (Ghaziani 2014b; 2015a), in this essay I will use my experience with studying them as an opportunity to reflect on five methodological problems that they pose for researchers: how to sample hidden populations; how to interview in ways that capture the interactional tone of life on city streets; how to position demographic statistics in a cultural context; how to move beyond binary conceptions of urban spaces as gay or straight; and how to identify indicators of sexual geographies. For me, these inquiries collectively capture the spirit of "queer methods" (Brim and Ghaziani 2016), and I use them to offer advice to students and established researchers alike: once you embrace fluidity, multiplicity, and silences, you will realize that the systematic and the chaotic are compatible in queer spatial analysis.

Census Conventions

Gayborhoods are not tightly sealed and walled-off districts; their boundaries are fuzzy. Existing studies in a number of disciplines have managed this problem by relying on census data to make inferences about the size of the gay and lesbian population and to identify the density of same-sex households in specific geographic regions. One common strategy is to create an "index of dissimilarity." The statistic represents the proportion of minority group members (same-sex partner households, in this case) who would have to exchange places, usually census tracts, with majority group members (different-sex households) in order to achieve an even residential distribution: a neighborhood that replicates the sexual composition of the city overall. The index measures residential segregation and spatial isolation (Massey, Rothwell, and Domina 2009). Its values range from zero to one hundred, where zero represents total integration and one hundred signifies conditions of extreme segregation. Research shows that male and female same-sex households have become less segregated from all different-sex households between the 2000 and 2010 census counts (Spring 2013).

Scholars also use census data to create a "gay index" that ranks regions based on their density of same-sex households. Developed by Gary Gates and his colleagues, the index is expressed as a ratio of the concentration of same-sex couples in a geographic area relative to the overall population (Gates and Ost 2004). A value of 1.0 indicates that a same-sex couple is as just likely as a randomly selected household to live in the respective area. A value of 2.0 means that couples are twice as likely to locate in the area, while values less than 1.0 indicate that they are less likely to do so when compared to a randomly selected household. Studies that use the gay index show that same-sex couples are much more likely to live in cities like San Francisco, California; Seattle, Washington; Austin, Texas; and Portland, Oregon; along with smaller towns like Provincetown, Massachusetts; Wilton Manors, Florida; Palm Springs, California; and Northampton, Massachusetts. City officials have taken a keen interest in this index because scholars who are visible beyond the academy, like Richard Florida, argue that it predicts economic competitiveness in a globalizing world (Florida 2002).

The 2010 census was the first in which government officials allowed respondents to identify themselves as married to a person of the same sex (Massachusetts pioneered legal same-sex marriage in the United States in 2005). Studies that use data from that particular census still produce low estimates of the gay and lesbian population, however, because the survey only counts *coupled* households. It excludes those who are not partnered (about a quarter of gay men and two-fifths of lesbians are in relationships at any given time). Those who do not live with their partner, those who are unwilling to self-identify as gay or lesbian, those who self-identify as bisexual, and those who self-identify as transgender also remain uncounted (Doan 2007; Doan and Higgins 2011; Hayslett and Kane 2011). These limitations raise vexing questions: What does it mean that same-sex marriage makes some of us measurable while concealing others? If we know where same-sex couples live, does that tell us where *all* queer people live? That the census renders an incomplete portrait is not up for debate—the survey still doesn't ask about individual sexual orientation, sexual behavior, or sexual attraction, after all—yet it remains one of the few probability samples that we have about the national gay and lesbian population.

Having considered two common techniques that scholars use to describe the gay and lesbian population and its geographic expressions, let's now think about possibilities for methodological innovations. I organize the advice that follows around a series of problems that I encountered as I was researching and writing my book *There Goes the Gayborhood?* I should note that these districts are generally white (Nero 2005), male (Browne 2007; Ghaziani 2015b), and middle-class in composition (Barrett and Pollack 2005). Thus, it goes without saying that we can generate even more principles based on the study of lesbian spaces and those inhabited by people of color, trans individuals, ball and drag subcultures, queer youth, suburban and rural migrations, and an examination of ephemeral spaces rather than those that are more enduring. What I offer here is an incitement to imagine a thing called queer spatial analysis.

Misalignments, Mutability, Diversity

Because they are a hidden population (Salganik and Heckathorn 2004), gays and lesbians are impossible to randomly sample. You can address this problem in three ways. First, remember that sexual orientation is a composite concept; what you learn depends on what you ask. Your options include questions about attraction or arousal (the desire to have sex or be in a romantic relationship with one or both sexes); behavior, acts, and contact (any mutual and voluntary activity that involves genital or bodily contact, even if an orgasm does not occur); or identity (socially and historically meaningful labels that guide how we think about sexuality). Here's why measurement matters: if you define homosexuality by same-sex behavior, then you will omit gay virgins while including self-identified straight men who have sex with other men. If instead you define homosexuality by an identity label like "gay" or "lesbian," then you will exclude those people who experience same-sex arousal or behavior but do not identify as such. You'll also overlook those who identify as bisexual or queer, along with individuals who use language that is not tied to mainstream terms (e.g., "aggressive," "in the life," or "same-gender-loving"). Did you know that in the biological and health sciences, a single instance of same-sex behavior automatically can place an individual in the "homosexual" category regardless of the frequency of sex and whether the person enjoyed it (Savin-Williams 2006)? Following queer theoretic commitments to misalignments, the corresponding principle of queer methods is to be mindful about the components of sexual orientation—do not ignore, conflate, or reify them—and make conclusions based on the type of data that you gather.

My second advice is to use sampling strategies that approximate probability theory. I adapted a technique, developed by Matthew Salganik and his colleagues, called respondent-driven sampling (RDS). This method of data collection uses a variation of chain-referral, or a snowball mechanism that is sensitive to community structure, geo-graphic clusters, and social networks. Krista Gile, Lisa Johnston, and Matthew Salganik (2015, 242) explain how it works:

> RDS data collection begins when researchers select, in an ad hoc manner, typically 5–10 members of the target population to serve as 'seeds.' Each seed is interviewed and provided a fixed number of coupons (usually three) that they use to recruit other members of the target population. These recruits are in turn provided with coupons that they use to recruit others. In this way, the sample can grow through many waves, resulting in recruitment trees. . . . The fact that the majority of participants are recruited by other respondents and not by researchers makes RDS a suc-cessful method of data collection.

RDS is useful if your inferential objective is to understand how people who are connected assign meaning to their lives in specific spatial con-texts, rather than calculating central tendencies that you hope to gener-alize beyond your sample. The logic of this approach to data collection is to study networks within a population, each of which is heterogeneous in its contacts yet still geographically clustered. The chain of friends and acquaintances in each network should be large enough to generate on-going recruitment efforts, even if some seeds prove fruitless for you as you seek additional referrals. Multiple waves provide access to parts of the network that you may have missed otherwise, and they avail the small world problem of short network distance between any two people.

I started with twenty seeds. This number is larger than the one that Gile, Johnston, and Salganik advise, but I wanted to cap the upper end of my sample to around one hundred people rather than the thousands that are common in big data studies. Four of the seeds did not produce additional waves of recruitment. The other sixteen snowballed into a total of 125 interviews with gay and straight residents and business own-ers of two neighborhoods in Chicago. I lived in the city for ten years before I did my fieldwork, yet I knew only one out of the twenty-five straight residents of Boystown; six out of the twenty-five lesbians and gay men in Boystown; two out of the twenty-five straights in Ander-sonville; and seven out of the twenty-five lesbians and gay men who lived in Andersonville. Thus, you don't need to be preoccupied with random sampling since the procedure assumes that a given population is fixed and unchanging. Chain-referral techniques are compatible with an understanding of queerness as mutable and group membership as fluctuating.

A third strategy is to maximize your efforts at representation by not relying exclusively on the census as your primary source of data. Andrew Whittemore and Michael Smart (2016) examined the street addresses of rental and for-sale properties advertised over twenty-six years in a weekly LGBTQ newspaper in Dallas. This type of data has its own limitations—"not all of this population can express their preferences in a capitalist land market," they acknowledge (193)—but it can track change over time, provide more precise data points than the decennial census, diversify your data beyond business listings, widen your analytic scope beyond traditional enclaves, and dismantle the tyranny of the couple that the census promotes. If you decide to use this method, keep in mind that property listings are skewed toward trendy and profitable areas, and these often attract heterosexuals as well. If you rely too heavily on advertisements as a proxy for queer people, then you will underrepresent racial and ethnic minorities, women, people with lower levels of education, and economic variation. The more you can diversify your data the better.

Interview Like an Ethnographer

Unlike conventional accounts that rely on demographic data and statistical techniques, I exploited the unique strengths of qualitative approaches, especially interviews, to explain why queer spaces are changing and to predict what will happen to them in the future. My decision was controversial. Some scholars argue that interviews capture ex post facto explanations for what people have already thought or done (Vaisey 2008). Others decry an attitudinal fallacy: what people say is a poor predictor of what they will do (Jerolmack and Khan 2014). Surveys can capture the prevalence of an attitude or snap judgments—in a feelings thermometer about sexual integration, for example—but these data exist at an individual level, and they are abstracted from lived experiences. When ethnographers encounter interview data like mine, they wonder about the situated nature of social life. What does it feel like to be a straight person living next door to a lesbian or a gay man? Or to walk along rainbow-lined streets next to same-sex couples who are holding hands?

I think that interviews can capture interactional tones if we ask questions about specific groups of people and the situations in which they interact, even if we weren't around when the action occurred. For instance, I organized my conversations around a set of newspaper articles that presented common scenarios in gayborhoods across the country. One story from the *San Francisco Chronicle* was entitled "SF's Castro District Faces an Identity Crisis: As Straights Move In, Some Fear Loss of the Area's Character." The article included a photograph of a woman, whom the reader assumes is straight, pushing a baby carriage on Castro Street with a rainbow flag visible behind her. Sitting next to my interviewee, I read aloud the following passage:

> To walk down San Francisco's Castro Street—where men casually embrace on sidewalks in the shadow of an enormous rainbow flag—the neighborhood's status as a 'gay Mecca' seems obvious. But up and down the enclave that has been a symbol of gay culture for more than three decades, heterosexuals are moving in. They have come to enjoy some of the same amenities that have attracted the neighborhood's many gay and lesbian residents: charming houses, convenient public transportation, safe streets and nice weather. (Buchanan 2007)

I then asked open-endedly, "What are your reactions to this headline, this photograph, or this story?" The question always generated a rich exchange.

Drawing on the principle of triangulation, I followed the same procedure with a second article. This one, published in the *New York Times*, was entitled "TURF: Edged Out by the Stroller Set." The piece also included a photograph of a woman pushing a baby stroller, whom we again are to assume is straight, with two presumably gay men on either side of her who have been wedged apart by her stroller. I read this passage out loud:

> It was supposed to be a kind of homecoming. Last year, Chris Skroupa and John Wilson sold their apartment in Hudson Heights, in northern

Manhattan, and moved to Chelsea, where, as a gay couple, they already spent most of their time socializing. But they soon discovered that the neighborhood was changing faster than they expected. Home prices were rising, and many of their friends were moving to Hell's Kitchen, a few blocks west of Times Square. In restaurants that used to be almost exclusively gay, they noticed an influx of straight customers, often with children in strollers. On a recent Saturday, Mr. Skroupa and Mr. Wilson went out for brunch and 'literally less than one-third of the restaurant was gay,' Mr. Skroupa said last week, pausing between bench presses at a New York Sports Club on Eighth Avenue. (Rich 2004)

The final story that I used to structure my interviews came from the *Huffington Post*. It was entitled "Boystown Gay Bar Bans Bachelorette Parties":

Bar owner Geno Zaharakis sat one busy evening at the window of his gay nightclub, watching as groups of straight women celebrating bachelorette parties made their way along a strip of bars in Chicago's gay-friendly 'Boystown' neighborhood. That's when he made a decision now posted for all to see: 'No Bachelorette Parties.' Though the small sign has been there for years, it's suddenly making a big statement amid the national debate over gay marriage. While most gay bars continue to welcome the raucous brides to be, Zaharakis's bar Cocktail is fighting for what he sees as a fundamental right, and his patrons—along with some peeved bachelorettes—are taking notice. 'I'm totally losing money because of it, but I don't want the money,' Zaharakis said. 'I would rather not have the money than host an event I didn't believe in.' Gay bars are popular with bachelorettes, both for the over-the-top drag shows that some offer and for the ability to let loose in a place where women are unlikely to be groped or ogled. (Associated Press 2009)

We can use this type of data to learn about the subtleties of queerness and capture the interactional texture of city life. To do this, you need to organize your conversations around *specific actors*, *concrete situations*, and *resonant symbols*. Once you've done that, you then work with your respondents to unpack the meanings of these analytic elements. Using media documents in this way is also innovative because it reduces the threat of social desirability bias; my respondents were able to offer comments about the characters in a story without implicating themselves personally. This helped them to open up in ways that they may not have been able to do otherwise, thereby enhancing the validity of my findings. Be careful, though, about which vignettes you select. Although queerness can challenge reproductive logics, remember that many same-sex couples also have children. We need to acknowledge that the symbols we study acquire significance in particular places, times, and for certain groups of people—and that they do not have singular meanings. In the passages that I read aloud during my interviews, strollers and bachelorette parties were symbols that journalists regularly used as anathema to queer spaces. They were meaningful, richly resonant, and emic cultural codes that my respondents shared at the time of my data collection. As the times change, so too will the symbols.

Statistical Silences, Cultural Meanings

A lot of research on queer spaces and spatial practices uses census data to create an index of dissimilarity. As a qualitative researcher, I knew that statistical scores were silent about attitudes and motivation. This motivated me to ask a different question: What is behind the drop in sexual segregation that demographers and geographers have documented? A bird's-eye view of statistical desegregation is a powerful place to start, but it left me with little more than a numerical description of a phenomenon that demands a fuller explanation. Sociologists have a saying that we call the "Thomas theorem": If people believe something is real, then it is real in its consequences. In other words, perceptions about sexuality should matter a great deal to you when you conduct a queer spatial analysis. In my book, I developed a qualitative counterpart to the dissimilarity index—a "dissimilarity meanings measure"—which I used to explain why lesbians, gay men, and even straight people choose to live in an area of the city that is widely recognized as a gayborhood. The lesson may be simple, but it is still worth saying: What a neighborhood means is more than the sum of the bodies that inhabit it or the central tendencies that describe it.

In addition to thinking about the cultural meanings of sexuality and space, rather than just the statistical distribution of same-sex households across census tracts, I would also encourage you to broaden your view of the city beyond a binary conception of gay or straight spaces. Consider that gay neighborhoods formed in North America after World War II. Many gays and lesbians were discharged from the military at this time for their real or perceived homosexuality, and rather than return home disgraced, some remained behind in major port cities. These spatial clusters grew rapidly in the 1970s and 1980s. Gays and lesbians perceived these emerging concentrations as beacons of tolerance that offered some reprieve from heterosexual hostility (Weston 1995). Today, there is an emerging consensus among academics, journalists, and even residents that the significance of the gayborhood is changing. The wisdom that connects these observations spanning several decades is about the relationship between oppression and space: gayborhoods are "a spatial response to a historically specific form of oppression" (Lauria and Knopp 1985, 152). When the nature of oppression changes, so too should the spatial response. This is a key hypothesis of queer spatial analysis.

By making this move, you can uncouple sexuality from specific spaces, since gayborhoods, along with queer-friendly areas (Gorman-Murray and Waitt 2009) and queered straight districts, can exist anywhere in and even beyond the city. One surprising finding from my research is that cities with the highest percentage of same-sex couples who are raising children include Albuquerque, Salt Lake City, and Bismarck. This outcome should remind you of arguments from queer theory: power operates through the imposition of binaries like gay or straight, male or female, and masculine or feminine. These binaries have always inadequately mapped onto people's lives. In early twentieth-century New York, a man could have sex with another man without anyone questioning whether he was "normal." A world of "trade," "husbands," and "wolves" existed in a highly gender-segregated bachelor subculture alongside "fairies," "third-sexers," and "punks" (Chauncey 1994). The same thing is happening today with the rise of "dude sex" between straight-identified white men (Ward 2015) and "sexual fluidity" in women (Diamond 2008) and men (Savin-Williams 2017). When we apply this framework from sexuality studies to the city, we begin to see "cultural archipelagos" (Ghaziani 2014b, 133): the plural expressions of queer geographies.

Indicators of Queer Space

If the phrase "queer culture" denotes the ways of life of queer individuals, and if those ways of life are merging with the mainstream as society embraces increasingly liberal attitudes toward homosexuality, then how can we detect distinct urban sexual cultures? The very idea of measuring queer cultures is thwarted in an era of acceptance, inclusion, and integration. What can indicate the presence of queer ways of life in a historical moment that is characterized by the dilution of cultural distinctions? What does queerness even mean in a context of "cultural sameness" or being "post-gay," as I have called it in my other research? How can we think about the gayborhood as an observable analytic entity in a time when same-sex households are dispersing across the city?

My final advice is to be creative about the indicators that you use to identify queer spaces. Urban sexual cultures are observable, despite the integration of gayborhoods, through placeholders like anchor institutions and commemorations (Ghaziani 2014a). Anchors are organizations and businesses, such as bookstores, bars, and community centers that have a special resonance among queer communities. They are the primary engines of community building since they locate the material culture of queer people in a symbolically charged place. One resident told me, "Businesses are an important part of anchoring the gay neighborhood and defining it in the same way that ethnic businesses would help define an ethnic neighborhood." Another added, "As long as those businesses are still here, that's a big thing that keeps the perception in people's head that Lakeview is still gay."

Commemorations are a second analytic device that researchers can use to identify queer spaces. These range from municipal markers like rainbow crosswalks to recurring ritual events such as Pride parades and Dyke Marches. In a nationally unprecedented move, the city of Chicago in 1997 installed tax-funded rainbow pylons along North Halsted Street to celebrate the area's queer character. Bernard Cherksov, formerly the CEO of Equality Illinois, explained why this was a historic decision: "With these pylons we're saying, 'This is our community space.' People move in and out of this neighborhood for different reasons, but the community isn't moving. Boystown is still here." A professor at a local university agreed with this image of territoriality: "It is a political victory, an urban political victory to have any metropolitan or municipal authority allow you to fix identity to space. So many struggles are really about contestations of space. So, when you are allowed to plant your flag anywhere, I think it's a victory for lesbigay identity politics because it says we are here or we were here: this is an important dimension of the city."

Chicago is not alone in its efforts to install commemorative markers. In 1999, the Newcastle City Council became the first in the United Kingdom to announce that it wanted to actively build a gayborhood by designating a section as the "Pink Triangle." In April of 2007, Philadelphia became the second American city to mark one of its neighborhoods as gay by renaming a portion of the Washington Square West district in Center City as "the Gayborhood." The city added thirty-six rainbow flags underneath street signs that bordered the area, which extends from 11th to Broad and from Pine to Locust Streets. Finally, in 2013, Vancouver installed permanent rainbow-colored crosswalks in its Davie Village gayborhood. This was the first such permanent installation in Canada. Other North American cities that have installed rainbow crosswalks to mark and celebrate their local gayborhood include Austin, Texas; Key West, Florida; Long Beach, Sacramento, San Francisco, and West Hollywood, California; Northampton, Massachusetts; Philadelphia, Pennsylvania; Seattle, Washington; Toronto, Ontario; and Victoria, British Columbia, among others.

Compared to racial and ethnic groups, queer communities lack a clear sense of ancestral linearity (Sedgwick 1990). The absence of awareness—who are my people?—induces collective amnesia about our lives. This is one of the most insidious and painful forms of homophobia. During my third year of undergraduate study, I remember feeling astonished when I learned that the history department was offering a course on "Gay and Lesbian History." I had never imagined that such a class could ever exist. The narrowness of my worldview reflected the burden of queer communities in that historical moment, and still to this day, I think. Anchors and commemorative devices protect against the temptation or coercion to forget. They, like other preservation strategies (renaming city streets to honor queer activists, for example, or building LGBTQ museums), fossilize the culture of a group in space and enable a sense of permanence amid the inevitable realities of demographic migrations, gentrification, and development. That said, even those queer cultures that are based in a gayborhood involve more than a collection of organizations, businesses, and municipally sanctioned installations. Queer ways of life also encompass the symbolic meanings associated with the closet; genres of television, music, and literature; ritual events like Pride; the iconography of drag; camp; diverse family forms; and countless other measures that showcase unique subjectivities, aesthetics, and styles of socialization. None of this trivializes the analytic power that inheres in anchor institutions and commemorations, of course, since no single mechanism can explain the full range of variation in urban sexual cultures. What we need to do is to innovate our methodological portfolio in ways that increase the degree of precision in our observations about urban sexualities.

The Birth of an Intellectual Movement

Queer studies is in the midst of a methodological renaissance, as Matt Brim and I noted in our introduction to this volume. David Halperin's books *How to Do the History of Homosexuality* (2002) and *How to Be Gay* (2012), along with the 2010 *Queer Methods and Methodologies* volume edited by Kath Browne and Catherine Nash indexed this shift toward methods by reframing fatigued questions like "*What* is queer?" and "*What* is queer theory?" to the fresh and lively inquiry "*How* do we do queer theory?" The principles that I have shared with you in this chapter offer several possibilities for queer spatial analyses. First, we need to retain our skepticism as we respectfully question the concepts and categories of conventional social science. The dissimilarity index and the gay index are valuable but not without inferential limits. An effort to queer existing protocols requires us to embrace misalignments, mutability, diversity, interactions, and silences. Remember as well that sexual orientation is a composite concept, implement chain-referral sampling techniques, access multiple data sources, and supplement statistical analysis with an understanding of what sexuality means and how it feels for your study participants. Second, queer methods are powerful because they clarify the conditions that make life livable (Brim and Ghaziani 2016). In this regard, I have offered innovative ways of interviewing that can capture the interactional tones of the city, the interstices where life is empirically rich. Finally, queer methods create space for the coherent and the chaotic. Concepts like cultural archipelagos, anchors, and commemorations are powerful because they enable you to conceptualize gayborhoods and other queer-friendly districts as analytically observable entities without naively denying the realities of residential and commercial change.

The volume in which this essay appears births an intellectual movement that has only just begun to develop in the humanities and social sciences. A new generation of scholars is interested in identifying queer protocols and practices that have been eclipsed by advances in queer theory. We share a concern with how to link an account of a situation (or "theory") with a set of guidelines for gathering evidence about it (what I would call "methods"). The resulting notion of "queer methods" is paradoxical, provocative, and productive—and maybe a little counterintuitive too. While the queer ethic is deconstructive and antipositivist, an emphasis on methods invokes a sense of order and identifiable patterns. The genius of this volume is in its imagining of a new horizon of inferential possibilities.

NOTE

1 The census first asked about same-sex households in 1990, offering hope for a revolution in how we study the gay and lesbian population. Unfortunately, the data suffered from validity problems because government officials recoded it. When a same-sex household identified as being married, the bureau changed the gender of the spouse to force it into the framework of a heterosexual married couple. Therefore, we need to be careful about how we interpret statistical data that use the 1990 census. For more on changes between 1990 and 2014, see Allen 2012.

WORKS CITED

Allen, Samantha. 2012. "Why LGBT People Are Moving to Red States." *Daily Beast*, March 9. www.thedailybeast.com.

Associated Press. 2009. "Boystown Gay Bar Bans Bachelorette Parties." *Huffington Post*. June 16.

Balk, Gene. 2014. "Seattle's Gayborhood Is Becoming Less Gay." *Seattle Times*, July 31. http://old.seattletimes.com/.

Barrett, Donald C., and Lance M. Pollack. 2005. "Whose Gay Community? Social Class, Sexual Self-Expression, and Gay Community Involvement." *Sociological Quarterly* 46 (3): 437–56.

Brim, Matt, and Amin Ghaziani. 2016. "Introduction: Queer Methods." *WSQ: Women's Studies Quarterly* 44 (3–4): 14–27.

Browne, Kath. 2007. "Lesbian Geographies." *Social and Cultural Geography* 8 (1): 1–7.

Browne, Kath, and Catherine J. Nash, eds. 2010. *Queer Methods and Methodologies.* Farnham, UK: Ashgate.

Buchanan, Wyatt. 2007. "S.F.'s Castro District Faces an Identity Crisis: As Straights Move In, Some Fear Loss of the Area's Character." *SF Gate, San Francisco Chronicle,* February 25. www.sfgate.com.

Chauncey, George. 1994. *Gay New York: Gender, Urban Culture, and the Making of the Gay Male World, 1890–1940.* New York: Basic Books.

Diamond, Lisa. 2008. *Sexual Fluidity: Understanding Women's Love and Desire.* Cambridge, MA: Harvard University Press.

Doan, Petra L. 2007. "Queers in the American City: Transgendered Perceptions of Urban Spaces." *Gender, Place, and Culture* 14 (1): 57–74.

Doan, Petra L., and Harrison Higgins. 2011. "The Demise of Queer Space? Resurgent Gentrification and the Assimilation of LGBT Neighborhoods." *Journal of Planning Education and Research* 31 (1): 6–25.

Florida, Richard. 2002. *The Rise of the Creative Class.* New York: Basic Books.

Gates, Gary J., and Jason Ost. 2004. *The Gay and Lesbian Atlas.* Washington, DC: Urban Institute.

Ghaziani, Amin. 2014a. "Measuring Urban Sexual Cultures." *Theory and Society* 43 (3–4): 371–93.

Ghaziani, Amin. 2014b. *There Goes the Gayborhood?* Princeton, NJ: Princeton University Press.

Ghaziani, Amin. 2015a. "'Gay Enclaves Face Prospect of Being Passé': How Assimilation Affects the Spatial Expressions of Sexuality in the United States." *International Journal of Urban and Regional Research* 39 (4): 756–71.

Ghaziani, Amin. 2015b. "Lesbian Geographies." *Contexts* 14 (1): 62–64.

Gile, Krista J., Lisa G. Johnston, and Matthew J. Salganik. 2015. "Diagnostics for Respondent-Driven Sampling." *Journal of the Royal Statistical Society: Series A (Statistics in Society)* 178: 241–69.

Gorman-Murray, Andrew, and Gordon Waitt. 2009. "Queer-Friendly Neighbourhoods: Interrogating Social Cohesion across Sexual Difference in Two Australian Neighbourhoods." *Environment and Planning A* 41 (12): 2855–73.

Greenspan, Elizabeth. 2014. "It's a New Day in the Gayborhood." *New Yorker,* August 8. www.newyorker.com/.

Halperin, David M. 2002. *How to Do the History of Homosexuality.* Chicago: University of Chicago Press.

Halperin, David M. 2012. *How to Be Gay.* Cambridge, MA: Harvard University Press.

Hayslett, Karen, and Melinda D. Kane. 2011. "'Out' in Columbus: A Geospatial Analysis of the Neighborhood-Level Distribution of Gay and Lesbian Households." *City and Community* 10 (2): 131–56.

Jerolmack, Colin, and Shamus Khan. 2014. "Talk Is Cheap: Ethnography and the Attitudinal Fallacy." *Sociological Methods and Research* 43 (2): 178–209.

Lauria, Mickey, and Lawrence Knopp. 1985. "Toward an Analysis of the Role of Gay
Communities in the Urban Renaissance." *Urban Geography* 6 (2): 152–69.

Massey, Douglas S., Jonathan Rothwell, and Thurston Domina. 2009. "The Changing Bases of Segregation in the United States." *Annual Review of Sociology* 626 (1):
74–90.

Nero, Charles. 2005. "Why Are the Gay Ghettos White?" In *Black Queer Studies*, edited
by E. Patrick Johnson and Mae G. Henderson, 228–45. Durham, NC: Duke University Press.

Rich, Motoko. 2004. "TURF: Edged Out by the Stroller Set." *New York Times*, May 27.
www.nytimes.com.

Salganik, Matthew J., and Douglas D. Heckathorn. 2004. "Sampling and Estimation in
Hidden Populations Using Respondent-Driven Sampling." *Sociological Methodology*
34: 193–239.

Savin-Williams, Ritch C. 2006. "Who's Gay? Does It Matter?" *Current Directions in
Psychological Science* 15 (1): 40–44.

Savin-Williams, Ritch C. 2017. *Mostly Straight: Sexual Fluidity among Men*. Cambridge
MA: Harvard University Press.

Sedgwick, Eve Kosofsky. 1990. *Epistemology of the Closet*. Berkeley: University of
California Press.

Spring, Amy L. 2013. "Declining Segregation of Same-Sex Partners: Evidence from
Census 2000 and 2010." *Population Research and Policy Review* 32 (5): 687–716.

Staver, Sari. 2015. "Castro Retail Survey Shows Neighborhood Could Be Getting Less
Gay." *Hoodline*, May 21. http://hoodline.com/.

Vaisey, Steven. 2008. "Socrates, Skinner, and Aristotle: Three Ways of Thinking about
Culture in Action." *Sociological Forum* 23 (3): 603–13.

Ward, Jane. 2015. *Not Gay: Sex between Straight White Men*. New York: NYU Press.

Weston, Kath. 1995. "Get Thee to a Big City: Sexual Imaginary and the Great Gay Migration." *GLQ: A Journal of Lesbian and Gay Studies* 2 (3): 253–77.

Whittemore, Andrew H., and Michael J. Smart. 2016. "Mapping Gay and Lesbian
Neighborhoods Using Home Advertisements: Change and Continuity in the
Dallas–Fort Worth Metropolitan Statistical Area over Three Decades." *Environment
and Planning A* 48 (1): 192–210.

PART II

Narrating/Measuring

5

To Count or Not to Count

Queering Measurement and the Transgender Community

PETRA L. DOAN

What methods are most appropriate for assessing the fluid subjectivities contained within LGBTQ+ populations (Brim and Ghaziani 2016)? This is an area of increasing attention at the intersection of social sciences and queer theory. Attempts to estimate the size of the queer population both challenges this fluidity and undermines heteronormativity and its exercise of what twentieth-century queer theorist Michel Foucault called "governmentality" (1978). If compulsory heterosexuality "others" queer populations, then counting them may undermine this "otherness" by demonstrating the legitimate needs of the LGBTQ+ population. For the transgender population, the urgent need for access to safe bathrooms and social services, including medical care, more than justifies the act of counting. Bathroom access enables trans and other gendernonconforming people to move comfortably through public spaces. Since politicians excel in counting votes, without more complete estimates of the number of trans and gender nonnormative people, public officials are unlikely to invest in safer and accessible public facilities. In recent years legislative efforts to keep transgender people out of bathrooms have intensified, making the counting issue even more critical to demonstrate that there are indeed significant numbers of people for whom narrowly defined and gendered bathrooms are a significant problem.

British sociologists Róisín Ryan-Flood and Alison Rooke (2009) suggest that queer methodologies require researchers and subjects to acknowledge the complexity of their subjectivities and lived experiences. Interactions between researcher and subject are easily compromised when respondents are categorized to facilitate the aims of the research.

For instance, drawing on his background in psychological research, Daniel Warner (2004) argues that most work on LGBTQ+ populations reifies subjects into fixed categories that are chosen by the researcher but do not reflect the lived realities of those respective subjects. Irish geographer Kath Browne's (2008) participation in a quantitative survey using "tick boxes" to identify various LGBTQ+ subjectivities risked "selling out" her identity as a queer researcher, but she did provide useful insights into the inequalities faced by some lesbian and gay subjects, which was an essential first step to ameliorating inequality and developing more just policies.

Clearly, the measurement of subjective categories can be tricky. American anthropologist Kath Weston (2009) suggests that measuring lesbian subjectivities requires the deconstruction of even the most basic approaches. For example, simply asking subjects about their identity is fraught, because self-identification is dependent on the ways that individuals interpret what it means to be a lesbian. Because such identities, including "ex-lesbians" and men who identify as lesbians, are often in flux, the lesbian category destabilizes the very process of research. Self-definition also permits anyone to lay claim to lesbian identity, and therefore the results can be at odds with commonsense understandings of the term. In a pop-culture example of the fluid boundaries of self-definition, a character on the television drama *The L Word* who was born male insisted that he identified as a lesbian and struck up a relationship with a female character who had a history of erotic involvement with other women (Weston 2009, 142). Measuring transgender identity is even harder to do since it is one of the least visible segments of the LGBTQ+ rainbow.

This chapter applies a queer theory lens that seeks both to destabilize categories such as "gender" and to avoid severing queer bodies from the environment in which they live, breathe, and excrete bodily fluids. Feminist and queer theory scholar Annamarie Jagose highlights the instability of identity by arguing that "queer is an identity category that has no interest in consolidating or even stabilizing itself. . . . [Q]ueer is always an identity under construction" (1996, 131). Judith Butler, in her classic analysis of gender in *Gender Trouble* (1990), extends this instability to the performance of gender that transcends the body, while women's studies professor Elizabeth Grosz (1992) stretches this conceptualization by adding that there is a complex feedback relation between bodies and environments. Queer theorists Robert J. Corber and Stephen Valocchi (2003) suggest that subjectivities arise not from within the self but from outside it. In addition, New Zealand geographer Robyn Longhurst (1997) notes that bodily experiences of gender both shape and are shaped by the nature of the spaces in which they occur. Finally, American geographers Michael Brown and Larry Knopp (2008) argue that the spatial contingency of queer populations means that analyzing their dimensions and characteristics can usefully reveal the workings of hegemonic power.

Applying a queer lens shows that transgender people are not a fixed group but rather reflect multiple subjectivities, thereby complicating the collection and analysis of data about them. Eminent transgender historian Susan Stryker provides an early definition of transgender as

> an umbrella term for a wide variety of bodily effects that disrupt or denaturalize heteronormatively constructed linkages between an individual's anatomy at birth, a non-consensually assigned gender category, psychical identifications with sexed body images and/or gendered subject positions, and the performance of specifically gendered social, sexual, or kinship functions. (1998, 149)

This broad conceptualization encompasses a variety of gendered positions, including cross-dressers, transsexuals, and a range of other subjectivities. However, even these constructions can be problematic, since according to David Valentine, a cultural and linguistic anthropologist at the University of Minnesota, an overarching transgender identity does not mesh with some people's conceptualization of their subjectivity or their lived reality due to their race and class positions (Valentine 2007). T. Benjamin Singer, a scholar at the University of Pennsylvania's Program in Gender, Sexuality, and Women's Studies, notes that the stilted transgender imaginary rules out some gender-nonconforming individuals (Singer 2015). For instance, many drag queens do not consider themselves transgender, although they may live most of the time as women, take female hormones, or have surgeries to help them present in a more feminine manner. Other individuals with limited income may struggle with gender identity issues, but because of the expenses of surgery and transition, they eschew the label "transgender" as not pertaining to them. However, for counting purposes, any regularly occurring cross-gendered performance places the performer in a category that might need access to safe bathrooms, at least when they are in performance mode. A parallel argument is sometimes made about the identity "gay," which is a social construction that does not include men who do not consider themselves gay even though they sometimes have sex with other men. According to John Williams and his research team in cultural psychiatry at UCLA, the MSM (men who have sex with other men) category was developed during the HIV epidemic in the 1980s to capture risky behavior rather than identity (Williams et al. 2004).

Stryker (2008) addresses this point directly by admitting that she applies "transgender" to groups who would not apply it to themselves. She argues that this is a device for telling the story of the history of a movement, or in the context of this chapter about social scientific interventions into queer methods, for counting as broadly as possible. For example, while not all intersex people are transgender, sometimes the transgender umbrella includes them. Intersex activist Cheryl Chase found support from the transgender community that helped her understand her own intersex status as an "experience of movement through pain to personal empowerment described by other intersex and transsexual activists" (1998, 198). Accordingly, intersex people whose gender identity and anatomical sex do not fit within a rigid dichotomy are sometimes included as transgender even though they may not so self-define.

While some queer theorists avoid the counting of highly vulnerable populations, other researchers continue to estimate and analyze people falling into each subgroup. One reason for counting is the need to provide appropriate services to a highly vulnerable community that suffers from broad-based discrimination, such as that enumerated by a path-breaking report produced by the National Center for Transgender Equality and the National Gay and Lesbian Task Force (Grant et al. 2011). Other studies by social science scholars suggest that transgender individuals suffer from high rates of interpersonal violence (Doan 2007; Kenagy 2005; Lombardi et al. 2002), suicide (Haas, Rodgers, and Herman 2014), and a lack of appropriate medical services (Bradford et al. 2013; Kenagy 2005). Unfortunately, many counts underestimate significantly the number of gender-variant and nonnormative people. This chapter begins by considering the traditional methods of counting the transgender population, including the medical model, and then uses a queer lens to expand the subjectivities that are included in these estimates. Recognizing the fluidity of gender and identity, I conclude by asking whether even the roughest estimates can truly represent the complexity of this burgeoning set of identities.

Traditional Methods for Counting the Transgender Population: The Medical Model

Traditionally, it has been very difficult to obtain information about the transgender community because some parts remain hidden from view. The standard source of demographic information in the United States, the decennial census, uses discrete tick boxes for male and female but does not allow for other gender identities, making it impossible to use this definitive source to count the transgender population. Accordingly, alternate methods are needed to estimate this population.

Transsexual Estimates

The standard estimates of transsexuals are based on reporting by psychiatrists in various clinics and private offices whose patients have requested surgery. The traditional medical determination of transsexual identity required patients to fit within precise conditions for approved sexual reassignment surgery (now sometimes called gender affirmation surgery). In the 1960s and 1970s, historian Joanne Meyerowitz suggests that doctors considered factors including whether individuals would be heterosexual after transition, whether they could successfully pass as their intended gender, and whether they were willing to move and/ or change jobs so that they would not be outed (Meyerowitz 2002). These criteria constitute a truncated tick-box approach since those not approved for surgery were not counted.

The *Diagnostic and Statistical Manual of Mental Disorders* (*DSM*) produced by the American Psychiatric Association reported that "for natal adult males, prevalence [of seeking sexual reassignment therapy] ranges from 0.005% to 0.014%, and for natal females, from 0.002% to 0.003%" (2013). For some people, the trauma of being labeled "transsexual" may have discouraged them from ever presenting themselves to the medical community. Other estimates by Dutch scientists (Bakker et al. 1993) suggest that when transsexual status is less stigmatized, the prevalence of transsexuals may be significantly higher at 1 per 11,900 males (0.008 percent) and 1 per 30,400 females (0.003 percent). Similarly, in Singapore, the noted psychiatrist W. F. Tsoi (1988) reported that prevalence is even higher, with 1 per 9,000 males (0.011 percent) and 1 per 27,000 females (0.004 percent). However, transgender researcher and retired University of Michigan professor Lynn Conway (2002) argued that these are old estimates and must be updated. She used estimates of sexual reassignment surgeries conducted in the United States and Canada to argue that the prevalence of male-to-female transsexual surgeries may be closer to 1 in 2,500 males (0.04 percent).

Not all transsexuals can afford the cost of surgery or desire a radical solution and may opt instead to transition without surgery. In Britain, a recent estimate conducted by a group of transgender researchers led by Bernard Reed found that the number of transgender people who had transitioned might be as high as 0.1 percent of the adult population (Reed et al. 2009). In New Zealand, psychology researcher Jamie Veale used data from the passport agency to illustrate that roughly 1 in 6,364, or 0.016 percent of the population, both male and female, had applied to change the sex markers on their New Zealand passports, although the author notes many trans individuals would not wish to make such a change, causing a substantial underestimation (Veale 2008). A conservative count based on Reed et al. estimates 0.1 percent of the adult population as transsexual, meaning they have taken steps to transition and live permanently in the gender that matches their identity.

Cross-Dresser Estimates

The above estimates necessarily exclude cross-dressers because they do not fit within the narrower transsexual box. However, some people choose to wear clothing associated with the opposite sex on an occasional or sometimes more frequent basis.[1] There is a high level of stigma attached to the term "cross-dresser," though it is vastly preferred to the older term "transvestite." No matter what term we use, it is very difficult to estimate the size of this segment of the transgender community, since cross-dressing largely takes place in private spaces, and many cross-dressers eschew therapy. Noted sexologists Vern L. Bullough and Bonnie Bullough (1993) have suggested that a rough estimate of the extent of cross-dressers in the population might be 1 percent of the adult male population.

Intersex Population Estimates

In assembling a count of the transgender population, it is important to consider physiological variations in the construction of gender. It is commonly assumed that there are only two sexes, but there is increasing evidence that there is much greater diversity in our physiological understanding of sex than previously believed. Ann Fausto-Sterling (2000) argued that from a biological perspective, there is a great deal of overlap in every characteristic that might be used to divide the sexes into a simple dichotomy. In particular, a significant number of babies are born with ambiguous genitalia and can be classified as intersex. Prior to 2006, invasive early surgeries were routinely recommended by pediatricians attempting to "fix" babies with nonnormative genitalia. These decisions were based on surgeons' perceptions of a baby's organs and *not* on the baby's incipient gender identity, since that cannot be known until a number of years later. Other intersex individuals whose conditions are linked to chromosomal differences may not appear visibly intersex until puberty or after. Considering intersex people as "errors" is extremely problematic. These children are not anomalies but rather represent errors in our conceptualization. While intersex is not precisely transgender, it is certainly a category that endures many similar societal sanctions for nonnormatively gendered people and therefore should be included under the umbrella. Suzanne Kessler, an ethnomethodological scholar, estimates that prior to changes in these pediatric protocols, doctors recommended "corrective surgery" for roughly 1 to 2 babies in every 1,000 live births (0.2 percent) to fix these sexual "anomalies" (Kessler 1998).

Traditional Estimates of the Transgender Population Derived by the Medical Model

A preliminary count of the transgender community in the United States that starts with the medical model of transsexuality and adds estimates of cross-dressers and intersex people is displayed in table 5.1.

TABLE 5.1. Estimates of the Transgender Population in 2014 Using Traditional Methods and Expanded Counts

	Ref. rate	Ref. pop.	Pop. 2014 est.
U.S. total pop.			314,107,084
U.S. adult pop.			240,329,426
U.S. adult males			116,799,121
Transsexuals	0.1%	U.S. adults	240,329
Cross-dressers	1%	U.S. adult males	1,167,991
Intersex	0.2%	U.S. pop.	628,214
Total trans pop.			**2,036,535**
Trans %			**0.65%**
Expanded transsexuals	0.5%	U.S. adults	1,201,647
Cross-dressers and gender fluid	2%	U.S. adults	4,806,589
Expanded intersex	1%	U.S. pop.	3,141,071
Expanded trans pop.			**9,149,306**
Expanded trans %			**2.91%**

Sources: U.S. 2014 population figures (total, adult, and adult male) from the U.S. Census. Estimated rates calculated by the author.
The census estimates the U.S. population as 314,107,084 in 2014, and the adult population as 240,329,426. The transsexual population (0.1 percent) can be calculated as 240,329 people. The population of adult male cross-dressers (1 percent of adult males) can be calculated as 1,167,991 people. The intersex population (0.2 percent of the whole population) can be calculated as 628,214 people. These estimates provide a total of 2,036,535 transgender people in the United States or 0.65 percent of the U.S. population.

Unfortunately, these traditional counts do not do justice to everyone who struggles with a rigidly dichotomous gender system. In the natural sciences, there is evidence that gender diversity is more complex than a binary model of male and female. In the ecological sciences, Joan Roughgarden (2004) provided numerous examples of species that exhibit a range of gendered behaviors and attributes that cannot be explained with a simple dichotomy. In the social sciences, feminist geographer Liz Bondi (2004, 12) suggested that "the binary construct of gender . . . [is] a superfluous and unnecessary distraction from the reality of the human condition." Within the trans community, a number of scholars have argued for a more flexible understanding of gender. These scholars use a queer understanding of gender to transcend the dichotomy and move past a binary conceptualization.[2] For instance, transgender theorist Kate Bornstein describes her discovery that gender transcends the binary as follows:

And then I found out that gender can have fluidity, which is different from ambiguity. If ambiguity is a refusal to fall within a prescribed gender code, then fluidity is the refusal to remain one gender or another. Gender fluidity is the ability to freely and knowingly become one or many of a limitless number of genders, for any length of time, at any rate of change. Gender fluidity recognizes no borders or rules of gender. (1994, 51–52)

Transgender activist and scholar Riki Ann Wilchins (2004) argues that the inequalities embedded in a highly structured gender system are the driving force toward the adoption of a nondichotomous vision of gender. My own experiences have provided insights into gender fluidity that I described in an auto-ethnographic description of a walk through a shopping mall (Doan 2010). This example prompted me to consider a Heraclitean frame of reference to situate the experience:

I experienced my gender as a kind of moving target, like one of those opposing moving sidewalks in modern airports. I was moving in one direction and the spectators were moving in the other, and somewhere in between, my gender was constructed and reconstructed with each fleeting moment. In this way not only was the gender I expressed subject to the fluidity of my movement through the mall, but the spatiality of this performance was also shifting with each instance of my performative interaction. (2010, 645–46)

The editors of the 2008 "Trans-" issue of *WSQ* reflect this shift to a more fluid understanding of gender by arguing that it was time for "bursting 'transgender' wide open, and linking the questions of space and movement that the term implies to other critical crossings of categorical territories" (Stryker, Currah, and Moore 2008, 12). The result has been a proliferation of subjectivities that are too numerous to name. As an illustration of the scope of this identity explosion, the National Transgender Discrimination Survey collected responses from 6,546 people, the largest data set ever assembled on the transgender community. The questions used to determine transgender status were carefully constructed to account for both gender identity and sex assigned at birth. They also used an open-ended component (Question 3) for "gender not listed" (GNL). The authors note:

Q3 garnered 860 written responses to GNL, many of them creative and unique, such as twidget, birl, OtherWise, and transgenderist. The majority of these respondents wrote in genderqueer, or some variation thereof, such as pangender, third gender, or hybrid. Still others chose terms that refer to third gender or genderqueers within specific cultural traditions, such as Two-Spirit (First-Nations), Mahuwahine (Hawaiian), and Aggressive (Black or African American). (Harrison, Grant, and Herman 2012, 14)

These 860 written responses constituted 13 percent of the survey, illustrating the breadth of the transgender subjectivities that were included in the count (Harrison, Grant, and Herman 2012). The authors indicate that of these 860 write-in answers, 73 percent were composed by individuals assigned female at birth, though for the entire sample, 60 percent were assigned male at birth. The lopsided nature of these conceptualizations from the perspective of sex assigned at birth is intriguing. It seems clear that some of these people assigned female at birth are choosing to define themselves in ways that are different from traditional female to male (FtM) identities. It is unclear what effect going forward this will have on the counts of male to female (MtF) versus FtM people.

Other evidence from the same source indicates that a number of respondents appear to no longer recognize binary gender as an identity, suggesting that gender itself has been splintered. On this same openended question, twenty-three respondents used words that indicate they refuse to acknowledge any gender, nineteen responses indicated completely fluid gender, sixteen answers suggested trigender or third gender, and ten individuals used the terms "gender-fuck" or "radical-fuck" for a total of sixty-eight or roughly 8 percent of the gender not listed respondents.

In another study, gender scholar Dana Stachowiak (2016) conducted qualitative interviews with genderqueer individuals and argued that their experiences reflect a process of continuous and simultaneous negotiation of gender in the face of external oppression. It is clear that these diverse identities represent creative experimentation with alternate subjectivities and at times a deep-rooted conviction that the current gendered system is not working. In the end, they trouble the waters of traditional counting processes.

Queering the Count for a More Fluid Transgender Community

After a strong storm, especially one with high winds, one often finds the tattered remains of blown-out umbrellas strewn along the sidewalks. The results from the National Transgender Discrimination Survey suggest that while it is time to discard this metaphor for queerness, there is no replacement terminology that includes and possibly shelters all the people gathered in the vicinity of this blown-out umbrella.[3] No matter what term we use, we need estimates of vulnerable people to demand that decision-makers respond and provide appropriate and safe bathrooms.

As indicated above, estimating the precise numbers of these vulnerable populations is fraught with complexity, since subjective identities within the trans population are quite diverse. Accordingly, a number of scholars who focus on transgender issues argue that many attempts to count this vulnerable population miss the mark by forcing fluid subjectivities into narrow gender boxes (Ingraham, Pratt, and Gorton 2015; Singer 2015; Thompson and King 2015). The following section expands traditional counting methods by queering the gender dichotomy and incorporating a broader range of subjective identities that express gender nonnormativity. In the interest of clarity, I refer to this expanded and complex population as the transgender community, even though not all those included would label themselves using this term.

Expanding the Definition of Transsexual

Transgender activists often criticize medical and therapeutic communities for their role as gatekeepers with a special kind of regulatory power (Foucault 1978). Many traditional estimates of the size of the transgender population are based on this gatekeeping. First, it is essential to examine the one-sidedness of many estimates of transsexuals. Evidence from several Swedish psychiatrists (Landén, Wålindel, and Lundström 1996) suggests that increasing numbers of FtM are requesting and receiving reassignment surgery, undermining the longstanding disparity in FtM and MtF surgeries. Current surgical procedures for FtM are unable to create a fully functional neophallus and are much more expensive than the surgical procedures for MtF individuals. As a result, counts based solely on surgeries performed will significantly undercount FtM individuals. Age may also be a factor here, since there are an increasing number of FtM individuals in the eighteen to twenty-five age cohort, though we have little direct evidence that it is disaggregated in this manner.

The traditional counts are also deeply flawed for both FtM and MtF people because the stigma attached to gender nonconformity and transgender status are likely to have inhibited many individuals from ever seeking professional advice. A significant number of transgender people, moreover, do not consider themselves ill or disordered, and they are unlikely to present themselves to the medical community as such. In addition, insurance policies often explicitly exclude any gender-identity-related treatment, making the high costs of therapists and the even higher costs of reassignment surgery simply unaffordable.

We must expand the count beyond those who have had surgery. More precise estimates of this population by two transgender scholars suggest that as many as 1 in 500 (0.2 percent) can be considered transsexual (Olyslager and Conway 2007). A different study by social epidemiologist Kerith Conron and others used data from the 2007 and 2008 Massachusetts Behavioral Risk Factor Surveillance Survey to estimate that 0.5 percent of adults between eighteen and sixty-four identified as transgender (Conron et al. 2012). The critical difference to note here is that individuals self-identified as transgender, not necessarily transsexual. The following prompt was used in this study:

> Some people describe themselves as transgender when they experience a different gender identity from their sex at birth. For example, a person born into a male body, but who feels female or lives as a woman. Do you consider yourself to be transgender? (Conron et al. 2012, 118)

This study is quite significant. It is one of few estimates derived from a population-based survey that specifically asks about self-identified transgender status and not transition or surgery.

Finally, a widely cited estimate by the Williams Institute at UCLA averages previous estimates (Conron et al.'s high estimate of 0.5 percent, Olyslager and Conway's 0.2 percent, and Reed et al.'s estimate of 0.1 percent) to argue that approximately 0.3 percent of the U.S. population is transgender (Gates 2011). Unfortunately, this average mixes apples and oranges, since the 0.1 percent estimate is for transsexuals who have transitioned, the 0.2 percent is an estimate of transsexual incidence, and the 0.5 percent is for people who self-identify as transgender. Since the purpose of this essay is to estimate transgender subjectivities, it is more appropriate to extrapolate from those who self-identify as transgender (0.5 percent) by expanding the Massachusetts survey data to the entire U.S. population (Conron et al. 2012). While there may be some concern that extrapolating a statewide survey conducted in Massachusetts to the national level will introduce errors, it seems less of a stretch than applying estimates from Great Britain (Reed's 0.1 percent) to the United States. The critical factor here is that the Massachusetts-based survey was the first to allow people to self-identify as transgender, thereby yielding a significant improvement in the data.

In analyzing these data, I made the decision not to conduct separate estimates for trans men and trans women. Although historical data suggests there may be disparities between the number of FtM and MtF individuals, recent estimates place these numbers much closer to parity. There certainly are a number of older individuals who were identified at birth as female and over time came to self-identify with other non-normatively gendered butch lesbians. It is possible, and perhaps even probable, that given a more expansive understanding of transgender to include nonbinary categories such as gender fluid, some proportion of these butch-identified women might more comfortably self-classify as somewhere on the trans continuum. For example, in a recent interview, Judith Butler suggested, "Sometimes I think that I am probably trans" (Tourjee 2015). This resonates with my own experience after conducting a workshop on trans issues where several older lesbian women approached me wondering that perhaps if they had heard this more expansive understanding of "transgender" when they were younger, they might have adopted trans as a part of their identity. No age-specific counts would account for these individuals, but they might be more easily included in the following category.

Counting the Gender-Flux Category

The cross-dressing category outlined earlier in this chapter is too narrowly construed and needs expansion. Although some men of a certain age (certainly baby boomers) might engage in cross-dressing, I wonder if younger people identified at birth as male may feel freer to express a wider range of gender behaviors in the twenty-first century. There is no reliable method for identifying all those who were identified as male at birth for whom this identity does not feel comfortable. The common element among both men who cross-dress and young people who express their gender as "genderqueer" or "gender-fuck" is the fluidity of their gender expression with respect to the sex that they were assigned as at birth.

But what about women who wear men's clothing? Since women can cross-dress at will with little to no consequences, this is a much more difficult estimate. Sexologists Bullough and Bullough suggest these numbers are even more elusive since female cross-dressers and gender benders are "quieter about their behavior" (1993, 315). A queer approach would ask: How should women who cross-dress be counted? It is difficult to sort out who is simply making a fashion choice and who is wearing men's clothes as an act of nonnormative cross-dressing or as a precursor to accepting a transgender subjectivity. A reexamination of the National Transgender Discrimination Survey found that 192 respondents of the total number of 6,456 responses (nearly 4 percent) were assigned female at birth but reported living part of their lives dressed as men (Harrison-Quintana, Glover, and James 2015). This implies that there are significant numbers of female-to-male cross-dressers. Other results from this same survey suggest that 73 percent of the 860 respondents who reported "no gender listed" were identified as female at birth. This suggests that a significant number of women report behavior that is gender fluid or explicitly nongendered.

There is no clear way to gauge the size of this gender-flux population, but if gender differences are experienced equally across the gender spectrum, then we should use equal percentages as well. Adding gender-flux people suggests that the traditional cross-dressing estimate of 1 percent of the adult male population is likely to be too low. For example, Lynn Conway (2002) shows that cross-dressing clubs typically estimate that 2 to 5 percent of the male population cross-dresses privately on an intermittent basis, and a proportion perhaps as high as 1 to 2 percent of this same population actively considers transition. These numbers suggest that we could use a higher percentage for men, perhaps 2 percent as a conservative estimate. Since estimates of individuals who experience and express gender fluidity must also include those who were identified as female at birth, it seems appropriate to apply this percentage to the entire adult population.

Expanding Intersex

Suzanne Kessler (1998) argues that a careful examination of individuals who identify as intersex challenges the notion that all gender is socially constructed. Intersex activist Cheryl Chase asserts that "insistence on two clearly distinguished sexes has calamitous personal consequences for the many individuals who arrive in the world with sexual anatomy which fails to be easily distinguishable as male or female" (1998, 189). As partial confirmation, Claire Ainsworth (2015) argues that for humans the idea of two sexes is simplistic, especially when we consider nondimorphic evidence from chromosomes. More rigorous analysis by UCLA and Michigan-based geneticists suggests that as many as 1 percent of babies born could to some extent be intersex or have what the scientific community now calls a disorder of sexual development (Arboleda, Sandberg, and Vilain 2014). These numbers suggest that a much higher percentage of the population than previously expected is forced to deal with some level of incongruity about societal expectations for normatively sexed people.

Expanded Transgender Population Counts

Using a more broadly defined understanding of transgender yields a significantly larger estimate of the population under the umbrella (see table 5.1). The estimate of 0.5 percent (Conron et al. 2012) of the U.S. population indicates that there might be 1,201,647 transgender people. Adding the cross-dressing population as 2 percent of the adult population (including both males and females) generates an additional 4,806,589 people. Finally, using the 1 percent figure for the expanded intersex population yields an additional 3,141,071 people.[4] Overall, these estimates produce a much larger total of people who experience some form of nonnormative gender identity. For the U.S. population in 2014, this amounts to 9,149,306 individuals who could broadly be counted among the transgendered, or nearly 3 percent (2.91 percent) of the U.S. population. This is almost a fivefold expansion from 0.6 percent.

Conclusions

Even with this large increase in transgender population estimates, it is important to ask whether it will ever be possible to precisely assess the number of nonbinary subjectivities since the transgender umbrella concept has burst wide open. From a methodological standpoint, it is not possible to extrapolate from the National Transgender Discrimination Survey to count the numbers of "gender not listed" or nongendered subjectivities on a national level. The survey provides a superb perspective on discrimination experienced by the transgender community, but the snowball approach that it used limits the ability to generalize to a wider population. It does, however, provide a rich assessment of the breadth of the transgender community in the second decade of the twenty-first century that is a significant improvement from the narrow medical model of transsexuality used previously.

Recognizing the vast array of nonnormatively gendered people who defy expectations for gendered behaviors is a crucial first step in expanding our understanding. Perhaps this proliferation of new genders represents the flowering of a thousand or more genders, as suggested two decades ago by Sandra Bem, an eminent feminist psychologist, who said:

> I propose that we let a thousand categories of sex/gender/desire begin to bloom in any and all fluid and permeable configurations and, through that very proliferation, that we thereby undo (or, if you prefer, that we de-privilege or de-center or de-stabilize) the privileged status of the two-and-only-two that are currently treated as normal and natural. (1995, 330)

The quotation raises questions linked to the enumeration of trans bodies and identities. Bem's exhortation about a thousand gender categories was intended to "turn up the volume" as a strategy for diminishing polarized gender roles, compulsory heterosexuality, and homophobia. But are we succeeding? Has the scope of the transgender community and all of its related gendered expressions become so vast that the metaphor of an umbrella is no longer functional? Has the proliferation of identities and subjectivities reduced the intelligibility and viability of gender as a category, as perhaps intended by Bem?

I think the most critical question is: How does the larger heteronormative community respond to the proliferation of genders? From my perspective, a university professor located in the midst of the Deep South, the issue remains an important one. The epidemic of violence against transgender people and especially trans women of color continues unabated throughout the nation and reminds us of the vulnerability of people who display nonnormative genders. Across the Southern Bible Belt, conservative pastors use words like "abomination" to describe gender-variant people both in church and at county commission hearings. Sometimes this fear-mongering enables them to achieve their heteronormative ends. The popular rejection of the Houston Equal Rights Ordinance in October 2015 is an example of painting the gender variant as "dangerous," raising the shibboleth of cross-dressed men assaulting women and children in bathrooms. The South Dakota state legislature passed a similar bill designed to limit transgender use of bathrooms in February 2016, but the governor ultimately vetoed it. Unfortunately, in March 2016 the North Carolina legislature succeeded in passing a sweeping measure that restricts bathroom usage to gender listed on birth certificates. The governor has signed this measure into law.

If a thousand genders bloom, how can society protect people who express nonbinary gender from harmful backlash? In the final analysis, bathrooms are a universal necessity, but they can easily turn into sites of political demagoguery that trigger physical threats to people whose gender does not conform to heteronormative expectations (see Browne 2004; Lucal 1999). In a world that still clings to a rigid gender dichotomy, those who do not fit within that system pose a conundrum for public policymakers. Planning for rapidly shifting identities is a real challenge. While some municipalities (for example, Philadelphia) are committed to including "all gender" washrooms in future building projects, how many such bathrooms do we need? In addition, how can universities, which are often at ground zero for the exploration of alternate subjectivities, assess the demand for more inclusive bathrooms?

Some queer scholars call for research to avoid quantitative assessments of sexuality and gender diversity because they constrain complex subjectivities into narrow boxes (Warner 2004). In this chapter, I have argued that failing to account for the entire transgender spectrum simply reifies outdated medical models that severely underestimate the size of this community. The large difference between the two summary counts calculated above (1.1 million versus 9.1 million) deserves further attention. There is a clear contrast between the overly conservative traditional approach and the more expansive approach that paints the transgender community with broad brushstrokes to increase awareness about a marginalized community that is often invisible and penalized by existing population estimates.

If the purpose of counting the transgender community is to make decisions about the allocation of scarce public funds for transsexual surgery, then erring on the side of caution might be justified and indeed required. For example, if health officials are trying to predict the potential costs to city or state governments of including gender reassignment as a covered condition for insurance purposes, then it might not make sense to include cross-dressers, gender-flux, and intersex individuals. However, I have argued that some cross-dressers will in fact choose to have surgery, and some intersex people may also require a surgical solution for affirming a gender identity that was not visible anatomically. More importantly, if the purpose of counting is to correct the longstanding neglect of the transgender community by trying to gauge the number of people who are subject to fear, discrimination, and potential gender-related violence, then the larger number is justified. If cities want their public bathroom facilities to be safe and accessible for everyone, then using the larger estimate is essential. Under such circumstances, counting can be a queerly radical act.

NOTES

1 While the American Psychological Association (2015) suggests that many individuals who cross-dress do *not* identify as transgender, in my experience as a person who for twenty-plus years identified as a cross-dresser and eventually accepted my transsexual identity, I have argued that most cross-dressers are indeed transgender but experience their cross-gender feelings episodically and perhaps less intensely than others under the transgender umbrella (see Doan 2007).

2 See Butler 1990; Feinberg 1996; Green 2004; Hines 2006; Rothblatt 1995; Stone 1991; Stryker 1994; 2004; Sullivan 2003; Wilchins 1997; 2004.

3 The big top or a circus tent might be a better shelter metaphor, but its potential
   to further "other" trans people by bringing to mind circus freak shows makes it a
   nonstarter. Other large shelter metaphors like bomb shelters, castles, and walled
   cities have equally unfortunate connotations of militarism and outright warfare.
4 Technically the 1 percent figure applies to babies born, but if we assume that
   intersex babies occur and have occurred at a fairly constant 1 percent over time, it
   makes sense to apply this number to the entire population.

WORKS CITED

Ainsworth, Claire. 2015. "Sex Redefined." *Nature* 518: 288–91.

American Psychiatric Association. 2013. *Diagnostic and Statistical Manual of Mental Disorders*. 5th ed. Arlington, VA: American Psychiatric Association. doi.org/10.1176/appi.books.9780890425596.

American Psychological Association. 2015. "Guidelines for Psychological Practice with Transgender and Gender Nonconforming People." *American Psychologist* 70 (9): 832–69.

Arboleda, Valerie A., David E. Sandberg, and Eric Vilain. 2014. "DSDs: Genetics, Underlying Pathologies, and Psychosexual Differentiation." *Nature Reviews Endocrinology* 10: 603–15.

Bakker, Abraham, Paul J. M. van Kesteren, Louis J. G. Gooren, and Pieter D. Bezemer. 1993. "The Prevalence of Transsexualism in the Netherlands." *Acta Psychiatrica Scandinavica* 87 (4): 237–38.

Bem, Sandra. 1995. "Dismantling Gender Polarization and Compulsory Heterosexuality: Should We Turn the Volume Down or Up?" *Journal of Sex Research* 32 (4): 329–34.

Bondi, Liz. 2004. "Tenth Anniversary Address: For a Feminist Geography of Ambivalence." *Gender, Place, and Culture* 11 (1): 3–15.

Bornstein, Kate. 1994. *Gender Outlaw: On Men, Women, and the Rest of Us*. New York: Routledge.

Bradford, Judith, Sari. L. Reisner, Julie. A. Honnold, and Jessica Xavier. 2013. "Experiences of Transgender-Related Discrimination and Implications for Health: Results from the Virginia Transgender Health Initiative Study." *American Journal of Public Health* 103 (10): 1820–29.

Brim, Matt, and Amin Ghaziani. 2016. "Introduction: Queer Methods." *WSQ: Women's Studies Quarterly* 44 (3–4): 14–27.

Brown, Michael, and Larry Knopp. 2008. "Queering the Map: The Productive Tensions of Colliding Epistemologies." *Annals of the Association of American Geographers* 98 (1): 40–58.

Browne, Kath. 2004. "Genderism and the Bathroom Problem: (Re)materializing Sexed Sites, (Re)creating Sexed Bodies." *Gender, Place, and Culture* 11 (3): 331–46.

Browne, Kath. 2008. "Selling My Queer Soul or Queerying Quantitative Research?" *Sociological Research Online* 13 (1).

Bullough, Vern L., and Bonnie Bullough. 1993. *Cross Dressing, Sex, and Gender*. Philadelphia: University of Pennsylvania Press.

Butler, Judith. 1990. *Gender Trouble: Feminism and the Subversion of Identity*. London: Routledge.

Chase, Cheryl. 1998. "Hermaphrodites with Attitude: The Emergence of Intersex Political Activism." *GLQ: A Journal of Lesbian and Gay Studies* 4 (2): 189–211.

Conron, Kerith J., Gunner Scott, Grace S. Stowell, and Stewart Landers. 2012. "Transgender Health in Massachusetts: Results from a Household Probability Sample of Adults." *American Journal of Public Health* 102 (1): 118–22.

Conway, Lynn. 2002. "How Frequently Does Transsexualism Occur?" *LynnConway.com* Blog. http://ai.eecs.umich.edu/people/conway/TS/TSprevalence.html.

Corber, Robert J., and Stephen Valocchi, eds. 2003. *Queer Studies: An Interdisciplinary Reader*. New York: Wiley-Blackwell.

Doan, Petra L. 2007. "Queers in the American City: Transgendered Perceptions of Urban Spaces." *Gender, Place, and Culture* 14 (1): 57–74.

Doan, Petra L. 2010. "The Tyranny of Gendered Spaces: Living Beyond the Gender Dichotomy." *Gender, Place, and Culture* 17 (5): 635–54.

Fausto-Sterling, Anne. 2000. *Sexing the Body: Gender Politics and the Construction of Sexuality*. New York: Basic Books.

Feinberg, Leslie. 1996. *Transgender Warriors: Making History from Joan of Arc to Dennis Rodman*. Boston: Beacon Press.

Foucault, Michel. 1978. *The History of Sexuality*, Volume 1, *An Introduction*. Translated by Robert Hurley. New York: Pantheon.

Gates, Gary. 2011. "How Many People Are Lesbian, Gay, Bisexual, and Transgender?" Los Angeles: Williams Institute Briefing Paper. http://williamsinstitute.law.ucla.edu.

Grant, Jaime M., Lisa A. Mottet, Justin Tanis, Jack Harrison, Jodie L. Herman, and Mara Keisling. 2011. *Injustice at Every Turn: A Report of the National Transgender Discrimination Survey*. Washington, DC: National Center for Transgender Equality and National Gay and Lesbian Task Force.

Green, Jamison. 2004. *Becoming a Visible Man*. Nashville, TN: Vanderbilt University Press.

Grosz, Elizabeth. 1992. "Bodies-Cities." In *Sexuality and Space*, edited by Beatriz Colomina, 241–54. New York: Princeton Architectural Press.

Haas, Ann P., Philip L. Rodgers, and Jody Herman. 2014. "Suicide Attempts among Transgender and Gender Non-conforming Adults." Los Angeles: American Foundation for Suicide Prevention and the Williams Institute.

Harrison, Jack, Jaime Grant, and Jody L. Herman. 2012. *A Gender Not Listed Here: Genderqueers, Gender Rebels, and OtherWise in the National Transgender Discrimination Survey*. Los Angeles: University of California Los Angeles, Williams Institute Working Paper. http://escholarship.org.ezproxy.gc.cuny.edu/.

Harrison-Quintana, Jack, Julian Glover, and Sandy E. James. 2015. "Finding Genders: Transmasculine Crossdressers in the National Transgender Discrimination Survey."

LGBTQ Policy Journal at the Harvard Kennedy School 4: 93–102. www.hkslgbtq.com/.

Harrison-Quintana, Jack, Jaime M. Grant, and Ignacio G. Rivera. 2015. "Boxes of Our Own Creation: A Trans Data Collection Wo/Manifesto." *TSQ: Transgender Studies Quarterly* 2 (1): 166–74.

Hines, Sally. 2006. "What's the Difference? Bringing Particularity to Queer Studies of Transgender." *Journal of Gender Studies* 15 (1): 49–66.

Ingraham, Natalie, Vanessa Pratt, and Nick Gorton. 2015. "Counting Trans* Patients: A Community Health Center Case Study." *TSQ: Transgender Studies Quarterly* 2 (1): 136–47.

Jagose, Annamarie. 1996. *Queer Theory: An Introduction.* New York: NYU Press.

Kenagy, Gretchen P. 2005. "Transgender Health: Findings from Two Needs Assessment Studies in Philadelphia." *Health and Social Work* 30 (1): 19–26.

Kessler, Suzanne. 1998. *Lessons from the Intersexed.* New Brunswick, NJ: Rutgers University Press.

Knopp, Larry, and Michael Brown. 2003. "Queer Diffusions." *Environment and Planning D: Society and Space* 21: 409–24.

Landén, M., J. Wålindel, and B. Lundström. 1996. "Incidence and Sex Ratio of Transsexualism in Sweden." *Acta Psychiatrica Scandinavica* 93: 261–63.

Lombardi, Emilia, Riki Anne Wilchins, Dana Priesing, and Diana Malouf. 2002. "Gender Violence: Transgender Experience with Violence and Discrimination." *Journal of Homosexuality* 42 (1): 89–101.

Longhurst, Robyn. 1997. "(Dis)embodied Geographies." *Progress in Human Geography* 21 (4): 486–501.

Lucal, Betsy. 1999. "What It Means to Be Gendered Me: Life on the Boundaries of a Dichotomous Gender System." *Gender and Society* 13 (6): 781–97.

Meyerowitz, Joanne. 2002. *How Sex Changed: A History of Transsexuality in the United States.* Cambridge, MA: Harvard University Press.

Olyslager, Femke, and Lynn Conway. 2007. "On the Calculation of the Prevalence of Transsexualism." Chicago: WPATH 20th International Symposium. http://ai.eecs.umich.edu/ people/conway/TS/Prevalence/Reports/Prevalence%20of%20Transsexualism.pdf.

Reed, Bernard, Stephanie Rhodes, Pietà Schofield, and Kevan Wylie. 2009. *Gender Variance in the UK: Prevalence, Incidence, Growth, and Geographic Distribution.* London: Gender Identity Research and Education Society.

Rothblatt, Martine. 1995. *The Apartheid of Sex: A Manifesto on the Freedom of Gender.* New York: Crown.

Roughgarden, Joan. 2004. *Evolution's Rainbow: Diversity, Gender, and Sexuality in Nature and People.* Berkeley: University of California Press.

Ryan-Flood, Róisín, and Alison Rooke. 2009. "Que(e)rying Methodology: Lessons and Dilemmas from Lesbian Lives: An Introduction." *Journal of Lesbian Studies* 13 (2): 115–21.

Singer, T. Benjamin. 2015. "The Profusion of Things: The 'Transgender Matrix' and Demographic Imaginaries in U.S. Public Health." *TSQ: Transgender Studies Quarterly* 2 (1): 52–76.

Stachowiak, Dana M. 2016. "Queering It Up, Strutting Our Threads, and Baring Our Souls: Genderqueer Individuals Negotiating Social and Felt Sense of Gender." *Journal of Gender Studies* 26 (5): 532–43.

Stone, Sandy. 1991. "The Empire Strikes Back: A Posttranssexual Manifesto." In *Body Guards: The Cultural Politics of Gender Ambiguity*, edited by Julia Epstein and Kristina Straub, 280–304. New York: Routledge.

Stryker, Susan. 1994. "My Words to Victor Frankenstein above the Village of Chamounix: Performing Transgender Rage." *GLQ: A Journal of Gay and Lesbian Studies* 1 (3): 237–54.

Stryker, Susan. 1998. "The Transgender Issue: An Introduction." *GLQ: A Journal of Lesbian and Gay Studies* 4 (2): 145–58.

Stryker, Susan. 2004. "Transgender Studies: Queer Theory's Evil Twin." *GLQ: A Journal of Gay and Lesbian Studies* 10 (2): 212–15.

Stryker, Susan. 2008. *Transgender History*. San Francisco: Seal Press.

Stryker, Susan, Paisley Currah, and Lisa Jean Moore. 2008. "Introduction: Trans-, Trans or Transgender." *WSQ: Women's Studies Quarterly* 36 (3–4): 11–22.

Sullivan, Nikki. 2003. *A Critical Introduction to Queer Theory*. New York: NYU Press.

Thompson, Hale, and Lisa King. 2015. "Who Counts as 'Transgender'? Epidemiological Methods and a Critical Intervention." *TSQ: Transgender Studies Quarterly* 2 (1): 148–59.

Tourjee, Diana. 2015. "Why Do Men Kill Trans Women? Gender Theorist Judith Butler Explains." *Sexuality Policy Watch*, December 16. http://sxpolitics.org/.

Tsoi, Wing Foo. 1988. "The Prevalence of Transsexualism in Singapore." *Acta Psychiatrica Scandinavica* 78: 501–4.

Valentine, David. 2007. *Imagining Transgender: An Ethnography of a Category*. Durham, NC: Duke University Press.

Veale, Jaimie F. 2008. "Prevalence of Transsexualism among New Zealand Passport Holders." *Australian & New Zealand Journal of Psychiatry* 42 (10): 887–89.

Warner, Daniel Noam. 2004. "Towards a Queer Research Methodology." *Qualitative Research in Psychology* 1: 321–37.

Weston, Kath. 2009. "The Lady Vanishes: On Never Knowing, Quite, Who Is a Lesbian." *Journal of Lesbian Studies* 13 (2): 136–48.

Wilchins, Riki Anne. 1997. *Read My Lips: Sexual Subversion and the End of Gender*. Ithaca, NY: Firebrand Books.

Wilchins, Riki Anne. 2004. *Queer Theory, Gender Theory: An Instant Primer*. Los Angeles: Alyson Books.

Williams, John K., Gail E. Wyatt, Judith Resell, John Peterson, and Agnes Asuan-O'Brien. 2004. "Psychosocial Issues among Gay-and Non-Gay-Identifying HIV-Seropositive African American and Latino MSM." *Cultural Diversity and Ethnic Minority Psychology* 10 (3): 268–86.

6

Counternarratives

A Black Queer Reader

MATT BRIM

In the church I come from—which is not at all the same church to which white Americans belong—we were counselled, from time to time, to do our first works over again. . . . To do your first works over again means to reexamine everything. Go back to where you started, or as far back as you can, examine all of it, travel your road again and tell the truth about it. Sing or shout or testify or keep it to yourself: but know whence you came.
—James Baldwin, *The Price of the Ticket* (1985)

Primer, n.
  2. a. An elementary school-book for teaching children to read.
     b. *fig.* Something which serves as a first means of instruction.
     c. A small introductory book on any subject.
—*Oxford English Dictionary*

Introduction: Black Queer Illiteracies

This is an essay about remediation, about learning what we should have already learned: to read black queer literature. It is an essay about a classroom experience of learning to read again, of collectively coming to terms with the enforced illiteracies and educational impoverishments that make minority pedagogies of rereading urgent. And this is an essay about a collection of stories and novellas—John Keene's 2015 *Counternarratives*—that both exposes this state of black queer illiteracy and functions as a primer for addressing it. My opening claim is that *Counternarratives* is a black queer reader, a book that helps us to "do our first works"—of reading, of teaching—over again. My opening invocation of James Baldwin, a crucial touchstone for Keene, helps me to err on the side of the literal in nominating *Counternarratives* as a black queer reader, for the collection teaches us to revisit some of our first work with language—making sense of the world through story—and thereby to reexamine ourselves as readers. Enacting a fugitive pedagogy, a practice of education that has at once been banished from normative instruction and at the same time flees from its constraints,[1] Keene puts counternarrative in the service of black queer literacies.

The "we" above is important. It assumes a general illiteracy and therefore advocates for widespread reform. I do not come to that position theoretically but rather through my experience teaching black queer literature at the College of Staten Island (CSI) in the City University of New York system and, previously, at an elite private college and at a flagship state university. No matter the institution, higher education does little to teach its charges black queer literature or literacies.[2] And if the students at CUNY, one of the most diverse educational systems in the country, have not been guided toward fluency in reading black queer texts; if my classes have had what we described to ourselves as black queer "illiteracy feelings," then the problem is not simply ours. In response to this epistemological crisis, black queer remedial reading should be understood as a general educational requirement.

All of the texts in my "Black Gay Male Literature" course in the spring of 2017 exposed this educational shortcoming, as had numerous works in other classes I have taught at CSI, including "The Lesbian Novel," "Queer Studies," "Writing HIV/AIDS," and "The LGBTQ Short Story."[3] *Counternarratives*, however, offers a flashpoint for illuminating and addressing the systemic failure to teach black queer reading practices, for it conducts a radical formal experiment in crafting literacies of black human being in the New World. Literacies of black human being can be understood as a set of abilities, taught to us by narrative or, rather, counternarrative, for comprehending what has been made an obscured and often unreadable intersection: black human. And in Keene, always, black queer human. That Keene situates his experiment explicitly in the "New World," beginning in 1613 and ending in the near futural twenty-first century, speaks to the "firstness" of the work he does over again and to the historical and geographical distances he is willing to travel to do it. Spanning four centuries, Keene's counternarratives formally encode black literacy practices that open out onto a capacious understanding of black meaning and worldmaking. Central to this embodied and learned black epistemological project, queerness becomes part of the very syntax, the organizational principle, for making black people meaningful. *Counternarrative*'s service to blackness therefore contributes to the larger project of queer of color writers "to know and be known," with special attention to the ways black bodily experiences and black intellectualism inform the creation of and access to knowledge.[4]

A reader, also called a primer, is typically understood as a text of first instruction. As primers go, *Counternarratives* is therefore unrecognizable. I should say this up front: in ways that are immediately obvious, *Counternarratives* is a difficult read. Fundamental matters of character, setting, and plot are only circuitously revealed, and even then textual questions are not easily answered without a rudimentary knowledge of Portuguese, of the history of the African slave trade in South America and the Caribbean, and of global black intellectual and creative culture in the late nineteenth and early twentieth centuries. My class was not familiar with the people and places that Keene, who is also a translator of Portuguese, French, and Italian, writes about, from Mannahatta and Juan Rodriguez to the *quilombos* of colonial Brazil to the Catskill creek where musician Robert Cole committed suicide in 1911. The narratives follow an exacting and indeed overwhelming chronology as dates abound and genealogies meticulously unfold. My class Googled furiously as we read. Who was Miss La La? Mário de Andrade? When was the Counterreformation? Was there really a United States Army Balloon Corps? Even the table of contents, which one would expect to serve as a key or legend for the thirteen stories that follow, defamiliarizes in its formal innovation. On the one hand, its shape suggests a highly intentional ordering and collection of its constitutive stories. While the titles of the first story and the final seven stories are very short (usually one or two words), the second, third, fourth, and fifth stories obey an entirely different titular logic. They are far longer and more convoluted:

On Brazil, or Dénouement: The Londônias-Figueiras
An Outtake from the Ideological Origins of the American
    Revolution

A Letter on the Trials of the Counterreformation in New Lisbon
Gloss, or The Strange History of Our Lady of the Sorrows[5]

As one of my students pointed out, with these longer titles stretched
wide across the top of the page, the table of contents forms the shape
of a cross. Or a bird in flight. Or a totem figure, possibly androcentric.
And while a cross makes sense thematically given the presence of Ca-
tholicism in the collection, any organizing principle revealed by this
shape is at least in part undone when, unannounced by the table of contents, Keene divides the body of the collection into three uneven parts:
I. COUNTERNARRATIVES, II. ENCOUNTERNARRATIVES, III.
COUNTERNARRATIVE (this last comprising of a single, nonlinear,
apocalyptic story, "The Lions"). As form breaks proliferate, *Counternarratives* seems intent on actively reimagining what is possible when writing and collecting short fiction together. Though Keene distributes maps
throughout the text, they are too small to read. If the promise of a map
is to orient, Keene's maps (as well as his musical and literary allusions,
his epigraphs, his typography) break that promise and instead become
tools of defamiliarization.

The somewhat familiar kind of readerly problem posed by historical fiction (as exemplified by my class's questions and the strange allusions in the long chapter titles) was compounded because we couldn't
recognize Keene's black queer historiographic method. He doesn't, for
instance, simply rewrite history, though putting narrative in the service
of black queer literacies means, in part, telling stories about black people
that have been suppressed or untold as a condition of colonial rule and
therefore as a condition of that master fiction, the Historical Record.
Keene's work of countering narrative goes further, undermining ideological assumptions of Western narrative: not just that the whole story
has been or can be told, or that extant stories cohere into a grand teleological narrative, but that we *already know how to read* stories both told
and untold. In fact, *Counternarratives* suggests that the stories we know
how to read actively proscribe our ability to read otherwise. Ultimately,
the black queer historiography of *Counternarratives*—its story-making
method—teaches us to read fiction that does not depend narratologi-
cally on an underlying storytelling principle of antiblackness and an-
tiqueerness. If *Counternarratives* is formally original even to the point

of disorientation, and indeed reviews of Keene's collection frequently position it as unique, "unlike anything I've read before," it is necessary to grapple with the context of that disorientation and its pedagogical implications. Only in the face of the widespread inability to read and teach narratives working in the service of blackness must Keene craft stories of such formal innovation so as to work the disorientations experienced in the absence of antiblack narrativity into counternarrative.[6] One of the lasting lessons of the primer for my class was that our educations have not taught us to read *for, toward, in the service of* queer blackness.[7]

Reading for Queer Blackness

If counternarratives put narrative in the service of blackness by writing black and racialized nonhistories back into the historical record, they also do so by countering some of the West's most familiar stories, revealing them to have often been told in the quiet service of whiteness. Counternarratives thereby show whiteness to have been a structuring concern of narrative in the Americas since the sixteenth century.[8] Keene tells readers something about the white stories we've been taught, something those stories have hidden in order to be told, something we have helped to hide by retelling and embedding them in the American literary canon.

Put in the service of blackness, counternarrative whiteness is not allowed simply *to be.* This does not mean that all of the white characters in the collection are "bad," as though telling the story of white traumatization of black bodies could be sufficient for rendering blackness intelligible. It means, to the contrary, that whether white characters are foregrounded, backgrounded, or absent from these stories, whiteness is made visible and thus newly intelligible, given narrative meaning and narrative consequences, and that the very connection between white legibility and white meaning is made from the perspective of the most skilled interpreters, those characters with the most urgent need of expertise in seeing and making meaning out of whiteness: characters who know the mundane banality and life-saving urgency of black literacies.

Arguably, Keene puts counternarrative whiteness in the service of blackness most powerfully in "Rivers," a story that accomplishes a breathtaking reorientation of perspective. This story, placed at the center of the collection's thirteen stories, marks the moment in *Counternar-ratives* when my students literally gasped. "Rivers," one student com-mented, was the story that the first six stories made possible to tell. The crucial epiphanic moment in "Rivers," discussed below, therefore be-comes a meta-epiphanic moment mid-collection, a moment where the unfamiliar fictions of the historical, geopolitical, and linguistic pasts of those earlier stories with long and confusing titles and plotlines meet the familiar fictional near-present in a renarration of Mark Twain's *Huck Finn*, told from the perspective of Jim.

Typical of the genre of short fiction, "Rivers" ends with an epiphanic moment that opens out onto dramatic interpretive possibilities. The pre-text for Jim's recollection, quoted at length below, is an interview about his service in the Civil War with a reporter who, standing in the place of the adoring American reader, would rather hear about "the time you and that little boy . . ." (219). Instead of that famous story, Jim, who as a free man has renamed himself James Alton Rivers, offers an untold one about the war:

> . . . [C]reeping forward like a panther I saw it, that face I could have identified if blind in both eyes, him, in profile, the agate eyes in a squint, that sandy ring of beard collaring the gaunt cheeks, the soiled gray jacket half open and hanging around the sun-reddened throat, him crouching reloading his gun, quickly glancing up and around him so as not to miss anything. . . . [A]nd I looked up and he still had not seen me, this face he could have drawn in his sleep, these eyes that had watched his and watched over his, this elder who had been like a brother, a keeper, a sec-ond father. . . . [I] raised my gun, bringing it to my eye the target his hands which were moving quickly with his own gun propped against his shoulder, over his heart, and I steadied the barrel, my finger on the trig-ger, which is when our gazes finally met, I am going to tell the reporter, and then we can discuss that whole story of the trip down the river with that boy, his gun aimed at me now, other faces behind his now, all of them assuming the contours, the lean, determined hardness of his face, that face, there were a hundred of that face, those faces, burnt, determined, hard and thinking only of their own disappearing universe, not ours, which was when the cry broke across the rippling grass, and the gun, the guns, went off. (235–36)

In the black queer counternarrative, Jim Rivers is something of a swindler and sexual libertine, not the Uncle Tom figure of Twain's novel. Using Roderick Ferguson's queer of color framework in *Aberrations in Black*, Jim reads as a model of black nonheteronormativity, a model of queer blackness.[9] More importantly, in the counternarrative queer black Jim does not try to protect Huck. He shoots him. And it seems, given that Jim narrates "Rivers," that when "the guns" went off Jim's bullet found its target, since Huck's clearly did not. More importantly, the counternarrative does not just kill Huck. It de-individualizes him. Huck's story changes from the prototypical narrative of an American boy's ambivalent entry into manhood to a dangerously typical narrative in which the decision to fight and kill for slavery and racial supremacy makes all Confederate white men into the same character, each assuming Huck's face. What, I asked my class, do we make of all those faces, all those soldier Hucks?

Initially, the class of thirty-five—only three of whom, myself included, shared Huck's white male face[10]—fell into the trap that black queer illiteracy sets for us. We read Keene as humanizing the Confederate soldiers by making their faces into mirrors of Huck's, the flawed, redeemable man-boy. Perhaps Jim sympathizes with them all or wishes it were possible to save them? But as Huck's face becomes imaginable as the face of the South, the counternarrative inverts this interpretation, revealing that we have used a strategic prowhite literacy to misread the boy protagonist by mishumanizing him. Huck is but one racist in the monstrous horde that wears his same face. Indeed, this is what he has always been. We have been willfully misreading that face as universal rather than as capable of "thinking only of [its] own disappearing universe." If Jim is to be real, the thing to be done with Huck has always been to kill him.

This counternarrative epiphany raises an important philosophical point, an ethical point, about our relationship as readers to narratives not countered. "Rivers" sets the stakes of its own absence and the absence of *Counternarratives*, the stakes of *Huckleberry Finn* existing alone in the world. In the absence of counternarratives, we can easily humanize Huck and dehumanize Jim by attributing to him superhuman sympathy rather than the human choice to kill. For those who love to read, including the room full of English majors with whom I read *Counternarratives*, to the extent that this new awareness causes us to revisit our literary love objects and our affect-laden histories of reading, the radical confrontation of racialized reading practices occasioned by encountering *Counternarratives* may well rise to the level of reading crisis. And liberation.

Counternarratives thus raises questions that seem at once remedial, as a typical primer does, and philosophical, as a typical primer does not: How do I read this book? What kind of book is this? What have I been reading? *How* have I been reading it? What does it mean to read as I have been reading? And what explains the informed illiteracy—or the ignorances created by dominant knowledge practices—at the intersection of black queer human that makes a black queer reader necessary in the first place?

Counternarrative and Black Queer Human Being

Why should "black queer human" fail to signify and thus need to be made readable by a book like *Counternarratives*? Robert Reid-Pharr's critique of humanism in *Archives of Flesh: African America, Spain, and Post-Humanist Critique* (2016) offers a partial explanation. Reid-Pharr argues that "[t]he Western philosophical traditions to which we have all been forced to pay obeisance represent not vessels of truth per se, but instead the quite specific discursive protocols and institutional procedures by which examination and discussion of human being has been delimited" (9). The "human" in humanism turns out to be not the expansive figure championed by "complex rhetorics of pluralism" but instead a narrow and filtered fellow, a mechanism of shrunken possibilities for thought. With "murky" inclusive language practices supplanting analyses of structural exclusions, "'the black' can be imagined much more simply and comfortably than he can be addressed" (7). To *address* "the black" in and through fiction would be to put literature in the service of blackness as part of a fugitive epistemological project that resists both exclusion from humanism and the general impoverishments produced by humanism's crude tools for thought.

Reid-Pharr reanimates protocols for knowledge-making that center the experiences of black human being. Helpfully for my present chapter, his study calls for the invigoration of "the African American Spanish archive" (11), a project I take to be near the heart of Keene's book as well. Tracing "rhetorics of flesh," a kind of embodied literacy that has been used by black people to "access alternatives to the most vulgar of the humanist protocols" (11), Reid-Pharr reveals "not only enslaved persons' awareness of their presumed status as chattel but also and quite importantly their resistance to this status, their self-conscious articulation of counternarratives of human subjectivity in which enslaved and colonized persons might be understood as both historical actors and proper subjects of philosophy" (9). Using the word "counternarratives" for a second time in his introduction, Reid-Pharr takes pains to "remind readers of some naughty truths. Slavery and colonization . . . produced any number of (un)bounded, (un)authorized counternarratives in which the many contradictions of racialism and capitalism were made patently visible" (12). Mikko Tuhkanen (2017) in his review essay of *Archives of Flesh* homes in on Reid-Pharr's sustained critical practice of undoing ideologies of race, describing his intellectual project as "*vulgarizing modernity.*" Reid-Pharr's vulgarizing method extends to bounded sexual identities and nomenclatures associated with modern knowledge production in the West that operate as markers not only of erotic imprecision but of the antiblack epistemological violence that co-creates them.

Like *Archives of Flesh*, *Counternarratives* indicts humanist philosophies as too thin to narrativize black intellectualism in the New World. It does so by providing a virtual catalog of fugitive epistemologies that emerge from the lived experience of black people under conditions of slavery, colonial expansion, and, in the U.S. context, "emancipation." Keene is ingenious in the number of ways he writes embodied black philosophies into *Counternarratives*. Real-life philosophers appear in several stories, and Keene boldly philosophizes via characters who are not philosophers by training. In "Our Lady of the Sorrows," the slave girl Carmel briefly considers her skills of divination in a moment of fugitive philosophizing: "In terms of my own will and gifts, . . . I had not yet developed a theory of knowledge by which to understand them. Or rather perhaps I had, but lacked a language to characterize and describe them. It struck me that the spells and the drawings themselves might be a language, but this seemed so exploratory and fantastic, that I set aside further consideration of it, and instead reflected, when the thought struck me, on the process of my experience and practice of those episodes" (145–46). Carmel understands her gifts as potentially having epistemological implications, but she defers exploration of a theory of knowledge and instead turns back to and invests value in the everyday phenomenological experience and practice of her supernatural gifts. Yet elsewhere, a black slave's repeated escapes from captivity represent the unrelenting, embodied articulation of a freedom that is simultaneously rendered illegible in political philosophy's classic terms of "the social order." Similarly, archival materials reproduced in close proximity (an advertisement for a runaway slave followed several pages later by an inset of the Declaration of Independence) suggest a fundamental incommensurability, in this instance between slave and man, at the heart of Western humanist philosophy.

Yet Keene does not simply jettison Western thought and replace it with an idealized, non-Western black thought. The fugitive epistemologies created in *Counternarratives* form not by rejecting Enlightenment philosophy wholesale but by engaging it. Philosophical ruminations on themes such as duty and freedom thus emerge from *within* black experiences of New World slavery and clearly in conversation with liberal rhetorics that shape it: "Under the circumstances, are there any benefits to dedication, devotion, honor—responsibility?" (90). And later, "Within the context shaped by a musket barrel, is there any ethical responsibility besides silence, resistance, and cunning?" (105). "Persons and Places" explicitly reminds readers of the long tradition of African American and Spanish American philosophical interanimation rather than isolation. The story is structured temporally, hinged on a moment, though that moment is only a fleeting one as Keene pairs black philosopher and future leader in Harlem Renaissance intellectual and artistic circles, W.E.B. Du Bois, and the American-educated Spaniard, George Santayana. These thinkers, with their overlapping but misaligned orbits, later morph into a more convivial interracial couple in "Blues," which extends the story of a moment glimpsed between Du Bois and Santayana into the story of an evening shared by self-described "poet low-rate" Langston Hughes, a virtual philosopher of black working classes, and Mexican poet and playwright Xavier Villaurrutia. Julian Lucas notes that this story is "a fantasy spun from the slenderest evidence: [Villaurrutia's] dedication of an erotic poem to Hughes and the knowledge that their time in New York and Mexico City overlapped" (2017). A half-longing, half-suspicious instant of eye-catching between black and brown (or, to use Reid-Pharr's preferred term, "off-white") men in "Persons and Places" becomes in the "Blues" counternarrative an evening of dinner then sex that indexes a fleeting genealogy of embodied homoerotic black intellectualism and cultural production in the West.

Resonating with Reid-Pharr's posthumanist philosophical intervention, Keene invents a counternarrative method of making queer black experience into vital knowledge. But if, as Reid-Pharr suggests, the protocols of black human being have not yet been fully collected and made legible as archives of flesh, it stands to reason that the work of counternarrative method will not be instantly recognizable either. Keene's counternarrative work must be shared and shouldered by what Reid-Pharr calls "the wide-awake reader" (2016, 11) of the new archives. I have framed that intersection where counternarrative invention and wide-awake reading practices resist traditional humanist (il)literacies as a site of pedagogy. And if introducing *any* work of literature into the classroom for the first time can feel like equal parts voyage out and con job, *Counternarratives* seems even more urgently to raise the pedagogical question: How do I teach this unrecognizable, highly original collection? I suggest that the book's uncommon originality can be understood as the very basis for its *common* value as a pedagogical text, for as a boundary object for black queer literacies it teaches new and *indispensable* ways of reading. In other words, we all should do the work of becoming wide-awake readers. Though not "an elementary school-book for teaching children to read," *Counternarratives* enters the pedagogical gap created by standard white and straight reading practices in order to teach readers to counterread both black narratives and the white racialized stories that have overwritten them. By framing *Counternarratives* as a black queer reader, I hope to stage an unsettling pedagogical confrontation between readers' current presumptions about their own literacies and *Counternarratives*' unintelligibility.

Secret Pedagogies and Inverted Worlds

My attention to the pedagogical implications of *Counternarratives* as a black queer reader and my discussion of the particular pedagogical scene in which I first taught the book play to my personal and scholarly interest in thinking about queer pedagogy as it intersects with minority race and class formations. But I am also pointed in that direction by a special characteristic of *Counternarratives*: it thematizes fugitive pedagogies. Secret educations and upstart knowledge practices help to structure this book. Slaves are polyglots, linguistic savants, self-educated readers. They invent sign languages and teach them to others, including their masters. In fact, roles of the learned Provost and the illiterate slave are reversed in Keene's counternarratives, and powers of mind do not exist under pale heads alone. Queer black and brown readers, writers, and scholars animate this text, appearing as characters within individual narratives and as authors of Keene's eclectic epigraphs. In short, the collection is explicitly concerned with black learning, fugitive study, and embodied epistemological struggle. My treatment of the book as a black queer reader attempts to gather together the various pedagogical moments of the text and then name the sum of the work they ask the reader to do: read in the service of black knowledge practices, including black thought, teaching, intellectualism, and genius.

The opening story offers a fitting preview of the fugitive pedagogical work of the entire collection in that it enacts a reading practice of entering language anew. Inverting official narratives of colonial exploration and expansion, "Mannahatta" tells the story of Jan/Juan Rodriguez, who in 1613 became the first documented non-native American to live on what is today called Manhattan Island in New York City. Rodriquez, born in one of the Caribbean's oldest cities, Santo Domingo, was part African and part Lusitanian/Portuguese. As told by Keene, Rodriguez's story not only subverts a specifically racialized history of "firsts" by making the first American immigrant black—and what an impact this simple detail could have on thinking about U.S. immigration today. It also reconceptualizes the logic of settler encounters with first people, in this case the Lenape, who were the original inhabitants of Manhattan Island. The Lenape envoy who serves as Rodriguez's primary contact "had, through gestures, his stories, later meals and the voices that spoke through fire and smoke, opened a portal onto his world. Jan knew for his own sake, his survival, he must remember it. . . . [H]e could see another window inside that earlier one, beckoning. He would study it as he had been studying each tree, each bush, each bank of flowers here and wherever on this island he had set foot. He would understand that window, climb through it" (4–5). Rodriguez the settler refuses the role of colonial explorer. He plans, rather, to desert the Dutch colonizer's ship on which he serves as translator for trading with the Lenape. Rodriquez thus allows Keene to conceive of multiple modes of translation happening parallel to imperialist language practices. Rodriguez will not use his linguistic talents to extract value from the first people. They have offered language as a portal, a series of portals, through which he might pass and, so passing, perhaps commune. The metaphor of passing through windows, of being swallowed up into the language of another, replaces colonial metaphors of contact, spread, and influence.[11]

Counternarratives further upends colonial narrative practices by thematizing the methods by which fugitive narratives are produced by technologies that range from the mechanical to the fantastical. *How* stories come to be told is of paramount importance, and in Keene's experiment in black literacies knowing how to read means knowing the history of a story's emergence. Keene inscribes the mechanisms of communication into his fine-tuned histories, richly detailing how narratives are recorded, transcribed, transmitted, handled, received, revealed, and read. Literacy technologies enable black resistance and produce black human being.

In "Counterreformation," the fugitive cipher symbolizes the power of counternarrative technology to invert worlds. Using the colonizer's own technology of encoded communication—a letter hidden within the binding of a book—the black fugitive writes not just in the language of the Portuguese colonizer but in the *secret* language practice of the colonizer. And it is via that secret language practice, moreover, that he *readdresses* the colonizer, personified here as a regional leader of the Catholic Counterrformation, in epistolary form. The letter, dated June 1630, begins:

DOM FRANCISCO,
I write you in the expectation that you will soon discover this missive, concealed, as you regularly instructed the members of the professed house in Olinda, during the period that you led it, within the binding of this book that has been sent to you and which you, having discovered the letter, have just set down. . . . The most valuable of all, however, is this written missive, as you will certainly soon agree. As you also shall see, you will gain full access to it only by the application of another trick

you conveyed to those in your care, underlining how well your lessons took root, like cuttings, even in the distant fields. Thus the special care I have taken. If you should see fit, do let the lit candlewick linger upon this document once you have read it, as that would be in the utmost order, though it is of no matter to me, for it should be declared that I am beyond the reach of those laws, earthly or divine, that would condemn you, on the very fact of possession of the written account I shall shortly begin. (45–46)

Dom Francisco, located at the seat of knowledge, is here confronted by his multiple ignorances. Who is the author? How does he know the priests' tricks for secreting missives? Though we soon learn that "[t]his letter sails to you, in its clever guise, out of an abiding desire to convey to you the truth of what occurred at [the outpost monastery in] ALA-GOAS" (47), the unknown author begins with a rumination on the technology by which that ignorance is presently being exposed.

Exhibition of detailed knowledge of a technique for encoding story soon gives way to the story itself, "that series of events, unforeseeable at least to some of those who lived them, that inverted worlds" (47). As events build to the climactic inversion of worlds, the "civilized" priests who run the monastery in colonial Brazil and who are the local caretakers of the Catholic Counterreformation are revealed to be the rapists and torturers of the "uncivilized" African slaves, who themselves stand accused of all manner of sexual perversion and sodomitic abomination. The inversion of the civilized/uncivilized binary is personified in the narrator, who ultimately reveals himself as N'Golo BURUNBANA Zumbi, one of the former African slaves at the monastery at Alagoas. Because Burunbana, a Jinbada spirit worker, is "such a one who is both" (80), who sometimes appears male and sometimes female and whom "[s]ometimes the spirits fill and mount . . . as one and the other" (80), he offers an easy target for the priests' accusations of defiling the monastic order through the performance of lasciviousness acts and diabolical rituals. Yet, in Burunbana's gender multiplicity, his status as "such a one who is both," we see the collapse of the distinction between his role as narrator and vessel for knowledge. He calls himself his people's "instrument, their conduit and gift" (83). Burunbana has the ability to counternarrate his own story, to manipulate the communications technology and thereby invert the function of the colonizer's cipher to serve his own purposes. He explicitly stakes out his own narrative position: "I ask only that you understand given all that has transpired since you last spoke face to face with any of those at that now accursed house, that some who have been condemned to the most foul contumely do reside, nevertheless, in Truth, and so this missive proceeds from *that strange and splendid position*" (48, emphasis mine). In this expanded system of black literacy, fugitive Truth narrative stands not on the periphery of knowledge or in simple opposition to it or even outside of it altogether but rather at its fullest point of saturation. Burunbana knows, for example, that the new Provost of the monastery, Juaquim D'Azevedo, also goes by a false name, one that hides his Jewish identity and his true intentions, the secret education of Jewish boys in the town whose families are also passing as Roman Catholics. Fugitive literacies intersect as, reading future and past, Burunbana oversees D'Azevedo's escape from the monastery so that he can return to the practice of his faithful pedagogy.

When Burunbana reveals his identity to Dom Francisco at the letter's close, he does so with an impossible reference: "for as my sister will write in the distant future, 'it is better to speak / remembering / we were never meant to survive'" (83). Burunbana speaks Truth here with the words of Audre Lorde, black, lesbian, mother, warrior, poet, whose lines from "A Litany for Survival" are pulled back in time from the twentieth century to the early seventeenth century. Keene's reference to Lorde reiterates the earlier message that the "strange and splendid position" from which Burunbana counternarrates his story is not only black but also queer—and also literary. Through *Counternarratives*, queerness becomes part of the textual fabric of the emergent black meaning-making project. Lorde's poem also enables Keene to set the stakes of this short story by linking the word to survival. The fugitive narrative is always also a story of its own survival. Black queer story is never, simply, there.

Conclusion: Pedagogies of Queer Black Literacy

How does a black queer story make its way into being and then survive? My class had been thinking about that question a good deal throughout the semester as we read or viewed other works by black gay men. A narrative does not survive without readers who can make sense of it. And to make sense of black queer literature, as Keene's fantastic use of Lorde attests, one needs *other* works of black queer literature.

By contextualizing Keene's book, which my class read at the end of the semester, within a black queer literary tradition, we were able to rearticulate our "illiteracy feelings," those affective experience of not being "wide-awake" readers with which *Counternarratives* forces a pedagogical confrontation. Following Sharon Holland, I have elsewhere explored the utility of using "tradition" as a framework for understanding gay, same-gender-loving, and queer black men's writing.[12] Here, I do not argue that this is the only or even the best way to contextualize Keene's collection, but I do want to suggest that positioning it this way enabled my class to key into particular black queer reading practices. We were familiar, for example, with what Valerie Traub calls the opacity or obstinacy of sexual knowledge,[13] having made the name of our course, "Black Gay Male Literature," into an obstacle that could be productively used for rethinking racialized and sexualized epistemological standpoints. Black queer naming practices had been a steady source of debate in the course (*Tongues Untied* [1989] and the short documentary *Passing* [2015]), as had encoded writing strategies (Harlem Renaissance poetry); the contestations around masculinity and same-sex desire (*Moonlight* [2016]); the power of white, middle-class hetero- and homonormativity to put brown and gender nonconforming bodies at lethal risk (Baldwin, *Giovanni's Room*); and the need to create life-giving historiographies of queer black lived experience (*Looking for Langston* [Julien et al. 1989]).

Following Traub, the sex/ "sex" we saw in *Counternarratives* stood in often ambiguous but productive relation to the sexual knowledge we had produced earlier in the course. Keene sets many of his counternarratives prior to the development of late nineteenth-century sexual and racial taxonomies. A bachelor plantation owner lounges between the thighs of his seated Haitian slave, who elsewhere in the story "moved through the house as if it were his" (98). Near the end of a long list of items found in the master's trunk, Keene—without explanatory comment—places a "large carved and polished rosewood implement, like an arm-length squash, that smelled vaguely of the outhouse" (94). A young white mistress mistakes her slave's dutifulness for devotion and, instrumental-

izing her property, "would practice her affections" upon the slave. A
black man in the service of a Union engineer during the Civil War flies
an army hot air balloon from Washington, DC, back to his black male
sweetheart in Philadelphia. The fetishized queer black female body, object not only of the common white male gaze but of the intertwining categorical compulsions of scientific racism and sexology in fin-de-siècle
Western Europe, is pushed higher up her acrobat's rope (represented by
a slim vertical line of text) as much by the stares as by the voices of the
men in the carnival audience below. The perspective will be reversed at
the story's close by another vertical line of text. This time "Miss La La,"
whose real name was Anna Olga Albertine Brown, stares down the rope,
fixing her eyes on the artist frantically sketching her, "Degas, le blanc,
down there" (247).[14]

In all of these textual instances and many others, my class saw imper-
fect analogs to many of the sexual/racial issues we had been discussing
all semester. But one particular relationship between *Counternarratives*
and another work of black gay male literature enabled us to shake off
our illiteracy feelings and instead position ourselves as competent black
queer readers. Earlier in the semester we had read large portions of the
collection *Brother to Brother: New Writings by Black Gay Men* (2007).
Conceived by Joseph Beam, completed by editor Essex Hemphill, and
originally published by Alyson Publications in 1991, the book represented the flourishing of writing by same-gender-loving black men in
the 1980s and 1990s. Like Beam and later Hemphill, and like significant portions of their black gay male readership, many of the writers in
Brother to Brother died of AIDS. The book fell out of print. To imagine
the absence of *Brother to Brother* was a powerful exercise for many of my
students in recognizing AIDS as a tool of un-knowledge, an intentional
obfuscation that made black gay male sex resistant to understanding.[15]

The survival of this collection of black queer narratives, poems, and
essays was not guaranteed. But Lisa C. Moore, who founded Redbone
Press in 1997, recognized the immense value of the collection to queer
black literacies and lives, and she reprinted the volume in 2007. Moore
visited our class at CSI to tell the story of how the new edition came into
being, of the challenges of securing permissions when authors have died,
of the struggle to find next of kin when some families have abandoned
their queer children. She told of locating men who had stopped writing

or not, moved or stayed, lived in one way or another. Some of *Brother to Brother*'s authors were easy to find. John Keene was one of them.

Keene comes out of a history of writing by black queers where survival was not guaranteed and, as Lorde attests, not intended. His presence in *Brother to Brother* cemented for my class the connection between Keene's work in *Counternarratives* and Moore's work at Redbone Press. Their projects are bound together by a shared knowledge that black queer stories are not meant to survive and cannot survive if we do not put the books in each other's hands and begin teaching ourselves and others, once more, to read.

NOTES

1 First published by the Feminist Press in 1982 and republished in 2015, the document that best theorizes and operationalizes fugitive pedagogy continues to be *All the Women Are White, All the Blacks Are Men, But Some of Us Are Brave: Black Women's Studies*, edited by Gloria T. Hull, Patricia Bell-Scott, and Barbara Smith.

2 I use the term "literacy" in its general sense, "the ability to read and write."

3 Implicitly I recognize the incredible burden shouldered by those educators, especially queer people of color, who teach queer black literacies at sites across the curriculum, for they teach against the active presence of antiblack, antiqueer educational histories and student preparations.

4 Ernesto Martinez suggests that queer of color writers have had "a recurring preoccupation with intelligibility, . . . a concern with the everyday labor of *making sense of oneself* and of *making sense to others* in contexts of intense ideological violence and interpersonal conflict" (2012, 13; emphasis in original).

5 This last title, it turns out, is an abbreviated—or rather, aborted—form of an even longer title that appears on the first page of the story itself: "Gloss on a History of Roman Catholics in the Early American Republic, 1790–1825; or The Strange History of Our Lady of the Sorrows." The reason for this discrepancy emerges formally on the second page of the "gloss," or superficial, historical narrative that opens "the" story, when the reader is redirected by way of a footnote to the "strange" story beneath. The footnote, extending for the next seventy-two pages, becomes the true story.

6 Aida Levy-Hussen, in *How to Read African American Literature: Post-Civil Rights Fiction and the Task of Interpretation* (2016), offers another model for disrupting normative practices for reading African American literature and, in particular, slave narratives.

7 In their 2017 collection *Who Writes for Black Children?: African American Children's Literature before 1900*, editors Katharine Capshaw and Anna Mae Duane pose a related set of questions about blackness, reading, and the white supremacist historical record.

8 The connection between white need and story has been most convincingly articulated by Toni Morrison in *Playing in the Dark: Whiteness and the Literary Imagination* (1992).

9 Jim and Huck have a longstanding critical association with nonheteronormativity, beginning with Leslie Fiedler's influential 1948 essay, "Come Back to the Raft Ag'in, Huck Honey!"

10 The counterreaders in this class, like most of my classes at CSI, were brown and black and ethnic white, mostly women and gender nonconforming, mostly working class or working poor, many first-generation and immigrant, all commuter students taking a three-and-a-half-hour night class, often coming from work earlier in the day.

11 Alexis Pauline Gumbs's consideration of philosopher Sylvia Wynter's notion of "the poetic" is apt in this regard (2014, 240–41).

12 See Sharon Patricia Holland's *Raising the Dead* (2000, ch. 4), and my *James Baldwin and the Queer Imagination* (2014, ch. 1).

13 In *Thinking Sex with the Early Moderns*, Traub argues that the epistemological value of sex, especially over time, lies precisely in its inscrutability: "[T]he opacities of eroticism—not just those aspects of sex that exceed our grasp, but those that manifest themselves as the *unthought*—can serve as a productive analytical resource. . . . [T]hese structures of occultation and unintelligibility *are also the source of our ability to apprehend and analyze them*" (2016, 4).

14 For more on Degas's gaze, see "The Modern Woman Explores the Male Gaze," by Robin Laurence (2010). For more on scientific racism and the construction of homosexuality, see Siobhan Somerville (2000). For more on the objectification of female carnival performers, see Rosemarie Garland-Thomson (1997).

15 Martin Duberman, in his 2014 dual biography of Michael Callen and Essex Hemphill, notes that "[t]elling Essex Hemphill's story proved more difficult" in part because "Essex's temperament was considerably more guarded than Mike's" but also because of the paucity of material he left behind (2014, 10). Such absences in the black gay archival record are a result of the same racist, homophobic, and classist sociocultural conditions that create AIDS as a "tool of un-knowledge."

WORKS CITED

Baldwin, James. (1956) 2000. *Giovanni's Room*. New York: Delta.

Baldwin, James. 1985. *The Price of the Ticket: Collected Nonfiction, 1948–1985*. New York: St. Martin's.

Brim, Matt. 2014. *James Baldwin and the Queer Imagination*. Ann Arbor: University of Michigan Press.

Capshaw, Katharine, and Anna Mae Duane. 2017. *Who Writes for Black Children?: African American Children's Literature before 1900*. Minneapolis: University of Minnesota Press.

Duberman, Martin. 2014. *Hold Tight Gently: Michael Callen, Essex Hemphill, and the Battlefield of AIDS*. New York: New Press.

Fiedler, Leslie. 1948. "Come Back to the Raft Ag'in, Huck Honey!" *Partisan Review* (June).

Garland-Thomson, Rosemarie. 1997. *Extraordinary Bodies: Figuring Physical Disability in American Literature and Culture*. New York: Columbia University Press.

Gumbs, Alexis Pauline. 2014. "Nobody Mean More: Black Feminist Pedagogy and Solidarity." In *The Imperial University: Academic Repression and Scholarly Dissent*, edited by Piya Chatterjee and Sunaina Maira, 237–59. Minneapolis: University of Minnesota Press.

Hemphill, Essex, ed. (1991) 2007. *Brother to Brother: New Writings by Black Gay Men*. Washington, DC: RedBone Press.

Holland, Sharon Patricia. 2000. *Raising the Dead: Readings of Death and (Black) Subjectivity*. Durham, NC: Duke University Press.

Hull, Gloria T., Patricia Bell-Scott, and Barbara Smith, eds. 2015. *All the Women Are White, All the Blacks Are Men, But Some of Us Are Brave: Black Women's Studies*. 2nd ed. New York: Feminist Press.

Julien, Isaac, Nadine Marsh-Edwards, Essex Hemphill, and Bruce Nugent. 1989. *Looking for Langston: A Meditation on Langston Hughes (1902–1967) and the Harlem Renaissance*. London: Sankofa Film & Video.

Keene, John. 2015. *Counternarratives*. New York: New Directions.

Laurence, Robin. 2010. "The Modern Woman Explores the Male Gaze." *Straight*, June 7, 2010. www.straight.com/.

Levy-Hussen, Aida. 2016. *How to Read African American Literature: Post–Civil Rights Fiction and the Task of Interpretation*. New York: New York University Press.

Lucas, Julian. 2017. "Epic Stories That Expand the Universal Family Plot." *New York Times*, September 1. www.nytimes.com/.

Martinez, Ernesto. 2012. *On Making Sense: Queer Race Narratives of Intelligibility*. Stanford, CA: Stanford University Press.

Moonlight. 2016. Dir. by Barry Jenkins. New York: A24.

Morrison, Toni. 1992. *Playing in the Dark: Whiteness and the Literary Imagination*. Cambridge, MA: Harvard University Press.

Passing—Profiling the Lives of Young Transmen of Color. 2015. Dir. by Lucah Rosenberg Lee and J. Mitchell Reed. San Francisco: Frameline.

Reid-Pharr, Robert. 2016. *Archives of Flesh: African America, Spain, and Post-Humanist Critique*. New York: NYU Press.

Tongues Untied. 1989. Dir. by Marlon Riggs. San Francisco: Frameline.

Somerville, Siobhan. 2000. *Queering the Color Line: Race and the Invention of Homosexuality in American Culture*. Durham, NC: Duke University Press.

Traub, Valerie. 2016. *Thinking Sex with the Early Moderns*. Philadelphia: University of Pennsylvania Press.

Tuhkanen, Mikko. 2017. Review of *Archives of Flesh: African America, Spain, and Post-Humanist Critique*, by Robert Reid-Pharr. In *American Literary History Online Review Series XI*, June 13. http://academic.oup.com/.

7

Measurement, Interrupted

Queer Possibilities for Social Scientific Methods

ZANDRIA F. ROBINSON AND MARCUS ANTHONY HUNTER

In June 2017, people representing Black Lives Matter and the more expansive Movement for Black Lives demonstrated against Pride parades in cities across the United States as part of black organizers' longstanding attempts to build an intersectional coalitional politics simultaneously attentive to race, gender, sexuality, ability, nationality, and immigration status. Black activists, many of whom were queer, declared "no justice, no pride," highlighting what they saw as white queer people's tacit acceptance of police brutality against black people across sexuality and gender identity. Indeed, many white Pride marchers carried "Black Lives Matter" signs or donned clothes and pins; some expressed awareness of the work that still needs to be done by white lesbian, gay, bisexual, gender-nonconforming, and trans people to stand in solidarity against all forms of oppression, including racial oppression.

Others saw Pride as not the place for this "interruption," as it was characterized by some white marchers and media outlets reporting on the event, instead embracing a willful ignorance of the black and Latina origins of the movement and its resistance to police brutality. In the usual intersectionality fail, some whites seemed unaware that it was entirely possible to be both black and queer. Although black political scientist Cathy Cohen (1997) had argued beautifully and persuasively for a coalitional, radical, queer resistance politics some two decades previous, at that year's Pride parades, it was evident that there was still quite a distance to go to realize her vision.

These tensions were especially palpable, materially and symbolically, in the original chocolate city,[1] Washington, DC. Now a "latte city" (Hyra 2017), DC's racial inequities and displacement of black people made it a staging ground for place-based demonstrations against police brutality, economic exploitation, and the exclusion of black queer people from the core the LGBTQ community in the city. In the nation's capital, black people, who had once been the majority there, demanded a redistribution of urban resources and an immediate rectification of the violent policing of black people and black communities. As they have been in many U.S. justice movements, black queer people were at the helm.

The social sciences have provided us with a wealth of data about the experiences of lesbian, gay, bisexual, and transgender people, and increasingly gender-nonconforming people, in the past twenty years. Social scientists, and gender scholars in particular, have been charged to conceptualize power and domination in ways that recognize how heteropatriarchy and cisnormativity disadvantage queer people and privilege straight folks. From quantitative data on employment discrimination and disparate health outcomes, to qualitative data on how people navigate marginalized sexual and gender identities and how sexuality shapes family formation, our contemporary scholarly understandings of queer experience owe much to the theoretical and methodological orientations of social scientists.

This research, with important exceptions, has generally been about white people and often about white men, which has severely limited the scope and veracity of our data, claims, and findings. It has also limited the questions that we have been able, or have known, to ask. It has further distanced us from the kind of coalitional politics of liberatory resistance Cohen imagined.

The field of social science, and sociology specifically, has struggled methodologically and epistemologically with the basic premise of queer theory, which at least nominally undergirds this research. Queer theory asks us to begin with decentering "normal," to interrogate it, to point out the relations of domination imbedded in an invisible normal, and to ultimately obliterate the very idea of normal. Yet, in a field that requires by nature of its methodological approaches a *norm*, if not a *mode*, it would seem that the liberatory aims of queer theory and the constraining form of social scientific methods are incongruous (Brim and Ghaziani 2016). Aware of this, gender and sexuality scholars work diligently to innovate methodologically in ways that gesture toward queer theory's call for change within the confines of the usual kinds of data we can access, collect, and analyze.

This methodological conundrum, that of the tension between liberatory theory-making and the constraints of social scientific method, is not unique to sexuality studies and queer theory. The concept of intersectionality, a black feminist perspective that sees systems of power and oppression—patriarchy, racism, sexism, heteropatriarchy, cissexism, ableism, and, as theorist Judith Butler called it, "the embarrass[ing] etcetera" (Butler [1990] 2007, 196)[2] —has also been the subject of much theoretical and methodological handwringing about how to make the conversation between theory and our existing social scientific methods more deliberately and authentically dialectical. It is because of this work, for instance, that we can measure, in dollars or callbacks for rental units or jobs, how much more disadvantaged a black woman might be than a white woman or a black man, or a black man with a felony versus a white man with one, and so on.

We can use an intersectional perspective to measure how inequality is distributed through institutions—the labor market, the housing market, health care, criminal justice, and politics. The "methodological complexity" (McCall 2005) and "definitional dilemmas" (Collins 2015) of intersectionality make the concept difficult to tame, as it were, and put in service of the kinds of data and research social scientists produce. Moreover, its roots in black feminist critical analyses and black women's social movement work put it at odds in some ways with the quantitative turn in social science that holds all research, qualitative or otherwise, up to the same measurement standards. How can we measure the impact of inequity so that we might effect policy change, or even liberation, without losing the diversity and nuance of human experience that might exist outside of the norms we have defined for the sake of social scientific expediency and legitimacy?

One way to think through this is to throw measurement away altogether, acknowledging that its tyranny is incorrigibly heteropatriarchal, ableist, and white supremacist, and recalling what black feminist poet Audre Lorde ([1979] 2004) told us about not using the master's tools to dismantle his house. This strategy, however, forgets how marginalized people have harnessed measurement to liberate themselves from enslavement, challenge and upend the status quo, and rewrite history. Alternatively, then, following queer theory's aims to tear down and reimagine, we might decenter measurement and the way it has come to be defined in neoliberal and social scientific terms and focus instead on people and stories. We also might relocate this kind of measurement, demoting it below other kinds of investigatory methods. At the very least, we must queer and thus expand the possibilities of what counts as a "measure" and what counts as "data." Not simply deductive versus inductive pathways to theory and knowledge, this approach asks us to consider other kinds of data—stories, feelings, popular culture events, Twitter timelines, songs, blogs—and to continue to develop ways to systematize their collection. To decenter or relocate measurement is to place queer theory into conversation with cultural sociologist Stuart Hall's ([1980] 1998) call for an investment in the popular as a site of investigation, to begin there and move forward, backward, around, and underground. It is to acknowledge that theory is lived and begins with the people.

We might do well to deploy queer methodologies that reinvigorate social science's early commitment to the spirit sciences, or *Geisteswissenschaften*, a wide range of humanistic and interdisciplinary social science fields that sought to explore the human condition comprehensively. The notion of a spirit science undergirds pioneering black sociologists W.E.B. Du Bois's (1903) theoretical treatise "Of Our Spiritual Strivings" and Zora Neale Hurston's folk investigations in her hometown of Eatonville, Florida, and in Haiti. Queering measurement with spirit, the seemingly immeasurable, is the first necessary goal of queering our disciplinary practices.

This is the methodological approach we took in *Chocolate Cities: The Black Map of American Life* (2018), which began in an *Annual Review of Sociology* article that argued for "chocolate city sociology" (2016). Weary of the deficit epistemology of most social scientific research about black urban life, we argued for an asset approach, focusing on how black folks theorized, shifted, and changed the American urban landscape. This is of course not a novel idea; it is one that black people, and indeed marginalized people of all sorts, have deployed for as long as they have been oppressed. In the neoliberal articulation of the social sciences, however, this approach was and is foreign. Deficits are, after all, how we both justify research that highlights the inequity of the status quo and reify the status quo to continue to justify our research.

It is also the approach we took, albeit without the moniker of "chocolate city sociology," in our respective monographs and research programs before *Chocolate Cities*. In *Black Citymakers: How "The Philadelphia Negro" Changed Urban America* (2013), Hunter reverses and effectively queers the narrative of black urban displacement by focusing on how black people made place, in this case in the city of Philadelphia, from the pioneering sociological work of Du Bois to the choices of everyday black Philadelphians who created robust black communities. Similarly, Robinson's work in *This Ain't Chicago: Race, Class, and Regional Identity in the Post-Soul South* (2014) decenters traditional measurement and instead draws on the popular, including film, television, and music, to make scientific claims when there was little social scientific data, quantitative or qualitative, on the intersection of race, class, gender, and region in the contemporary urban South. In each of our books, we pushed at the boundaries, assumptions, and epistemologies of urban sociology to attend to race, place, and oppression through an asset lens.

Black people occupying multiple disadvantaged positions in society, including black women and femmes, black queer, trans, and nonbinary people, disabled black people, undocumented black people, and combinations of the aforementioned, are rightly skeptical of social science, a wariness often exacerbated by their experiences at intersecting positions of marginalization. For these groups, asset-based epistemologies are central. Black women organized against the assertions of the federally commissioned Moynihan Report (1965) to argue for the special resilience of black families and black mothers; black queer men focused on strong communities and gay families in light of discourses that situated them as sociopathic sexual deviants; black lesbian women conjured histories of themselves where there were none, like black feminist filmmaker Cheryl Dunye's *Watermelon Woman* (1997); black trans women asserted not only their rights to womanhood but also their contributions to more liberatory notions of womanhood; and black disabled people created discourses of pride in their intersecting identities where popular discourses rendered them invisible or where ableist black people encouraged them to downplay their experiences as disabled in order to put forth a respectable face for the race. To decenter measurement, we must look to the ways that multiply marginalized groups—whether they are in "double jeopardy" (Beal [1969] 2008) or multiple jeopardy (King 1988), are under "triple constraints" (Barnett 1993), or are in the long list of "embarrassed etc." (Butler 1990)—have used an asset-based approach to theorize their own lives and imagine new worlds for themselves.

Here, we offer a retrospective on research on black queer urban experiences, highlighting work operating at the intersection of race, urban sociology, and sexualities research that decenters measurement. These works offer new ways of thinking about queer theory, queer methods, and queer life in the United States, and though they will be familiar to most readers, we hope that revisiting them through a queer urban asset-based approach that decenters measurement resituates this work in lineage of queer methodological practice. We also review approaches to black queer theory and black urban theory as epistemological, methodological, and theoretical interventions into queer theory and urban theory writ large. We put this work in conversation with our work on chocolate city sociology with an aim to distill some methodological approaches to queering/quaring urban life.

Intersectionality, Queer Theory, and Epistemology

Although it became a fashionable and hypervisible terminology quite recently as a result of the work of black women on Twitter, intersectionality, as the term's coiner, black feminist legal scholar Kimberlé Crenshaw (1989), notes, is rooted in black women's theorizations of their experiences simultaneously inhabiting at least two disadvantaged sites of oppression—race and gender—and most often three—race, gender, and class. Enslaved black women understood their societal positions relative to white women as neither free nor "woman" or "lady," so they used rhetorical strategies to lay claim to the rights of womanhood when they could and resistance strategies to subvert capitalist aims to exploit the productive and reproductive value of their bodies. Some of the earliest social scientists, including Anna Julia Cooper, Ida B. Wells, and W.E.B. Du Bois, recognized that both race and gender intersected to socioeconomically disadvantage black women, and their research carefully demonstrated how these intersections functioned.

Black women's movements, from the club movement to civil rights and Black Lives Matter, have always focused on dismantling interlocking systems of racism and patriarchy, and often for black women this work has also meant dismantling capitalism. Through movement organizing in the civil rights era, queer black women and black trans women confronted heteropatriarchy in work with homoantagonistic and transmisogynist black women and men; racism in white women's organizing spaces, white lesbian spaces included; and sexism, homoantagonism, and transmisogyny in organizing spaces dominated by patriarchal leadership. Queer and trans black women's visibility increased in the third and fourth waves of the black feminist movement, in concert with a national turn in attitudes toward LGBTQ persons but also as the result of queer black women's usual vigorous naming of themselves and creating space for themselves. Alicia Garza's extensive "Herstory" (2014) of the Black Lives Matter organization is explicit about the work she did with fellow Black Lives Matter activists Patrisse Cullors and Opal Tometi to found the organization. Her purposeful and thorough history is explicitly positioned to prevent the "theft of black queer women's work," both within and beyond black communities.

In short, because black women have always existed at the intersection of race, gender, and class disadvantage, they have always already been engaged in intersectional theorizing. Crenshaw's (1989; 1991) essential early work in this area contributed to the naming of a centuries-old theoretical practice and the institutionalization of this theoretical work in the academy, from law to the humanities and later to sociology and other social sciences as well (Robinson 2016; 2017). These perspectives still ground much of black women's organizing and black organizing in general, as activists work to challenge all systems of oppression.

Queer theory, too, emerged from a movement tradition, and one that was aligned and often in solidarity with black feminist movements and leftist movements. The Stonewall riots were led by black and Latina trans women Marsha P. Johnson and Sylvia Rivera, and Garza's "Herstory" of Black Lives Matter certainly recalls the lesson of Johnson and Rivera's erasure, as well as the erasure of scores of transgender, lesbian, and gay activists who were not white, from the history of LGBT liberation. Johnson and Rivera's organizing, most notably the Street Transvestite Action Revolutionaries (STAR), set the agenda for and made possible subsequent organizing, including the AIDS Coalition to Unleash Power (ACT UP) and later Queer Nation.

Just as the organizing work and writings of SNCC members set the stage for black writing and research across disciplines in the academy in the 1970s, so too did STAR's work, including its pamphlets, serve as the foundation for modern queer theory, writing, research, and practice. Because they existed at disadvantaged race, class, gender, and sexuality positions, these women's theory and organizing was also necessary and endemic to their lived experiences. As such, their lived experiences and labor, whether we recognize their spirit or not in our queer and queering work, should be acknowledged as present in our research and writing. Decentering measurement allows us to know and to show in our work upon whose ground we stand.

Marginalized scholars, community organizers, and activists rarely have control over if and how their ideas are institutionalized in the academy, the media, and popular discourse. The paths of intersectionality and queer theory, as well as the methods used in conjunction with them, tell us much about how, once disconnected from their history, liberatory principles are stripped of the practices and perspectives that make liberation possible. Intersectionality has been shorn of its black feminist origins in many spaces, existing in a race × class × gender formulation used to understand degrees of disadvantage. In a race to *not* compete in the so-called "Oppression Olympics," some people have deployed intersectionality as a theory of identity and lived experience rather than one of interlocking systems of oppression.

Queer theory similarly has been shorn of its black and Latina, trans, and radical leftist origins. Both theoretical ideas gained traction in academic discourse just as "people," "bodies," and "oppression" were being replaced by the poststructural language of "identities," "signifiers," and "difference." That is, when people who had experienced the most material disadvantage, the most physical violence and brutality, made it into the academic mainstream, the academy had moved beyond the material to the poststructural and nearly posthuman. While sociology can claim some immunity from this largely humanities-based turn, it was not unaffected by its tendency to obscure. This language and its accompanying methodological shadowboxing distances us further and further from the roots of organizing for liberation of all dispossessed persons.

Black feminist and black queer theorists have carved out space for themselves and their work by drawing on their lived experiences to delineate distinct epistemic positions. These spaces are not responding to normative theoretical articulations—"white" feminism or "white" queer theory—but rather existed all along and have become visible, for better or worse, as interventions into white-dominated scholarly spaces. In their important edited volume *Black Queer Studies*, performance studies theorist E. Patrick Johnson and literary scholar Mae G. Henderson begin with an explicit declaration about the collection's purpose: "[To stage] a dialogic and dialectic encounter between [black studies and queer studies], two liberatory and interrogatory discourses" (Johnson and Henderson 2005, 2). The editors also make some critical notes about discipline and method, which still resonate more than a decade and a lifetime of social media later. We quote here at length from their conversation about the volume's essays vis-à-vis discipline, method, and liberatory possibilities:

> Although these essays span diverse disciplines and deploy multiple methodologies, they only begin to mine the rich theoretical terrain of black studies as it intersects with queer studies. Notably, many of the authors included in this volume are in the humanities as opposed to the social sciences, a bias that is a reflection of the background of the editors rather than a deliberate omission. Our goal, however, is to make disciplinary boundaries more permeable and thereby encourage border crossings between the humanities and social sciences. As such, the focus of inquiry here tends to be less on the formal disciplinary training of our contributors and more on the interdisciplinary intellectual content of their scholarship. Nevertheless, while some authors write from paradigms reflecting a perspective and training in the social sciences and/or the humanities, others deploy social science methodologies despite their affiliation with the humanities. *Moreover, much of the interventionist work in the areas of race and sexuality has come out of the humanities and not the social sciences.* Indeed, social sciences fields such as sociology have often been antagonistic toward African American culture and nonnormative sexualities in ways that have, according to Roderick Ferguson, "excluded and discipline those formations that deviate from the racial ideal of heteropatriarchy. (Johnson and Henderson 2005, 2–3, emphasis mine)

Although we might gladly take exception to the critique because of our disciplinary training and concomitant loyalties, there is no lie to be found here. Black queer and black feminist work has certainly increased and advanced in the social sciences since the publication of *Black Queer Studies*; however, the continued marginalization of black feminist and black queer perspectives in the epistemology and methodology of queer social scientific work has rendered interventionist, liberatory work all the more difficult in the social sciences more broadly.

Issues of method are foremost issues of epistemology. Johnson's groundbreaking essay outlining the contours of a black queer theoretical field is important precisely because it is concerned with the epistemology that precedes theory and method. "Queer" is not enough; "'quare,' on the other hand, not only speaks across identities, it *articulates* identities as well" (Johnson, 2005, 127). Here, Johnson highlights a distinct set of ways of knowing that are rooted in black experience, vernacular traditions, and importantly, place. Our epistemic positions shape the questions we ask, where we see gaps, and which ways of interrogation and rectification we see as appropriate. The question, then, becomes: How do we devise methods that are rooted in the epistemologies of the people about whom we seek answers while also interrogating structures and systems of power that affect their lives on a macro scale? How can measurement be relocated into and repurposed for the liberation arsenals of marginalized groups, whose intersecting theories about racism, heterosexism, and class oppression are forged in activist struggle?

Mapping the Gaps in the Sociological Study of Black Queer Life

Sociological investigations of black life have several gaps that inhibit our ability to innovate methodologies toward the ends of equity and justice. Three such gaps are of interest to us in this discussion. First, most sociological work on black people deploys a deficit perspective, examining how structural inequities have affected the behaviors and choices, lumped under the umbrella of "black culture," of black folks in the United States (Hunter and Robinson 2016). This epistemic practice is a feature of the discipline's and its major departments' engagements with and creation of white supremacist logics in tandem with the dramatic change in urban America's racial landscapes in the first half of the twentieth century (Baldwin 2004). Engaging with black people as a "problem" endures, and neoliberal language continues to obscure the fact that asking marginalized people "How does it feel to be a problem?" is still an especially wrong question. We address this gap by both employing an asset perspective and, when necessary, pointing directly to the parties and policies responsible for inequitable material realities.

Second, most research about black life takes places in urban, suburban, and exurban spaces, locating all black people, and people of color more generally, in city spaces. Indeed, most people live in metropolises, and people of color are more likely to live in inner cities than other groups. Still, black people are overrepresented in rural areas and small towns, which are not prominent sites of investigation in sociology. To address this epistemic gap and bring it more in line with how black people theorize and map their histories and lives, our definition of "chocolate city" does not literally denote the urban sociological and standard demographic definitions of "a city." Instead, we theorize any spaces that black people create and generate culture and make and do place as a city. This then includes neighborhoods of Harlem and Bronzeville; Clarksdale, Mississippi, the "big city" of the Mississippi Delta; the Central District and now suburban Kent in Seattle; and even the chocolate city of Black Twitter. In short, anywhere two or more black people are gathered, there is a chocolate city in progress.

Third, research on black life in sociology has often used a heteronormative lens, and has thus been largely unconcerned with the experiences of black queer people vis-à-vis the city. This work situates different-sex family formation patterns and the absence of men earners and jobs for men earners as one of the central problems of black urban life. As black sociologist Mignon Moore (2015) notes in her theoretical and methodological reflection on locating and rendering visible black queer populations in urban research, "most ethnographic approaches to the study of city life are biased toward the experiences of people who claim heterosexuality" (245), pointing out that the vast majority of work about queer experiences in cities emerges from the field of history. In calling for more work on queer persons of color in the city, Moore argues that such work "would help us theorize more effectively the role of urban communities in changing society" (246). A chocolate cities approach to black queer city life heeds Moore's call for increasing the amount of work on black queer folks in cities and also investigates how black queer and trans people have created and made space in cities both alongside and separate from black straight and/or cis people.

Across sexuality, gender identity, and gender expression, black Americans map the nation, and indeed the globe, in ways that are contrary to our traditional understandings of the geography of black life. One of these traditional understandings replicated in social science research is a linear, progressive one of black people's enslavement, freedom, and migration from the rural South to the cities of the West, Midwest, and Northeast. This understanding largely ignored the continuing existence of black people in the South, despite the fact that over half of the black population resided in the South for most of American history. Sociologists focused on black people as disruptions in the urban landscapes of Chicago, Philadelphia, and Detroit, and later on their deficiencies as a result of hypersegregation. This view of geography situates whiteness as the norm and white people as the persons always already present before black people "arrived." This is a convenient geographic history that obscures the white settler-colonialism that violently displaced indigenous populations; the entire nation's massive dependency on economies of enslavement; and the repressive violence of white supremacy that compelled black people to leave their lives and kin in the South.

We reject geographies of "moving" to freedom or opportunity, even as we recognize that by some quantitative measurements, black "outcomes" might be better in this place rather than that one. Instead, we draw on black people's collective understandings of the South as articulated in the prose of James Baldwin, the investigative journalism of Ida B. Wells, the ethnography of Zora Neale Hurston, the soul stylings of Erykah Badu, and the funky future posited by Parliament Funkadelic—in short, the narrative of black cultural workers—to remap the United States into multiple Souths. Like Malcolm X and other thinkers before us, we move the Mason-Dixon Line up to the U.S.-Canadian border, and frankly on up to the Arctic Ocean, given that Canada is hardly free of histories of antiblack and settler-colonialist violence. We call the resulting geography the Chocolate Map, a living cognitive and cultural understanding of space and place that centers the movement, politics, histories, and perspectives of black Americans as consequential to patterns of change, inequality, and development from the nineteenth century to present.

Our approach queers what counts as social scientific data and de-centers the questions of measurement—representativeness, reliability, generalizability, replicability, and validity—that can skew our under-standing of what matters most to a group of people who are chronicling their assets in the face of discourses that measure their lives only in terms of deficits. This is why we have taken a case approach—Ida B. Wells and W.E.B. Du Bois; Mary Shadd Cary and Mos Def; stories about our own parents and grandparents; narratives from San José, California, and Clarksdale, Mississippi—to illustrate sets of social facts about black life. This is not a new approach, but because it begins with an understanding of black popular culture, as it played out from nineteenth-century prose and media to the gifs and memes of Black Twitter (Clark 2014) as key data entry points, it is outside of accepted social scientific practice. We encourage scholars, especially those from intersecting marginalized identity groups, to take the cultural practices of their in-groups not simply as an escape from academic work, but rather as the popular liberation practices of people working every day, in one way or another, to get free.

In presentations of this work to sociology audiences, we have been asked, "What is the method/data/sampling regime [we used in *Chocolate Cities*]?" We make use of traditional data sources, including national and regional health, educational, and economic data; census data and demographic data about black population movement over time; and ethnographic data. These traditional sources constitute the background of our methodological approach. However, we also use case studies, oral histories, music, literary arts, and visual art from black culture workers to bring the Chocolate Map to life through the eyes of black people.

We have refused to contort the work of black cultural understand-ings into traditional social scientific methodological practice. We called this a "chocolate cities" approach simply because it begins with black folks as the central architects and philosophers of the social world. This requires the same tearing down and reimagining, the same decenter-ing of measurement that is needed in queer theory. To do our work of destroying and reimagining for chocolate cities, we draw on the late ge-ographer Clyde Woods's notion of "blues epistemology," which he used to describe the "ethno-regional epistemology" of black folks in the Mis-sissippi Delta, who had developed a "distinct perspective on who they are and where they are, on their predicament, and on who is responsible" (Woods 1998). Woods himself was drawing on a long tradition of Africana scholarship that situated the blues as the epistemological center of black life in the United States, from the work of blues singers to their various literary interlocutors and archivists to the people who lived and inspired the blues in the everyday. We do not suggest that there is one genealogy, one set of tools with which to destroy and rebuild. But a broad and robust archive of queer methods that decenter measurement is a necessary precursor to knowing what genealogies are available and which ones will be suited for which jobs of rethinking and reimagining.

We see our work as the beginning of an intervention in urban sociology that is invested in moving toward a liberatory urban practice in line with movement organizing for urban equity and justice. It requires, though, an epistemic shift from deficit to asset; rigorous interdisciplinary engagement, particularly with critical black geographies, American studies, cultural studies, and performance studies; and a queering of what counts as data in social science. This work also necessitates generating a black queer urban archive that is not just located *in* places but that is *of* places, one in which place is integral to our understanding of black queer experience in and beyond the city. Our approach is not without generalizations and the usual methodological hiccups that earn sociologists critiques both warranted and otherwise. However, we base our findings on a survey of black people's varied popular and public articulations of black geography and black life. We see black people as the best informants on their own lives and see their collective cultural creations, fraught and contentious, as the best data possible for use in service of black liberation.

In the next section, we follow a black queer urban archive from the traditional urban triumvirate of New York, Chicago, and Los Angeles to other kinds of chocolate cities in New Orleans, the Mississippi Delta, and across the South. We focus on how epistemology influences research design and research methods to underscore the importance of pushing beyond the boundaries of normative understandings of data and science. We see this work as constituting a historically important pathway to emergent work on black queer space, movement organizing, and equity and liberation.

Toward a Queer Chocolate Cities Archive

Cultural anthropologist William Hawkeswood's ([1991] 1996) work on black gay men in Harlem remains an important model for how work on black queer communities can and should be done. An exemplary urban anthropologist, Hawkeswood created scholarship out of his own lived experiences, his observations of black gay life in Harlem, and activism in Harlem around HIV/AIDS. His place in the community and impact on Columbia University's anthropology program and beyond ensured that his work moved from dissertation to book, from possibly buried archive to the surface of scholarship after his death. Now out of print, *One of the Children* is archived in the University of California Press's electronic library.

Hawkeswood's work offers a blueprint for an asset perspective research program in black communities. With beautifully comprehensive portraits of his research participants, he problematized existing social scientific tropes of black men that had been popularized both by the Moynihan Report and urban sociological research in the late 1980s and early 1990s. He rendered black gay men visible and simultaneously highlighted alternative ways to understand black masculinity that were applicable to black men across sexuality.

In addition to its pioneering status in the areas of black masculinity and family life, Hawkeswood's research is especially important foundational work for black queer life in cities. He observes that the black gay men in his study live in the black spaces of Harlem, rather than New York's largely white gay neighborhood, highlighting the men's status as sexual minorities in a racially homogeneous community. Importantly, Hawkeswood does not dwell on his respondents' exclusion from the gayborhood but rather focuses on how they create community and life within the space of Harlem and how they transform the social and family landscape of the neighborhood in the process. He does, however, issue a warning to HIV/AIDS educators and activists that education about the disease must increase to prevent unnecessary deaths. Hawkeswood was of course devastatingly right; the racism of white HIV/AIDS organizations and the silence around HIV/AIDS in black communities cost many black gay men their lives.

Though traditional "gayborhoods" are currently undergoing shifts in form as a result of years of people moving out of them (Ghaziani 2014; 2015), for black gay people, this shift is only important insofar as movement from gayborhoods contributes in some ways to the urban displacement of black people of all sexualities. While Hawkeswood may not spend time questioning the whiteness of Greenwich Village's gayborhood, rhetoric scholar Charles I. Nero (2005) considers the question outright in his essay "Why Are the Gay Ghettoes White?" The method here is of interest. Nero first offers an epistemological critique of existing research on gayborhoods, focusing on geographer Lawrence Knopp's (1997) work on gay gentrification in New Orleans's Faubourg Marigny neighborhood. In Nero's view, Knopp fails to engage how wealth and racism shaped Faubourg Marigny into an exclusively white and male gay community that was hostile to adjacent black neighborhoods. In general, Nero is struck by the fact that the significance of "racialization through processes of inclusion and exclusion . . . for the formation of gay neighborhoods is seldom discussed" (2005, 243).

Next, Nero constructs a skillful asset approach that highlights the richness of black queer communities and networks in New Orleans. He does so by drawing on his own lived experience coming of age, being educated in, and working in New Orleans as data for critique of the absence of rigorous engagement with race and power in Knopp's work. Nero says, "I have used my own knowledge about New Orleans, supplemented by further research" (232), which situates his experience as a legitimate data point in this research. He then turns to critical readings of television shows, films, and theater productions, demonstrating how white hostility toward black masculinity is rooted in enduring "controlling images" of black men, and gay black men in particular. Layering this analysis over engagements with Michael Omi and Howard Winant's (originally 1986) theory of racial formation (2014) and Melvin Oliver and Thomas Shapiro's (2006) work on housing and wealth inequality, Nero creates a multifaceted, multidisciplinary, multimethod examination of how material and discursive white supremacy create segregated gayborhoods. His work proceeds by offering an epistemological critique, centering the importance of black knowledges and personal experiences, and then drawing on a range of data types to bring black experiences, as well as the racist and homophobic white imaginary, into view. The result is work that both critiques the broader LGBTQ movement's gestures toward social justice and pushes toward black liberation across sexuality.

Hunter's (2010) work on social practices in black nightlife, which he terms "the nightly round," is another example of work with a methodology that begins with an important epistemological critique. Examining a "gay night" and "straight night" at one club in Chicago, Hunter offers a cross-sexuality intraracial analysis of how black people use the social space of nightlife and the practice of clubbing to garner social support and create networks of care in a segregated city. This is black queer urban work that renders black gay and lesbian people visible within cities, within leisure spaces, and within black communities. He shows that because of the racism embedded in the spatial and social organization of the city, black nightlife becomes more than a leisure space, but a place through which black gays and lesbians in Chicago can acquire the resources that they are denied during the "daily round." Inverting day and night, white and black, straight and queer, Hunter offers a queer method that begins with where and when the people enter—in this case, their weekly night at the club.

Creating visibility, then, is a central methodological practice for queer chocolate cities researchers, even as social scientific visibility can invite unwanted and detrimental attention to communities. Visibility is its own manner of decentering measurement, since social science or any other science cannot measure what it refuses to see. Sociologist Mignon Moore's extensive corpus is an archive of making black lesbians visible in New York City and Los Angeles, and a methodological tour de force that highlights insider/outsider researcher challenges as well as practices for balancing social scientific methodological mores while honoring the epistemic contributions of black communities. Moore's primary interventions change how we think about family and family life in sociology; she makes black lesbian women and families visible in a research literature landscape that is heteronormative, deficit-based, and focused on male absence.

Her methodological work on access and working in cities is central to building a queer chocolate cities archive and queer method that renders black queer families, and black queer people more generally, visible in the city. She reflects on this work in an issue of *City and Community*, American sociology's premier urban journal, with an epistemological critique and a direct call: "It is time for urban scholars to incorporate into their research the experiences of LGBT populations and the ways they relate to urban spaces, taking into account other identities around race, ethnicity, religion, social class, gender presentation, and age" (2015, 246). She continues this call with specific methodological advice to urban researchers, and urban ethnographers in particular: "[R]eturn to your data. You may have detailed snippets in your fieldwork about sexual minority community members that never made it to the final drafts of your manuscripts. Go back and review those data, build on that work, and publish it to provide a blueprint for future scholars looking to understand how sexual minorities fit into urban spaces" (248).

As Nero (2005) questions the erasing of racism and wealth disparities in research on gay neighborhoods, Moore questions the erasure of sexuality in studies of urban life, and black and Latinx urban life in particular. Like other scholars working in what we are calling this queer chocolate cities archive, their epistemic claim to black queer knowledges is central and primary. We want to push these epistemic and methodological interventions to examine what kinds of black queer *place* knowledges are possible—across all kinds of chocolate city types. After all, a map of black gay and lesbian households in the United States demonstrates that the original Black Belt across the Southeast has the highest percentage of such households, and not all of those places are "cities" by sociological definition.

E. Patrick Johnson's work on black gay men and black lesbian women in the South is an example of work outside the traditional urban triumvirate, those places to which queer people of all races escape. Escape for the South is a common narrative in black literature as well as in social scientific understandings of blackness, and this is certainly the case for some black queer southerners. Titus Andromedon, a character on the Netflix series *The Unbreakable Kimmie Schmidt*, is one such person. We learn his backstory several episodes into the series when his abandoned wife, Vonda Jean, travels to New York to find him, where he has assumed a new name and is hilariously pursuing a career in theater. Born Ronald Wilkerson in Chickasaw County, Mississippi, Titus's narrative about sexual repression and homophobia in the small-town South is a familiar if stereotypical one. Most black queer Southerners in the small-town South are unable to leave, and if they are, the "big city" for them is not New York, Los Angeles, or Chicago, but perhaps Atlanta, Georgia; Jackson, Mississippi; Memphis, Tennessee; Charlotte, North Carolina; or Birmingham, Alabama. It is these kinds of spaces that a queer chocolate cities archive must bring into view to understand how black queer people make and shape life in these places as well.

Johnson's work offers two key lessons about the importance of place and reconceptualizing the urban in black queer research. First, he makes black queer life visible in the South, challenging the easy stereotype of the South, and the small-town South in particular, as especially homophobic. Drawing on performance studies and ethnography, Johnson sketches a space in which the mores of politeness, hospitality, and performative worship mitigate homoantagonism and change the traditional understandings of in and out of "the closet." As a black gay Southerner, Johnson moves throughout the South to tell a regional story about black gay life. This regional perspective is essential to understanding the limitations and possibilities of a black queer archive, as well as how we might collect data for it.

Johnson's research on black lesbian women in the South contains an important methodological lesson for thinking about gender and black queer life in urban space. While Johnson might not characterize his research collecting oral histories of black gay men in the South as "easy," by his own estimation, it was less difficult relative to locating Southern black lesbian women willing to participate in his research. Yet, Johnson returns to his own personal archive—his grandmother's discourse, black queer women with whom he grew up—to craft a "quare *and* feminist" method to build rapport with participants. Further, performance is central to his methodological practice. In an implicit critique of social scientific concerns with objectivity, Johnson argues:

[N]o method of documenting queer desire is without its challenges. My research on black quare women of the South is no different. Repeatedly, however, I have called on my own interdisciplinary home of performance studies to bring a different perspective to traditional disciplinary approaches to queer culture making and history. While performance is certainly not without its own theoretical and methodological quagmires—for it, like history writ large, cannot escape the politics of representation—it does in the instance of oral history carefully traverse several minefields through its capacity to view history as processual. It thereby holds in tension the discursive and the material, while exposing the trappings of teleological approaches to everyday life, which cannot always be rendered through the gaze of "objectivity." (2016, 63–64)

A queer chocolate cities archive would do well to follow this example of presenting and collecting data in ways that not only center black people's voices but also acknowledge them as *the* voice and authority on their own lives.

This archive is also being constructed consciously through movement and policy work in black communities. The Movement for Black Lives (M4BL), a coalition of organizations including Black Lives Matter, has forwarded an extensive platform that centers the liberation of all black people and all black lives. Its policy foci span environmental justice, prison abolition, addressing violence against trans women, fostering employment and income equity for queer people and families, labor justice, immigration, and reparations. Like Black Lives Matter, this youth-led coalition has prominent queer leadership and works diligently to advocate for black lives across ethnicity, nationality, immigration status, gender, gender expression, ability, and class. Importantly, it locates its work in places, conceptualizing how place enables and constrains the possibilities for black people, as well as how places affect how they might organize for justice.

Although some view its focus on land acquisition as marginalizing indigenous history and people in settler-colonialist ways, there is still room for a coalitional politics that advocates for indigenous rights and reparations as well as black liberation. The M4BL asserts that inclusive black liberation will facilitate the liberation of all marginalized groups. The call to Fund Black Futures and divest from policies, places, and practices that harm black communities that is embedded within the work of the Black Youth Project (BYP) and M4BL is a significant epistemic turn in the national resistance discourse that names the sources of oppression and demands rectification.

The #SayHerName initiative of Kimberlé Crenshaw's African American Policy Forum (AAPF) is another model of epistemic intervention in a national conversation. The AAPF has consistently advocated for an intersectional approach to black life, focusing on how black cis and trans girls and women experience disproportionate violence, as their cis and trans men counterparts do. Crenshaw's work offers a queer challenge to the national focus on violence against black men, and like the founders of Black Lives Matter, resists the erasure of black het, cis, trans, and/or queer women.

The works we have reviewed herein constitute one way into a queer chocolate cities archive, but they are certainly not the only ways. We see locating and building a queer chocolate cities archive, which first requires a decentering and relocation of measurement, as of key importance to understanding black queer life vis-à-vis place, organizing, and resistance, and we encourage an expansive understanding of data and method to arrive at such an archive.

Black Queer Justice in the Chocolate City

We have argued here for a decentering of measurement as *the* central way we come to know about something, in particular, a marginalized community. In the tradition of queer theory's call to question and upset all centers and all norms, as well as to dismiss them as centers or norms, we move traditional conceptions of measurement from the center, relocate them outside of the core of our inquiry, and elevate and make visible what measurement so often obscures—an asset-based perspective generated from the radical resistance politics and epistemologies that emerge from marginalized communities like black queer communities. When measurement regimes are relieved of their capital-S Science power, other kinds of data, and other forms of measurement that have not been visible to us before as researchers, will shine through.

In order to queer the black urban present, we must recover, name, and render visible the black queer chocolate city archive. This requires that we boldly move across disciplines in our conversations, reading, and research, that we abandon traditional notions of social scientific data, and that we move with liberation in mind. It also necessitates that we not simply "listen to" and "center" black people, but that we move out of the way save for to render visible the work that has already been done, the models that have already been created, for that liberation. To decenter measurement in work on cities and sexualities, we encourage moving beyond the traditional queer urban spaces to all places and spaces black queer people exist in history, online, and "IRL." We must follow the lead of the people who are making black queer places—from black lesbian Twitter to the backyard juke joints of the Mississippi Delta—to construct this archive with an eye toward justice.

Queering chocolate cities is just one example of a queer method that destroys and rebuilds, queries and questions, decenters and relocates measurement, and reimagines place, race, and sexuality intersections through the radical vision of communities that have historically been at the forefront of social change. Moore has called for researchers to go back to their data and look for the experiences of lesbian, gay, non-binary, and trans individuals, which is one project of queering social science methodologies to render seen the unseen. We must extend this project, innovating ways to reconnect theory with activism, and more importantly, scholarly practices with liberatory ones (see also Brim and Ghaziani 2016). This is more than a call for more policy recommendations at the close of scientific papers, but a question: How can we do our work such that we aid and abet folks who can already see a new world, and who are ready to queer this one, to decenter, then deconstruct, then destroy it, and build it anew? Queer methods that are true to their radical, diverse, rupturing, decentering origins are essential to any social science interested in being part of that future.

NOTES

1 Although widely used colloquially as a phrase to characterize urban spaces that had significant black populations, the phrase "chocolate city" rose to mainstream prominence with the release of Parliament Funkadelic's 1975 album *Chocolate City*. *Chocolate City* was about Washington, DC, which by virtue of its designation as such by George Clinton and the other members of Parliament Funkadelic was the "original CC." When Washington, DC's demographics shifted such that the percentage of the city's population that was black declined, media covered the change with reference to the decline of the chocolate city. Our work on chocolate cities moves beyond DC to the other kinds of places Clinton references on the album's title track, chronicling any place where there are communities of black people from small-town Mississippi to Kent (an increasingly black suburb in Seattle) to Harlem.

2 Butler writes in an oft-quoted passage from *Gender Trouble*: "The theories of feminist identity that elaborate predicates of color, sexuality, ethnicity, class, and able-bodiedness invariably close with an embarrassed 'etc.' at the end of the list. Through this horizontal trajectory of adjectives, these positions strive to encom-

pass a situated subject, but invariably fail to be complete. This failure, however, is instructive: what political impetus is to be derived from the exasperated 'etc.' that so often occurs at the end of such lines? This is a sign of exhaustion as well as of the illimitable process of signification itself." Here, Butler is offering both a critique of feminist theory and also an implicit critique of signification.

WORKS CITED

Baldwin, Davarian. 2004. "Black Belts and Ivory Towers: The Place of Race in U.S. Social Thought, 1892–1948." *Critical Sociology* 30 (4): 397–450.

Barnett, Bernice McNair. 1993. "Invisible Southern Black Women Leaders in the Civil Rights Movement: The Triple Constraints of Gender, Race, and Class." *Gender & Society* 7 (2): 162–82.

Beal, Frances M. (1969) 2008. "Double Jeopardy: To Be Black and Female." *Meridians: Feminism, Race, Transnationalism* 8 (2): 166–76.

Brim, Matt, and Amin Ghaziani. 2016. "Introduction: Queer Methods." *WSQ: Women's Studies Quarterly* 44 (3–4): 14–27.

Butler, Judith. (1990) 2007. *Gender Trouble: Feminism and the Subversion of Identity.* New York: Routledge.

Clark, Meredith D. 2014. "To Tweet Our Own Cause: A Mixed-Methods Study of the Online Phenomenon 'Black Twitter.'" PhD diss., University of North Carolina at Chapel Hill.

Cohen, Cathy. 1997. "Punks, Bulldaggers, and Welfare Queens: The Radical Potential of Queer Politics." *GLQ: A Journal of Lesbian and Gay Studies* 3 (4): 437–65.

Collins, Patricia Hill. 2015. "Intersectionality's Definitional Dilemmas." *Annual Review of Sociology* 41: 1–20.

Crenshaw, Kimberlé. 1989. "Demarginalizing the Intersection of Race and Sex: A Black Feminist Critique of Antidiscrimination Doctrine, Feminist Theory, and Antiracist Politics." *University of Chicago Legal Forum*, 139–67.

Crenshaw, Kimberlé. 1991. "Mapping the Margins: Intersectionality, Identity Politics, and Violence against Women of Color." *Stanford Law Review*, 1241–99.

Garza, Alicia, 2014. "Herstory." *Black Lives Matter.* www.blacklivesmatter.com/.

Ghaziani, Amin. 2014. *There Goes the Gayborhood?* Princeton, NJ: Princeton University Press.

Ghaziani, Amin. 2015. "'Gay Enclaves Face Prospect of Being Passé': How Assimilation Affects the Spatial Expressions of Sexuality in the United States." *International Journal of Urban and Regional Research* 39 (4): 756–71.

Hall, Stuart. (1980) 1998. "Notes on Deconstructing 'the Popular.'" In *Cultural Theory and Popular Culture: A Reader*, edited by John Storey, 442–53. New York: Pearson.

Hawkeswood, William G. (1991) 1996. *One of the Children: Gay Black Men in Harlem.* Berkeley: University of California Press.

Hunter, Marcus Anthony. 2010. "The Nightly Round: Space, Social Capital, and Urban Black Nightlife." *City & Community* 9 (2): 165–86.

Hunter, Marcus Anthony. 2013. *Black Citymakers: How "The Philadelphia Negro" Changed Urban America*. New York: Oxford University Press.

Hunter, Marcus Anthony, and Zandria F. Robinson. 2016. "The Sociology of Urban Black America." *Annual Review of Sociology* 42: 385–405.

Hunter, Marcus Anthony, and Zandria F. Robinson, 2018. *Chocolate Cities: The Black Map of American Life*. Berkeley: University of California Press.

Hyra, Derek. 2017. *Race, Class, and Politics in the Cappuccino City*. Chicago: University of Chicago Press.

Johnson, E. Patrick. 2001. "'Quare' Studies, or (Almost) Everything I Know About Queer Studies I Learned from My Grandmother." *Text and Performance Quarterly* 21 (1): 1–25.

Johnson, E. Patrick. 2005. "'Quare' Studies, or (Almost) Everything I Know about Queer Studies I Learned from My Grandmother." In *Black Queer Studies: A Critical Anthology*, edited by E. Patrick Johnson and Mae G. Henderson, 124–57. Durham, NC: Duke University Press.

Johnson, E. Patrick. 2016. "Put a Little Honey in My Sweet Tea: Oral History as Quare Performance." *WSQ: Women's Studies Quarterly* 44 (3): 51–67.

Johnson, E. Patrick, and Mae G. Henderson, eds. 2005. *Black Queer Studies: A Critical Anthology*. Durham, NC: Duke University Press.

King, Deborah. 1988. "Multiple Jeopardy, Multiple Consciousness: The Context of a Black Feminist Ideology." *Signs: Journal of Women in Culture and Society* 14 (1): 42–72.

Knopp, Lawrence. 1997. "Gentrification and Gay Neighborhood Formation in New Orleans." In *Homo Economics: Capitalism, Community, and Lesbian and Gay Life*, edited by Amy Gluckman and Betsy Reed, 45–49. New York: Routledge.

Lorde, Audre. (1979) 2004. "The Master's Tools Will Never Dismantle the Master's House." In *Sister Outsider: Essays and Speeches*, 110–13. New York: Ten Speed Press.

McCall, Leslie. 2005. "The Complexity of Intersectionality." *Signs: Journal of Women in Culture and Society* 30 (3): 1771–800.

Moore, Mignon R. 2011. *Invisible Families: Gay Identities, Relationships, and Motherhood among Black Women*. Berkeley: University of California Press.

Moore, Mignon R. 2015. "LGBT Populations in Studies of Urban Neighborhoods: Making the Invisible Visible." *City & Community* 14 (3): 245–48.

Nero, Charles I. 2005. "Why Are Gay Ghettos White." In *Black Queer Studies*, edited byE. Patrick Johnson and Mae G. Henderson, 228–45. Durham, NC: Duke University Press.

Oliver, Melvin, and Thomas Shapiro. 2006. *Black Wealth, White Wealth: A New Perspective on Racial Inequality*. 2nd ed. New York: Routledge.

Omi, Michael, and Howard Winant. 2014. *Racial Formation in the United States*. 3rd ed. New York: Routledge.

Robinson, Zandria F. 2014. *This Ain't Chicago: Race, Class, and Regional Identity in the Post-Soul South*. Chapel Hill: University of North Carolina Press.

Robinson, Zandria F. 2016. "Intersectionality." In *Handbook of Contemporary Sociological Theory*, edited by Seth Abrutyn, 477–99. New York: Springer.

Robinson, Zandria F. 2017. "Intersectionality and Gender Theory." In *Handbook of the Sociology of Gender*, 2nd ed., edited by Barbara Risman, Carissa Froyum, and William J. Scarborough, 69–80. New York: Springer Publishing.

Robinson, Zandria F., and Marcus Anthony Hunter. 2018. *Chocolate Cities: The Black Map of American Life*. Berkeley: University of California Press.

Watermelon Woman. 1997. Dir. Cheryl Dunye. First Run Features.

Woods, Clyde. 1998. *Development Arrested: The Blues and Plantation Power in the Mississippi Delta*. New York: Verso.

PART III

Listening/Creating

8

The Intersection of Queer Theory and Empirical Methods

Visions for the Center for LGBTQ Studies and Queer Studies

DAVID P. RIVERA AND KEVIN L. NADAL

Academia has a wide-reaching influence in society, impacting every-thing from educational preparation standards to public policy. The breadth and depth of this impact is largely supported by academic free-dom, a basic tenet of higher education. Although the term *academic freedom* is used quite frequently, there is confusion about its meaning and how it is exercised (Abdel Latif 2014). Contrary to the basic mean-ing of the word *freedom*, academic freedom is not consistently used to promote and celebrate the inclusion of diverse ideas and experiences, especially those of people from socially marginalized communities (e.g., LGBTQ people, people of color, and women). As a result, people from marginalized communities have to navigate systems that were not created to support their worldviews. LGBTQ scholars' response to this problem has been to create their own organizations and theories that allow them to express academic freedom in ways that are truer to their lived experiences and worldviews. This chapter will examine how LGBTQ scholars have queered the academy through challenging empiricism and creating their own queer spaces. The process of queer-ing the academy relies heavily on incorporating queer theoretical tenets into the methods we use to create knowledge and the systemic practices that govern academic institutions and organizations. Using a case study approach, we will use CLAGS: The Center for LGBTQ Studies to show how critical theories can queer the academy.

In 1991, the historian Martin Duberman and his colleagues founded the Center for Lesbian and Gay Studies (CLAGS) at the Graduate Center in the City University of New York (CUNY). The center has been at the forefront of creating queer frameworks, promoting the study of historical, cultural, and political issues that are vital to lesbian, gay, bisexual, transgender, and queer individuals and communities. CLAGS has sponsored groundbreaking public programs and conferences; it has offered fellowships and scholarships to academics, artists, and students; and it has functioned as an indispensable conduit of information. As the first university-based LGBTQ research center in the United States, CLAGS (which was rebranded in 2014 as CLAGS: The Center for LGBTQ Studies) has served as a national center for the promotion of queer and trans studies. For decades, CLAGS has been a haven for many queer theorists, from the founder Martin Duberman to Kessler Award winners Judith Butler, Jonathan Ned Katz, and Susan Stryker; to past board members José Esteban Muñoz, Lisa Duggan, and Gayatri Gopinath.

Queer theorists challenge conceptualizations of what is legitimate and acceptable. Similarly, CLAGS has also been a place where people question how we conceive what is "normal" in society (through gender binaries, sexualities, politics, behavior) while celebrating what is "queer" (applauding that which is different while validating experiences of the oppressed). Queer theorists recognize that systemic heterosexism, sexism, and transphobia are embedded throughout society, and that it is imperative to change the ways that scholars approach research so as to not condone heteronormative and cis-sexist male approaches as the only methods of inquiry. This means recognizing that everything in academia, from the empirical methodologies we use to create knowledge to the structure of the tenure process, was created primarily by heterosexual, cisgender White men who use it to promote their own particular realities and successes. An essential component of queer methods, therefore, is the recentering of academia on the lived experiences of LGBTQ people. Doing so can create new approaches to research that reflect and honor their lived experiences. This chapter will discuss the practical and philosophical roles that queer and critical theories can play in queering empirical research methods, as well as a series of associated institutional, administrative, and leadership structures and processes.

Queering Empirical Methodologies

Queer theorists challenge the meaning of empiricism (Brim and Ghaziani 2016), an idea that is grounded in Western European philosophies from the seventeenth and eighteenth centuries. With such a long history influencing mainstream conceptualizations of research, the basic tenets and influences of empiricism have largely gone unquestioned. Empiricism affects the nature of scholarly research, the mechanisms that support research, and decision-making in our everyday life. For example, funding agencies often have a preference for promoting empirical research. They rely heavily on traditional methods to make their decisions and to determine program effectiveness. The vast reach of empiricism can also be found in everyday decision-making processes, such as when we determine which brand of shampoo will promote healthier hair. Traditional academic empiricism, like this quotidian example, cannot fully analyze all types of phenomena, especially those experienced by people living in the borderlands of society. From the academic to the everyday, the logic is the same: just as there is not one type of shampoo that leaves all types of hair healthy, the analysis of social life requires a more nuanced approach and perspective. Our example illustrates the wide reach and insidious nature of empiricism, and how it is relevant beyond the academy. Queer theorists question, challenge, deconstruct, restructure, revaluate, and create meanings that attempt to more accurately understand phenomena from the perspective of the socially marginalized. In doing so, queer theorists develop epistemologies that both augment and redefine traditional empiricism.

The work of Judith Butler, a philosopher and gender theorist, is regarded as foundational to queer theory. Butler was among the first to challenge widely held, binary, and essentialist conceptualizations of sex, sexuality, and gender (Butler 1988). The theory of gender performativity asserts that gender is a social construct. The repetitive performance of gender creates and reinforces an understanding that it is a naturally occurring feature of our identity. Butler's landmark text *Gender Trouble: Feminism and the Subversion of Identity* ([1990] 2011) further elucidated these concepts and even challenged feminist ideologies of womanhood, as Butler believed that the feminist movement inadvertently perpetuated gender essentialism and the gender binary by categorizing and defining the concept. The work of Judith Butler helped lay a critical foundation for queer theory, which included breaking away from the rigid definitions and ideologies of gender, sex, and sexuality by theorizing that these concepts are socially constructed and thus not immune to alteration or even outright dismissal. This opened the doors for future generations of queer theorists, academics, and activists to frame their work in similar areas.

The work of early queer theorists inspired a wave of academics who sought to challenge the historical methods of inquiry that were regarded as the backbone of knowledge creation. The late performance studies scholar José Esteban Muñoz was concerned with the nature of empirical evidence (Muñoz 1996). He pondered the quality of observable material evidence, phenomena that scholars first observe and later code into "data" that aggregates into a set of "empirical results." Muñoz argued that manifestations of phenomena experienced by marginalized people are not seen in the same way as phenomena experienced by people from dominant cultural backgrounds. Just as societal and institutional structures were built to maintain and uplift the privileged, the same is true for how traditional empirical methods were created to illuminate the experiences of those living comparatively privileged existences. This insight prompted Muñoz to ask: Can traditional empirical methods capture phenomena experienced by people living with marginalized identities?

Building off concepts from performance studies, Muñoz offers a compelling theory to address his question. It starts with the premise that people who are forced into the margins of society are rendered invisible. If a person is not seen by society, then it is nearly impossible to fully observe their experiences in ways that lead to capturing data via traditional empirical methods. Because queerness or having a queer identity exists in the margins of society and in many ways also exists in isolation, Muñoz argues that its manifestation is often fleeting and does not always materialize in solid form. This makes it difficult to assess by traditional empirical methods and thus challenges the entire concept of an observable and measurable phenomenon. Given the fleeting nature of queerness and observable queerness in particular, Muñoz offers the concept of *ephemera material* as a unit of observable phenomena that we can use when we investigate the experiences of queer people. This theory challenges the meaning of empirical methods—what is considered valid data—and it offers queer scholars more flexibility in how they conceptualize and capture data from their queer participants.

In addition to queer scholars who intentionally foreground sexuality and gender in their work, other scholar-activists and social movements have also impacted the field of queer studies and empirical methods of inquiry. Ideas from intersectionality theory, for example, align with and inform tenets of queer theory. Just as queer theory emerged from the crucial need to make visible hidden LGBTQ experiences, women of color called for intersectional theorizing of their lived experiences, which differed from the primarily White, middle-class women that led the mainstream feminist movement (Crenshaw 1989). The work of legal scholar and critical race theorist Kimberlé Crenshaw and others took an important step toward examining the synergistic relationship between various aspects of identity as situated in social contexts. The writings of the Combahee River Collective ([1977] 2007), a group of Black lesbian feminists, provided some of the first arguments for taking an intersectional approach to systems of privilege and oppression relating specifically to gender, sexual orientation, and race. These scholars called for feminists to abandon their singular, generalized focus on cisgender women and instead explore how gender interlocks with sexuality, class, and race. This approach is very similar to the motivations behind the work of queer theorists. As we consider the current state of queer theory and how to strengthen and advance its methodological influence, the intersectionality framework can make queer theory more inclusive of the lived experiences of multiply marginalized communities.

Recognizing that identity is complex, integrated, and synergistic, scholars are becoming increasingly concerned with developing a methodological portfolio that can capture a person's multiple identities rather than retain a singular focus (e.g., sexual orientation only or race only). The field of psychology has made a significant contribution in this area by questioning the utility of traditional empirical methods for the study of multiple identities and suggesting best practices for conducting intersectionality research (see DeBlaere et al. 2010; Parent, DeBlaere, and Moradi 2013). This work is pertinent to queer studies in its concern with sexual orientation and gender identity. Researchers in this area understand that sexual orientation does not exist in a vacuum and cannot be separated from other aspects of identity, such as gender, gender identity, race, ethnicity, and social class, when we attempt to understand how our identities shape our lived experiences.

Critical race theory (CRT; Delgado and Stefancic 2012) is another framework that aligns well with queer theory; both are rooted in critical theory (Sullivan 2003; Turner 2000). Both frameworks call for analyzing the oppression/privilege relationship on a structural level and elevating queer voices. While each focuses on a particular social identity category, both theoretical perspectives call for the inclusion of intersectionality and for complicating the dynamic nature of racial and queer identities. CRT offers a number of tenets that aid in making a queer theoretical perspective more intersectional in nature.

The CRT framework has five defining elements. These include (1) the centrality of race and racism; (2) the challenge to dominant ideology; (3) a commitment to social justice and praxis; (4) the centrality of experiential knowledge; and (5) a historical context and interdisciplinary perspective (Solórzano, Villalpando, and Oseguera 2005). CRT theorists more commonly endorse an intersectional approach to race and racial dynamics, and they articulate inarguable differences between lived experiences based on different social identities (Crenshaw 1991; Delgado and Stefancic 2012; Ladson-Billings and Tate 1995; Roberts 1995). CRT also posits that while those from marginalized groups share the experience of being oppressed, the quality of this shared oppression differs based on their respective intersectional configurations and social contexts (Delgado and Stefancic 1993). Critical race theory adds to queering empirical methods by offering storytelling and counter-storytelling as methods of describing qualitative and mixed-methods studies. Doing so centers marginalized voices in retelling stories that are typically expressed by dominant and mainstream voices, leaving the reader with a narrative that more closely matches the lived experiences of the marginalized and focuses in particular on issues of privilege and oppression.

Similarly, queer scholars support and promote research about concepts that are typically viewed as pathological in non-LGBTQ communities yet may be quite normative in LGBTQ communities. Just as it is necessary to use a critical queer theoretical lens to reconceptualize the research process, it is also necessary to include research topics that are relevant to LGBTQ communities—even if they challenge normative research topics. These include a variety of behaviors and processes related to sexuality, such as sex work for survival, polyamory, hookup culture, and BDSM. These topics are not only limited to sexual practices, however. Hetereonormativity also influences other phenomena and processes that are not solely or directly linked to sexual behaviors, such as healthcare needs, familial structures, and consumer behaviors. Thus, a queer theoretical lens can redefine "normative" research topics to make them more applicable to LGBTQ experiences.

Without a commitment to queering our research methods, there would be a dearth of academic literature on LGBTQ lives. If scholars in gender and sexuality studies, including those involved with CLAGS for the past twenty-five years, had merely focused on conventional scientific methods as ways of testing null hypotheses, we would have very little knowledge about the social, cultural, and political experiences of LGBTQ people. Participant samples would not be large or systematic enough, resulting in low effect sizes, and few of these analyses would be considered scientifically robust by communities of mainstream practitioners. If previous researchers had limited themselves to measures centered on samples of White, heterosexual, and cisgender men, it is likely that LGBTQ people would continue to be stereotyped as abnormal, inferior to the dominant groups, or both.

Queering Administration and Leadership

The theoretical perspectives and methodological approaches that we have discussed thus far can also be applied to organizational structures as a way of queering processes that were created to maintain systems of privilege and oppression. The essence of what we call "queering administration and leadership" entails implementing queer and critical theoretical perspectives in determining the practices that honor and validate the lived experiences of queer people. Marginalized people continue to be underrepresented in positions of power and in many industries. In academia, LGBTQ people make up roughly 1 percent of college and university presidents and chancellors (LGBTQ Presidents in Higher Education n.d.; U.S. Department of Education, National Center for Educational Statistics 2016). Representations of LGBTQ people in any given organization, as well as people from other marginalized communities, send messages about who is welcome and who is likely to succeed in that organization. Although representation is necessary for the inclusion of LGBTQ perspectives, we also need to queer the structures of an organization to ensure that material practices, such as recruitment, retention, and promotion, support LGBTQ people and scholars of queer studies. The work of CLAGS and similar queer- and trans-oriented organizations can provide concrete directions for how to do this—in other words, how academic institutions can queer their methods of administration and leadership to be more inclusive and celebratory of LGBTQ identities.

Over the years, CLAGS has offered several unique possibilities for queer methods. First, through its public programs, CLAGS encourages dialogue with people affiliated with the academy, as well as those who are not. In this capacity, CLAGS offers a type of queer education or "queer pedagogy," as editors Amin Ghaziani and Matt Brim describe in their introductory essay: its students learn not just from professors and textbooks but also from community members from multiple educational backgrounds, perspectives, and life experiences. CLAGS also queers education for individuals without scholastic opportunities, who now have access to learn about theoretical concepts that they might not be exposed to otherwise. Since 1998, the CLAGS Seminar in the City series has allowed community members to take weekly classes taught by a professor on a topic related to LGBTQ studies. Often, the topic is one that is not offered by traditional academic institutions, such as "Queering the Crip/Cripping the Queer: Introduction to Queer and Disability Studies."

CLAGS has also reframed the narrative of LGBTQ research. Non-LGBTQ-identified researchers have generally studied individuals who they deemed to have nontraditional sexual orientations and gender identities in pathologizing and harmful ways. Scientists performed castrations, lobotomies, electroshock therapy, and other heinous acts to "cure" people of their "disorders." It was not until 1973 that homosexuality was removed from the American Psychiatric Association's *Diagnostic and Statistical Manual* (*DSM*) of psychiatric disorders. While no longer labeled "gender identity disorder," the current *DSM* still includes "gender dysphoria" among its list of disorders. CLAGS encourages research to be conducted *by* LGBTQ people (and non-LGBTQ people who are LGBTQ-affirming) and to focus on the various *strengths* of LGBTQ individuals and communities. While it is important for researchers to concentrate on LGBTQ disparities (such as HIV/AIDS, substance use, etc.) in the hopes of addressing, treating, and/or minimizing them, it is equally important to identify the protective factors that allow LGBTQ people to survive and thrive. Speaking more directly, LGBTQ researchers and administrators, as well as those taking a queer theoretical perspective, are more likely to uphold a strengths-based (rather than pathologizing) or assets-based (rather than deficit) approach in addressing and incorporating queer issues.

CLAGS facilitated the creation of the LGBTQ Scholars of Color Network in October 2014 with a group of scholars who were interested in supporting others who identify as LGBTQ and as persons of color. With funding from the Annie E. Casey Foundation, the Arcus Foundation, and the Andrus Family Fund, the first LGBTQSOC Conference was held in April 2015 at John Jay College of Criminal Justice–City University of New York. Based on overwhelming popularity and a successful first conference, the network hosted its second national conference in 2017 at the Graduate Center–City University of New York. Part of the success of both conferences was attributed to the inclusion of various queer identity perspectives and taking an interdisciplinary approach to organizing, facilitating, and evaluating the conferences. This meant intentionally reaching out to new constituencies and involving purposeful evaluation throughout and after the conferences. The evaluation process was twofold: it included a focus on content, as we would expect, and also a focus on the process that planners and attendees were engaged in throughout the experience. This second piece is often a missing component in mainstream academic conferences. Additionally, conference coordinators intentionally promoted a "resilience and persistence model," which celebrates the achievements of those who have navigated historic racist, heterosexist, and cis-sexist systems, instead of the "deficit model" in which LGBTQ people of color are usually framed.

Guided by queer theory, the conference organizers were mindful about not replicating mainstream structures and philosophies that lead to narrow inclusion criteria and content that does not adequately reflect queer experiences. The starting point was a reconceptualization of the meaning of "scholar." Academia has a long history of gatekeeping that prizes the doctoral degree as an essential qualification for inclusion in traditional academic circles, including scholarly conferences. This tradition fails to recognize the disparities in educational attainment for marginalized communities, including LGBTQ people of color. Upholding this standard maintains systems of educational inequities for LGBTQ people of color and greatly circumscribes the range of possibilities for queer knowledge creation and dissemination. To address this issue, network organizers broadly defined "scholar" to include queer people of color from diverse educational and employment backgrounds. As a result, attendees included people with earned doctoral degrees as well as those without one. Participants were employed in traditional academic settings, as well as in non-profits, governmental agencies, and the self-employed.

The LGBTQ Scholars of Color Network was established primarily because of the lack or nonexistence of queer spaces in and out of academia (Bailey and Miller 2016). LGBTQ people and people of color often find themselves as being the only one in their organizations, as well as experiencing discrimination (Bennett et al. 2011). The discipline of organizational psychology is concerned with the nature of an organization's diversity climate. Research from this area suggests that a positive diversity climate recognizes and addresses issues that can lead to employee disengagement, turnover, and compromised work behaviors (Goyal and Shrivastava 2013). While the LGBTQ Scholars of Color Network cannot directly solve the compromises in diversity climate across all institutions, the network provides a venue, both virtually and physically, for LGBTQ people of color to commune with others who have similar identities and worldviews. In structuring the conferences, the organizers honored this need by incorporating formal and informal time for attendees to connect with each other beyond attending academic sessions. The second conference was themed "Resist and Persist: Empowering LGBTQ Scholars of Color." The theme was created in response to the many adversities LGBTQ people of color experience. The organizers included interpersonal process-oriented group dialogues where participants were able to reflect on their personal experiences and learn how to persevere in unwelcoming and hostile spaces. Examples of these group dialogues included "Navigating Self-Care, Balance, and Wellbeing as an LGBTQ Scholar of Color" and "Navigating Systemic Racism, Heterosexism, Sexism, and Transphobia in Academia." Although still in its infancy, the LGBTQ Scholars of Color Network and conference convenings have met the overall goal of providing a home for queer scholars who often feel marginalized in their organizations and disciplines. The network has also inspired its members to transport its spirit to their own organizations, furthering the reach of the endeavor.

Organizations like CLAGS and the LGBTQ Scholars of Color Network fill voids created by institutions that render queer and trans people invisible due to structures and processes that were not created to support their existence and success. Documented and anecdotal evidence reveals that LGBTQ scholars are subject to heightened scrutiny of their research topics, accusations of being biased in their work, and charges of an overall lack of academic rigor (LaSala et al. 2008). In order to fully support LGBTQ scholars, academia can queer its structures and processes in a number of ways. For example, the processes of tenure and promotion can be queered to include an appreciation for more diverse research topics, methods of inquiry, and publication outlets that may not fit neatly within the narrowly defined dictates that formally and informally guide these processes.

Visions for CLAGS and Queer Studies

Through the years, CLAGS has fulfilled its mission of being a catalyst for social change. It has allowed people to learn about LGBTQ identities and experiences, encouraged and facilitated difficult dialogues about diverse sexualities and genders, and supported and mentored future generations of scholars. Despite this, there are many opportunities for CLAGS to use its research to advocate for social change on systemic and societal levels. CLAGS can continue to utilize queer methods, while also being open to integrating traditional research methods into our practices in new ways that may ultimately blur the line between queer and traditional modes of research.

CLAGS needs to be more interdisciplinary. While queer studies has roots in the humanities, there has been a significant increase in LGBTQ scholars in fields like psychology, public health, sociology, and medicine. While it is crucial for young LGBTQ people to read James Baldwin and Audre Lorde, it is just as important for them to understand the current state of health, economics, structural inequalities, and well-being for LGBTQ people today. Further, in the same ways that scholars have made efforts to understand how phenomena like intersectionalities or identity development are studied in the humanities, it is crucial for us to be familiar with the empirical methods used in the social sciences to investigate similar concepts. Perhaps the programming by CLAGS or its scholarships can encourage more research on topics in which LGBTQ people are understudied but overrepresented, including criminal justice, homelessness, and other areas.

Queer studies emerged from the humanities, and we will be indebted to the scholars who broke away from their traditional disciplines to create spaces for the illumination of queer experiences and narratives. Thus, it is not surprising that queer studies programs and departments are occupied by scholars in the humanities. It also is not surprising that scholars outside the humanities who are engaged in LGBTQ-oriented scholarship are not fully versed in queer theoretical concepts or aligned with queer studies programs and departments. An interdisciplinary approach can bridge this gap and create spaces for many more disciplines to be involved in developing the field of queer studies. In order for this to manifest, however, scholars need to be aware of the history of queer studies and disciplinary representations when we make decisions about the operations of queer studies programs and departments. Course offerings send messages, both overt and covert, about the topics and disciplines that are relevant to queer studies. If the courses are limited to certain disciplines, this will send a message to emerging scholars about the fields that belong in the family. In this example, offering courses that represent an array of disciplines and that are interdisciplinary in nature is needed to ensure that future generations of queer scholars uphold and maintain an interdisciplinary approach to their work. This must include the social sciences as well as the humanities.

An interdisciplinary approach to addressing issues salient to LGBTQ people is beneficial for several additional reasons as well. First, applying multiple disciplinary lenses to the same issue can promote a more complex understanding of the phenomena at hand. Each discipline has its own unique set of overarching theoretical perspectives that its practitioners use to guide the creation of knowledge. When studying the costs of discrimination, for example, a sociological lens can broaden the scope of impact to include issues on a societal level, while an economics lens can help explain nonpsychological forces that create financial structures to promote institutionalized discrimination. If scholars uphold the queer methodological tenet of ephemera as evidence (Muñoz 1996), multiple disciplinary lenses can aid in capturing more glimpses of the queer experience than what we would capture by only using a singular disciplinary focus.

Second, CLAGS should endorse more empirical research that incorporates queer theoretical and methodological perspectives, particularly to influence public policy. For instance, in *Hollingsworth v. Perry*, which legalized same-sex marriage in California (and influenced other states and the Supreme Court of the United States), attorneys relied on researchers like psychologists Gregory Herek and Ilan Meyer to discuss their work on topics such as minority stress, sexual orientation identity development, and the psychological effects of discrimination to support their case. Opposing counsel introduced biased religious researchers whose expertise was based on anecdotal experiences and problematic methods (e.g., studying narratives of survivors of abuse and generalizing it to the entire LGBTQ community), all of which were deemed inadmissible in court by the judge. These researchers provide a useful example of how queer scholars can use their positions to have influence outside traditional academia. If research can sway local, state, or federal court cases and eventually lead to changes in federal law, then perhaps CLAGS should also integrate more rigorous research methods to instill systemic change.

An interdisciplinary approach increases the breadth and depth of influence of queer studies on issues that impact LGBTQ people and their communities. The example above is a cogent demonstration of the applicability of one discipline (psychology) to another domain (the law). It also suggests the necessity of interdisciplinary work in creating the most compelling arguments for social change. Without such an interdisciplinary approach, it can be difficult to visualize and conceptualize the connections between queer scholarship and practice-based domains such as the law, health care, and education. Additionally, the most convincing evidence and arguments will materialize from research that is based on empirical methods influenced by queer theory. An interdisciplinary approach opens the doors of possibilities and brings with it the potential for increased creativity and innovation in developing solutions to the most intransigent social problems that affect LGBTQ people and communities today.

Third, many LGBTQ researchers know that there is very little funding—particularly federal funding—for the study of LGBTQ people. Even less funding is offered for those who use qualitative methods or anything not considered empirical or quantitative. Perhaps CLAGS should promote more mixed-methods approaches, or collaborations that would foster qualitative/quantitative cross talk so that LGBTQ research would be more competitive for funding. Many LGBTQ researchers prefer qualitative or observational designs, including the case studies and close readings for which queer theory is best known, because they seem more personal or less intrusive. Funders, however, prefer quantitative designs with large samples because of the perception that such samples lead to greater generalizability. Perhaps mixed methodologies can secure more funding, while staying truer to queer theory in challenging traditional approaches. If more funding would signify more resources for LGBTQ communities, then being open to new designs is worth considering.

Finally, as CLAGS's first executive director of color (co-author Kevin Nadal) since its inception, I would encourage CLAGS and queer studies to queer their methods even more by better integrating critical race theory, intersectionality, and transgender studies into all aspects of their philosophies. In the same way that LGBTQ people should not be an afterthought in mainstream teaching, race, ethnicity, and gender-nonbinary identities should not be an afterthought in queer studies. In recent years, CLAGS has done a phenomenal job in creating programs that examine race and LGBTQ identity (e.g., our recent Kessler Award lectures by Cheryl Clarke, Cathy Cohen, and Richard Fung) and in maintaining the most diverse board of directors in CLAGS's history. However, there is still much more to do to dismantle gender and sexuality binaries; to support transgender, genderqueer, and gendernonbinary people; and to encourage future generations of trans and queer leaders in academia.

Concluding Thoughts

Queering academia involves a critical examination of structures and policies across all levels of higher education. This chapter offers insights into how to queer traditional empiricism to reflect experiences that are relevant to LGBTQ communities. We also considered how to apply the tenets of queer and critical theories to queer administration and leadership. Queering the academy entails dismantling and creating new structures and processes that will allow LGBTQ scholars and queer studies to have integrated and centralized existences, as opposed to relegating them to the margins, if including them at all.

Queer scholars offer theories that challenge how we conceptualize and analyze our objects of study. Much of this has been in the domain of academic scholarship, but we also need to apply these innovative theories to analyze the operations of higher education so that LGBTQ experiences and worldviews become integrated in the structures and processes that maintain academia as a social institution. We have focused on the legacy and current work of CLAGS and the LGBTQ Scholars of Color Network as two examples of administration and leadership vehicles that play a role in queering academia and that also cultivate the careers of LGBTQ scholars. In the immortal words of Audre Lorde, "The master's tools will never dismantle the master's house" (Lorde 2012). And so it is with queerness, as Amin Ghaziani and Matt Brim demonstrate with force in this field-defining volume on queer methods: we need to create and use our own queer tools to truly queer academia.

WORKS CITED

Abdel Latif, Muhammad M. 2014. "Academic Freedom: Problems in Conceptualization and Research." *Higher Education Research & Development* 33 (2): 399–401.

Bailey, Moya, and Shannon J. Miller. 2016. "When Margins Become Centered: Black Queer Women in Front and Outside of the Classroom." *Feminist Formations* 27 (3): 168–88.

Bennett, Andrew K., Derrick L. Tillman-Kelly, Johari R. Shuck, Jasmine M. Viera, and Bethany J. Wall. 2011. "Narratives of Black and Latino Faculty at a Midwestern Research University." *Journal of the Student Personnel Association at Indiana University*, 46–61.

Brim, Matt, and Amin Ghaziani. 2016. "Introduction: Queer Methods." *WSQ: Women's Studies Quarterly* 44 (3–4): 14–27.

Butler, Judith. 1988. "Performative Acts and Gender Constitution: An Essay in Phenomenology and Feminist Theory." *Theatre Journal* 40 (4): 519–31.

Butler, Judith. 2011. *Gender Trouble: Feminism and the Subversion of Identity*. New York: Routledge.

Combahee River Collective. (1977) 2007. "A Black Feminist Statement." In *The Essential Feminist Reader*, edited by E. B. Freedman, 325–30. New York: Modern Library.

Crenshaw, Kimberlé. 1989. "Demarginalizing the Intersection of Race and Sex: A Black Feminist Critique of Antidiscrimination Doctrine, Feminist Theory, and Antiracist Politics." *University of Chicago Legal Forum*, 139–67.

Crenshaw, Kimberlé. 1991. "Mapping the Margins: Intersectionality, Identity Politics, and Violence against Women of Color." *Stanford Law Review* 43: 1241–99.

DeBlaere, Cirleen, Melanie E. Brewster, Anthony Sarkees, and Bonnie Moradi. 2010. "Conducting Research with LGB People of Color: Methodological Challenges and Strategies." *Counseling Psychologist* 38 (3): 331–62.

Delgado, Richard, and Jean Stefancic. 2012. *Critical Race Theory: An Introduction*. New York: NYU Press.

Goyal, Saumya, and Sangya Shrivastava. 2013. "Organizational Diversity Climate: Review of Models and Measurement." *Journal of Business Management and Social Sciences Research* 2 (5): 55–60.

Ladson-Billings, Gloria, and William F. Tate IV. 1995. "Toward a Critical Race Theory of Education." *Teachers College Record* 97 (1): 47–68.

LaSala, Michael C., David A. Jenkins, Darrell P. Wheeler, and Karen I. Fredriksen-Goldsen. 2008. "LGBT Faculty, Research, and Researchers: Risks and Rewards." *Journal of Gay & Lesbian Social Services* 20 (3): 253–67.

LGBTQ Presidents in Higher Education. n.d. Current Presidents and Chancellors. www.lgbtqpresidents.org/about-2/members.

Lorde, Audre. 2012. *Sister Outsider: Essays and Speeches*. Berkeley, CA: Crossing Press.

Muñoz, José Esteban. 1996. "Ephemera as Evidence: Introductory Notes to Queer Acts." *Women & Performance* 8 (2): 5–16.

Parent, Michael C., Cirleen DeBlaere, and Bonnie Moradi. 2013. "Approaches to Research on Intersectionality: Perspectives on Gender, LGBT, and Racial/Ethnic Identities." *Sex Roles* 68 (11–12): 639–45.

Roberts, Dorothy E. 1995. "Punishing Drug Addicts Who Have Babies: Women of Color, Equality, and the Right of Privacy." In *Critical Race Theory: The Key Writings That Formed the Movement*, edited by Kimberlé Crenshaw, 384–425 New York: New Press.

Solórzano, Daniel G., Octavio Villalpando, and Leticia Oseguera. 2005. "Educational Inequities and Latina/o Undergraduate Students in the United States: A Critical Race Analysis of Their Educational Progress." *Journal of Hispanic Higher Education* 4 (3): 272–94.

Sullivan, Nikki 2003. *A Critical Introduction to Queer Theory*. New York: NYU Press.

Turner, William B. 2000. *A Genealogy of Queer Theory*. Philadelphia: Temple University Press.

U.S. Department of Education, National Center for Educational Statistics. 2016. "Fast Facts: Educational Institutions." https://nces.ed.gov/fastfacts/display.asp?id=84.

9

The Map Where We Meet and Other Queer-Quare Stories

An Essay-as-Performance Set to a Double-Bass Score

TEXT AND SCRIPT BY ROMMI SMITH, 2016, 2017, 2018

ORIGINAL MUSIC COMPOSITION BY JENNI MOLLOY, 2017

Contextual Note

This essay-as-performance[1] develops out of what I am calling a "practice-steeped" doctoral research process, from which I emerge as a doctor of philosophy, via research within English and theater. To "steep," meaning to infuse, or to imbue something with a specific quality or energy: this kind of practice-led research can only exist because it is immersed within (and has had time to absorb) the long-held practice within which it is situated.

My desire is to queer canonical academic method and convey research findings in ways that challenge traditional, accepted modes of presentation because I aspire to expand the essay's capacities within an arts context. Inspired by the shifting, eclectic queernesses of the Black women blues and jazz musicians whom my research profiles, I employ a shifting cast of methods on the research stage: the lecture-as-performance, the lecture-as-protest-march performed on the stroke of midnight (in reference to Thelonious Monk's "'Round Midnight" (1952) and now the essay-as-performance. It seems entirely logical that an essay written by a practice-steeped researcher and evolutionary of an arts-led, process-driven, scholarly study can reflect both the researcher's art form and process. This essay observes academic citation and referencing protocols, just as the work of Black queer scholar Alexis Pauline Gumbs does. *Spill* (2016), Gumbs's brilliant genre-queer scholarly study, was an affirmative discovery for me just after I had written this chapter. In short, this essay queers the artificial and limiting binary between creative and critical, in order to reflect and delight in the dialectical practice-steeped process, via an essay that can only have arisen from this kind of process.

As I am a playwright and performer of text, my creative psyche is steeped in the conventions of playscript (complete with tech notes for a lighting designer). Thus, as a theater-maker I see the academic presentation for what it is: a script-in-hand performance of a monologue. I posit to the academic-unconscious that scholars (and, especially, arts-led scholars) presenting papers before a live audience are, in essence, delivering critical soliloquies; that the academic script is—even pedestrianly—performative. All scholars use sometimes muted, sometimes explicit, performative gestures: eye contact, muscle memory, vocality, pause, emphasis, and ad-libbed interjections, which, arguably, constitute improvisation. Scholarly text (just like creative text) is not just a vehicle for information but the conveyance of opinion, affect, and argument; similarly, the intention is to engage the audience within the world of a perspective in order to persuade, or generate understanding.

I present this essay in the form of multivoice dialogue. The aim is to decenter normative codes of academic presentation by facilitating multiple distinct (yet interlinked) speakers, each conveying a different facet or register of practitioner-thought. Singularly narrated modes of academic presentation are, arguably, canonical, privileging a didactic flow of knowledge (scholar to audience) and thus compounding traditional hierarchies of power. It is intended that class members (or a selection of class members) perform the script, collaboratively, for I posit that embodied knowledge (experiential learning born of participation, activity, and collective action) is realized in the body in a potentially more holistic way than text for which the body is purely recipient.

Further, in terms of textuality, the multivoice script is an attempt to depict praxis in action. The relationality between thought/experience and theoretical articulation has inspired the script's range of voices: internal (thought) and external (articulations). It seems logical that thought takes the form of poetry—the form I consider the most intimate and tender of all registers, the one I associate most explicitly with feeling and experience. I depict a rhizomatic, creative, multiple consciousness. Such a concept riffs off and reframes W.E.B. Du Bois's concept of double

consciousness. For Du Bois, the term described a mode of hyperaware-
ness manifesting in heightened self-surveillance, one impact of coping
with discrimination. I seek to reframe the "two unreconciled strivings;
two warring ideals in one dark body" (Du Bois 1994) by exploring not
only the concept of "selves" as a rich vantage point for creativity but (in
reference to my wider research inquiry) the idea that creativity is one of
many strategic responses to trauma. Indeed, jazz and blues constitute
two of the ingenious responses by Black Africans—displaced by slavery,
or Maafa—to trauma. Further, jazz and blues evidence the transformative power of utilizing creativity as a mode of agency.

Thus, multiple consciousness is a place of dialogue and self-
expression. In the realm of the imaginary the scholar-artist's cast of
selves (researcher, practitioner, collaborator, writer, poet, lighting technician, performer, etc.) are in conversation and flux. My desire is to
convey a practice-steeped research-state of perpetual wake and dream,
giving rise to a dialectic of poetry and theory, which aims to "challenge the schism in the Western intellectual tradition between theory
and practice and to valorize what I shall call 'praxis'" (Nelson 2013, 5).
Multiple consciousness resonates with my own intersectional identities
(Crenshaw 1989). My positionality as a working-class, queer, woman of
mixed heritage (I have a white English mother and a Black Nigerian father) is reflected in my nonbinaried, fluid choices in research methods.
This is an approach I consider "intersectionality-as-artistic-method." I'm
a writer whose collaborative practice has (for the last twenty-five years)
been to fuse written, spoken, and sung word with other art forms and,
especially, improvised jazz. Further, my methodological stance is a statement against the isolationist "policies" upon which prejudice thrives—
both within and outside of the academy. Conservative notions (perhaps,
fictions) that demand neat (and, it is implied, pure) methodological binaries and singular modes of presentation are oppressive to an imaginative process. If all the doors were open in the House of Methodology,
then one method could intersect with another leading to blurrings and
queerings and, of course then, to new possibilities. One delight of queering method is that, surreptitiously, a method can appear to be one thing
and then another: this is what Ezra Berkley Nepon calls "Dazzle Camouflage," a reference to "the way that . . . non-conforming people can
use [methods] to create awe and excitement, distracting from potential

attack" (Nepon 2016, 9). The desire is to dazzle and disorientate in order to orientate: Is this a lecture or play? Is this an essay or poem? Is this a song or political speech? How many ways are there to articulate one's practice inside the academy?

NB: This essay-script is intended to be read aloud. A different group member takes each of the performative roles in the essay cast list. There are several "researcher thoughts" and "researcher articulations"—each different number is a distinct role for one performer.

Tech Notes: Lighting Information
This essay-as-performance utilizes three states of illumination as method:
LX1[2]—Blue Wash: Tuning into Queer-Quare[3] Frequencies
LX2—Spotlight: Divining the Ghost-Document and Redaction-as-Revelation
LX3—Follow Spot: Rewriting-the-Record and Lecture-Keepsake

CAST
RESEARCHER THOUGHTS 1, 2, 3
RESEARCHER ARTICULATION 1, 2, 3, 4, 5, 6, 7, 8, 9, 10, 11, and 12
HEADINGS AND STAGE DIRECTIONS
DESIGNER PROVOCATION 1
SX CUE BASS TRACK 1, 2, 3, and 4
SX CUE VINYL

Text Note
A slash (/) denotes an overlapping of thought and articulation, reflective of the different parts of the self in conversation with one another during the creative process.

LX1—Blue Wash: Tuning into Queer-Quare Frequencies

SX Cue Bass Track: 1

RESEARCHER THOUGHT 1: *Dim lights to blue. Trace your finger the archive's length. The frequency between now and then is spirit-thin; the place they intersect queers spatial dimensions. Listen. You're tuning in to what you see and sense for pitch. What's clear? The past is palimpsest behind the present-tense/.*

Embodied Empiricism

RESEARCHER ARTICULATION 1: At fourteen, I began tuning in to some of the great historical, Black jazz and blues women: Bessie Smith, Billie Holiday. I learned that the journey to school was the length of six Billie Holiday songs on a Walkman. It was a journey that took me past a café frequented by skinheads, members of the National Front—a white supremacist organization prevalent in the U.K. in the 1970s and 1980s. A sardonic maths teacher remarked:

RESEARCHER ARTICULATION 2: "If you worked for your maths exam as hard as you listen to Billie Holiday, you'd get an A!"

RESEARCHER ARTICULATION 1: I scraped a C.

RESEARCHER ARTICULATION 2: My practice-steeped, transdisciplinary, auto-ethnographic doctoral research inquiry concerns re-presenting African American jazz and blues women as agents of social change and protagonists of twentieth- and twenty-first-century civil rights movements. As part of this project, I'm interrogating heteronormative representations of historic Black jazz and blues women, using both performance and poetics as tools. Further, I examine the impact of their body of auditory and visual performances upon the corporeal materiality of contemporary artists and scholars, evidencing the interplay between listening and constructions of selfhood, ontologies, and embodied or empirical knowledge.

RESEARCHER ARTICULATION 1: What is pertinent now (from the positionality of being an academic researcher) is that at a pivotal time in the awakening of my own queer consciousness, I began— *subconsciously*—tuning into the frequencies of historical Black, queer-quare, jazz and blues women . . .

Tuning In

RESEARCHER ARTICULATION 2: Tuning in is at once a serendipitous, yet strategic method that animates discussion regarding social relations, specifically in a context of marginalization and misrepresentation. Marginalized narratives are subject to white noise (Stoever-Ackerman 2010). Channeling W.E.B. Du Bois's concept of the "visual color line" (1994), Stoever-Ackerman defines white noise as the *Sonic Color Line*: a hegemonic, sub-aural frequency reflective of societal power dynamics, deciding what and whom is heard (Stoever-Ackerman 2010). Tuning in is a sonic, affective counter to white noise, providing a means by which one accesses both external and internal registers of pitch as survival strategy. One follows hunch, clue, intuition, and sensation (the key hallmarks of trace evidence) in search of the substance of soundwave and story (Hannula, Suoranta, and Vaden 2014; Harper 2005; Kershaw and Nicholson 2011; Muñoz 1996; Walker 1989). One might not quite understand one is tuning in (or, indeed, needed to tune in at a particular point in time), but one does by reflecting in the river of hindsight.

RESEARCHER ARTICULATION 1: Several leading Black jazz and blues women, from Ma Rainey to Big Mama Thornton, Nina Simone to Josephine Baker, Billie Holiday to Bessie Smith—were queer-quare women. They either had romantic relationships with other women or challenged gender binaries and, in some instances, did both (Baker and Chase 1993; Blackburn 2006; Davis 1999; Lieb 1981; Light 2016; Sporke 2014). For example, Ma Rainey wrote and recorded "Prove It on Me Blues" in 1928. The song's female singer-narrator tells us that she flirts with women, "wear[s] a collar and a tie"—and unashamedly expresses her butch identity:

> . . . I went out last night with a crowd of my friends,
> it must've been women, 'cause I don't like no men.
> Wear my clothes just like a fan,
> talk to the gals just like any old man,
> 'cause they say I do it, ain't nobody caught me,
> sure got to prove it on me. (Rainey 1928)

RESEARCHER ARTICULATION 2: On stage, through the mask of character, Rainey celebrated her own desires for other women. Rainey's
live and recorded performances are premonitory of several of the
"Seven Demands"[4] of the Women's Liberation Movement (1970–
1978). From the right to financial independence to a woman's right to
define her own sexuality, Rainey's performances were assertions the
WLM wouldn't articulate for five further decades (Davis 1999, 40).
Yet, victimology stereotypes have dominated historical representations of Black blues and jazz women. These stereotypes intertwine
with heteronormativity, producing images of downtrodden women
in codependent relationships with men.

However, in both domestic and public contexts Black queer-quare
women were performing resistance. They performed civil rights in
lyrics, as well as in recorded, live, and off-stage performances. By
virtue of their lives as successful working musicians, Rainey and
others articulated their political demands through the blues. In
doing so, they disrupted sociocultural expectations regarding the
status of working-class Black women. They sang sonic frequencies I
term "blue-lines." Blue-lines aren't only overt political messages, but
a form of what poet-scholar Fred Moten calls "an abundance that
accrues especially at moments . . . when things sound 'edgy maybe
garbled at points,' when 'ears literally burn with what the words don't
manage to say'" (Moten 2003, 122).

RESEARCHER ARTICULATION 1: Each of these women sang blue-
lines into being; composing them from the pitch of moonlight, the
color of change and the refrain of stars hung on staves of infinite possibility called night. Blue-lines constitute the blues beneath our feet: a
political guide. Their reverberations and manifestations can be found
within, for instance, the second wave of the official feminist movement, the Black Lives Matter movement, and the Pride march.
In planting blue-lines in the earth (as sonic undertone), historical
Black blues and jazz women were not only forerunners of later social
movements but guides for queer-quare, working-class, mixed-
heritage girls walking home alone from school down the long road
of prejudice. By tuning into these musicians, at fourteen I accessed a
cultural and political score that not only became my companion as I
navigated the terrain of early adulthood but also served to (sonically)

orientate me (Ahmed 2006). Sound came before sight: audibility fueling my own visibility.

LX2—Spotlight: Divining the Ghost-Document and Redaction-as-Revelation

SX Cue Bass Track: 2 (slow fade in)

> RESEARCHER THOUGHT 2: *Shine a light in this direction (where spatiality confers with ink and time), then see how the past might leave behind more than a clue, or trace: queer Black marks upon the straight White page . . .*

The Ghost-Document

> RESEARCHER ARTICULATION 3: My inquiry is concerned with invisible presences. It celebrates women whose voices are archived on vinyl wax, the medium through which they sing to us in the present tense. I come from a line of women who "sense things": a mother, an aunt, and a cousin who receive spiritual messages. Those attuned to the presence of the "invisible" are mediums, "channelers" of spirits. Our role is a duty of convincing often-disbelieving audiences of contested presences. The academic engaged in resurrecting repressed knowledge is like the medium: we speak to (and narrate) the ghost— the thing that is culturally, or intellectually, invisible. We facilitate the revenant's comeback, evidencing where it has been—declaring the significance of what it has to sing.

> RESEARCHER ARTICULATION 4: The ghost-document is the invisible presence inside the archive: the visceral document, perceptible to the gut; suggested by the intersection of two, or more, literal documents, for example: a diary, a notebook, a letter, a recording, a photograph, a newspaper article, a drawing. At the nexus between literal documents, the ghost-document is *felt*, sensed to be there; its existence, conjecture-as-explanation for the connection between physical documents. In poetic terms, the nexus or crossroads is metaphor. Adrienne Rich beautifully summarizes metaphor as "the crossing of trajectories

of two (or more) elements that might have not otherwise known simultaneity. When this happens a piece of the universe is revealed as if for the first time" (1995, 8). The ghost-document resonates with Phillip Brian Harper's "speculative rumination" (2005, 108); it is politically and historically charged, precisely because it is both a demand that the unseen is acknowledged—and a response to disappearance.

RESEARCHER ARTICULATION 3: Hélène Cixous posits that the craft of writing is a response to the experience of disappearance (qtd. in Sellers 2003, xxvi). Thus, writing is a method of rejecting invisibility; a protest statement against denial and absence; a witness statement of existence: I mark the paper, therefore, I'm here my dear oppressor. Listening, too, in a queer-quare (and intersectionally queer-quare) context, is linked to the experience of disappearance. Listening, or tuning in, is a method of protesting erasure. Tuning in requires that one rejects silencing, affirming existence. By tuning in, one listens not just to literal sound but to metaphorical sound: to the spaces in between, the unsaid that whispers in the gaps within the dominant archive. Such listening requires tuning into the submerged, suppressed, or distorted narrative held beneath the surface of history's hegemonic waters (Rich 2017).

RESEARCHER ARTICULATION 4: The poet is, metaphorically, a diviner (Heaney 1980). We follow the desire to name what is felt or sensed (Lorde 1984, 37). We name what we find in order to realize it, in order to make visible and testify to a presence. The writer is a conduit, a medium sensing the liquid shape of a narrative body; by tuning into the past tense, the writer becomes a resurrection technician.

RESEARCHER ARTICULATION 3: Yet, dominant knowledge accuses the ghost-document of lacking the rigor of which it is assured. Taking no account that "archives of queerness are makeshift and randomly organized, due to the restraints historically shackled upon minoritarian cultural workers" (Muñoz 1996, 6–7), demands are issued for stability, promise, and certitude—the very things that the ghost-document, inherently, cannot be. Indeed, dominant knowledge misconstrues the ghost-document's positionality: to queer what knowledge is or can be. A composite of sensation, ambivalence, whisper, rumor, and trace, the ghost-document is real by virtue of being apparitional and manifesting in many guises.

RESEARCHER ARTICULATION 4: In *Performing the Archive*, Simone Osthoff writes, "Artists' reflections of representation, vision, and the invisible often alter the conventional boundaries of fiction and non-fiction" (Osthoff 2009, 11). The ghost-document is the invisible, the vision that alters the boundaries between fiction and nonfiction. The knowledge of the existence of the ghost-document (resurrected from the dead and made flesh by the writer) is a reparative narrative: a narrative that repairs absence. To write the ghost-document is to contribute to the queer-quare imagination. So, how can we, as writers, realize ghost-documents within the archive?

Redaction-as-Revelation

RESEARCHER ARTICULATION 3: Historically, redaction is an archival technique whereby parts of the original meaning of a text are "blacked out" or concealed, often to protect information deemed a risk to institutional, or national security. Blackout poetry was made popular by writer Austin Kleon (2010). With a blackout poem, the poet utilizes redaction not only as a tool for achieving poetic compression but as a device to subvert newspaper articles.
Christina Sharpe (2016) identifies Black redaction's utilization by artists in service of what she terms "wake work" (113): work alive to, and keeping vigil for, Maafa's ever-present-tense trace upon the contemporary. In solidarity with Sharpe's ethos, I utilize redaction as a means of generating queer-quare readings of archival documents: opening up printed texts to multiple alternative readings and, at the same time, releasing them from "Compulsory Heterosexuality and [Queer-Quare] [in]Existence" (Rich 1994).

RESEARCHER ARTICULATION 4: Marginalization's adjective accomplice is immateriality. However, in my research I welcome the spiritual manifestation of the word (in its philosophical coat), an ethereal, ever-present force of transformation inside the intellectual house of debate.

RESEARCHER ARTICULATION 3: In utilizing midnight's sable-ink upon the moon-pale page to divine possible meanings (perhaps potential, unconscious desires) within a document, redaction becomes a method not of obfuscation but of revelation. Therefore, I propose a methodological term: "redaction-as-revelation." This method functions via paradox: by "blacking out" text, its aim is *not* to hide or delete (with all the word's ominous overtones in a context of oppression) but to rejoice in the transformative powers of the substance, or body of blackness, and its encounter with the white page. With redaction-as-revelation, black ink is protagonist "fleshing out" queer-quare narrative space within historical consciousness.

Billie Holiday and Tallulah Bankhead

RESEARCHER ARTICULATION 5:

RESEARCHER ARTICULATION 4: In January 1949, charged with opium possession, Billie Holiday, known as Lady Day (who, in March 1948 was released from prison after serving time for narcotics offenses), was suicidal, fearful of another prison sentence. The actor Tallulah Bankhead (Holiday's friend and purported sometime-lover) not only arranged and paid for the services of a psychiatrist for her, but she wrote to J. Edgar Hoover (then director of the F.B.I. and a family friend)[5] in an attempt to ensure Lady Day's continued liberty (Blackburn 2006, 137):

RESEARCHER ARTICULATION 3: I read Tallulah Bankhead's letter and sense another document behind it: the ghost-document. The ghost-document offers interpretations of Bankhead's motivation. Hoover is a man of status and power. For a woman who states in her letter she has met Holiday "but twice in my life," Bankhead appears to be going to a lot of trouble (evidencing affection, loyalty, and the emotional and professional risks she is prepared to take) for Holiday. Bankhead, appealing not only to Hoover's egotism but to his prejudices, deploys complex, yet strategically placed paternalistic imagery designed to denote collusion with—and thus deference to—Hoover, renowned for his Southern, White, racist beliefs. Infantilizing Holiday (whom she describes as "a child at heart"), she deifies Hoover, writing: "as my Negro mammy used to say, 'When you pray, you pray to God don't you?'" In writing to Hoover, Bankhead accesses the highest echelons of American political power in pursuit of mercy for Lady Day.

RESEARCHER ARTICULATION 4: My hunch that there is another story to Bankhead's letter leads me to biographer Julia Blackburn's book, *With Billie* (2006). The book contains a series of interviews with people who knew and worked with Holiday. Detroit Red (a dancer-friend of Holiday's) states that Tallulah Bankhead was a lesbian, though Bankhead self-referred as "ambisextrous" (Stern and McKellen 2009, 39). Blackburn considers the trace evidence of Billie and Tallulah's romantic relationship describing how "for several months Tallulah followed [Billie] wherever she could" (2006, 136), sitting on the front row every night of Billie's performances at the Strand Theatre in 1948. Jose Esteban Muñoz theorizes:

Queerness is often transmitted covertly. . . . [L]eaving too much of a trace has often meant that the queer subject has left herself open for attack. *Instead of being clearly available as visible evidence, queerness has* instead *existed as innuendo, gossip, fleeting moments, and performances . . .* , while evaporating at the touch of those who would eliminate queer possibility. (Muñoz 1996, 6; emphasis mine).

RESEARCHER ARTICULATION 3: "Queer possibility" is the love notes, the pillow talk, the "speech d'amour" between Bankhead and Holiday. By utilizing redaction-as-revelation, I can reveal the possibility of Bankhead's hidden "love note" to Billie, in order to provide a potential version of their story.

SX Cue Bass Track: 3 (fade low)

RESEARCHER ARTICULATION 5:

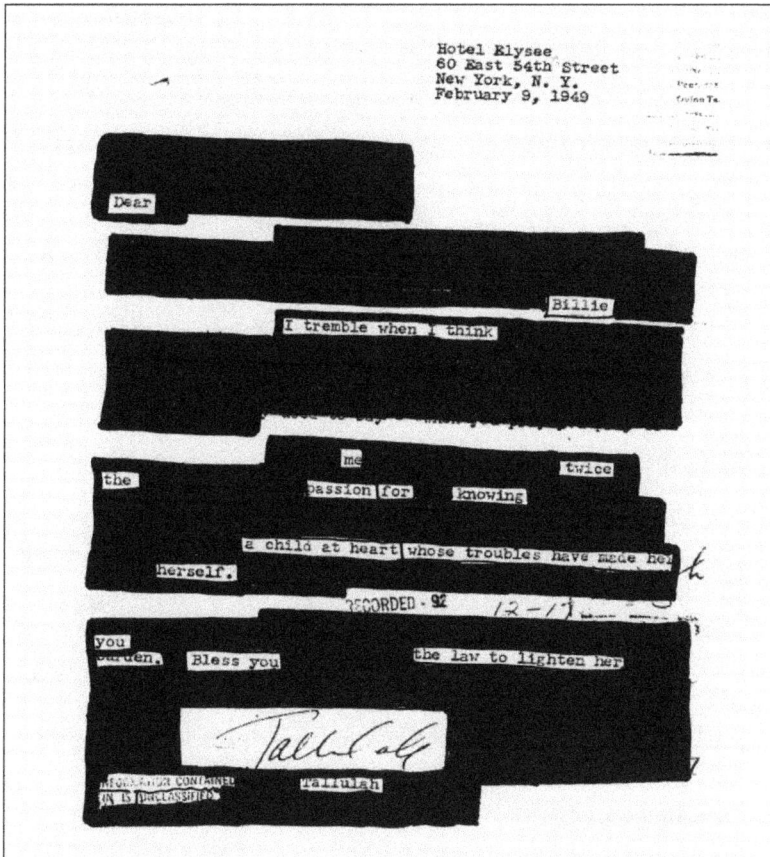

Dear Billie
I tremble when I think . . .
Me: twice the passion for knowing;
a child at heart whose troubles have made her, herself.
You: the law to lighten her burden.
Bless you.
(Smith 2016)

SX Cue Bass Track: 3 (fade out)

LX3: Follow-Spot—Rewriting-the-Record and Lecture-Keepsake

SX Cue Bass Track: 3 (fade in)

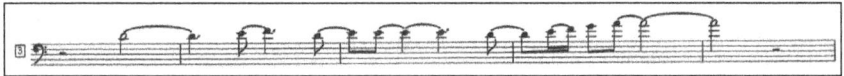

DESIGNER PROVOCATION 1: *What do you want the audience to take away with them?*

RESEARCHER THOUGHT 3: *You know that feeling, when what you're left with is a fragment of the story and when you touch it it's like a little follow-spot of light (just as a Midnight Special illuminates the dark)— and it reminds you (like an alibi), just what you witnessed? That feeling [pause], that feeling, yes—*

Rewriting the Record

RESEARCHER ARTICULATION 6: During an attic clear-out, I redis-cover a business card printed onto old vinyl. In the same time frame, director Juliet Ellis suggests I punctuate the lecture-as-performance with moments of vinyl played on a small, midnight-blue, portable Crossley record player. I reflect: matrix numbers are the ghost-script at the heart of vinyl. Dedications, dreams, or plain numeric code are marked on the "dead wax" at the center of each Black sound world; each compressed articulation a coded message, hidden. To read the code, the record has to be held to the light and deciphered. Matrix codes resonate, conceptually, with queer-quare methods and their fruit: queer-quare narratives. Thus, vinyl becomes inspiration for Mat Lazenby's design of a lecture-keepsake. The keepsake encourages audience contemplation and research, post-performance/.[6]

RESEARCHER ARTICULATION 7: The word "record" comes from the Latin, meaning "to pass through the heart again." The persistent, official "stuck record" of Billie Holiday's narrative body spins on the turntable of history, the pathological needle passing again and again through its heart. Each time the dominant, hegemonic "A side" of Holiday's narrative body sings, the needle is passing through the Black vinyl moon and she dies her socially constructed "pathography" of a death. Pathography is the clinical term meaning to write about illness. Joyce Carol Oates uses the word to mean a "diseased biography" (qtd. in Couser 2006, 162). A diseased biography is a psychopathologic study of its namesake's negative behavior, at the expense of profiling their accolades and achievements.

SX Cue Vinyl: Billie Holiday's recording of "Strange Fruit"

RESEARCHER ARTICULATION 8: The heteronormative image of Holiday portrays a Black woman dependent upon white, heterosexual, male insight; a political ingénue; an intellectual subordinate, coerced by white men into singing her most famous song, "Strange Fruit," because she was unable to comprehend its lyrics. Two sources illustrate this: in "Strange Record," a *Time* magazine article dated 12 June 1939 (cited in Margolick 2000,n.p.), Billie Holiday is described thus:

Billie Holiday is a roly-poly coloured woman with a hump in her voice. . . . [S]he does not care enough about her figure to watch her diet, but she loves to sing. . . . One number . . . she particularly wanted on wax. Called Strange Fruit . . . its lyric was a poetic description of a lynching's terrible finale. Billie liked its dirge-like Blues melody but was not so much interested in the song's social content.

RESEARCHER ARTICULATION 7: In *Soul Music, Strange Fruit*, a 2013 documentary for BBC Radio 4, the paternalistic stereotype is repeated:

According to Barney Josephson [the owner of Café Society], she didn't really get the song, it didn't really sink in . . . but she . . . agreed to sing it, because he wanted her to sing it. Before long, she fully embraced the song and everything it represented, and she took it extremely seriously.

SX Cue Vinyl: fade down "Strange Fruit"

RESEARCHER ARTICULATION 6: How can we play the unheard (or underheard) B-side of Holiday's narrative? How can we change the record, so that a different music can be heard?

SX Cue Vinyl: Billie Holiday's "Summertime"

RESEARCHER ARTICULATION 8: Holiday, a Black, working-class, queer-quare woman, is the teacher of presidents. President Barack Obama wrote:

Behind me, Billie was on her last song. I picked up the refrain, humming a few bars. Her voice sounded different to me now. Beneath the layers of hurt, beneath the ragged laughter, I heard a willingness to endure. Endure—and make music that wasn't there before. (2008, 212)

SX Cue Vinyl: "Summertime" (slow fade)

RESEARCHER ARTICULATION 6: Lady Day beguiled the ear of the forty-fourth president; she sang him the melody (not for a song called "Pathography" but) for a tune called "Endurance."

SX Cue Vinyl: Bessie Smith's "On Revival Day"

This singing of courage, these notes of resistance sung by the singer, are heard by the listener across the staves of the decades.

RESEARCHER ARTICULATION 8: In 1961, James Baldwin spoke of the time he arrived in the Swiss mountains, with two Bessie Smith records and a typewriter. Baldwin, struggling to finish his first novel, *Go Tell It on the Mountain*, said:

I finally realized that one of the reasons that I couldn't finish this novel was that I was . . . ashamed of the Blues . . . , of Jazz . . . , all of these stereotypes . . . the country inflicts on Negroes, that . . . we all do nothing but sing the Blues. . . . [A]s far removed from Harlem as anything

you can imagine, with Bessie Smith and me . . . I began. In this isolation, I managed to finish the book. . . . I played Bessie every day. . . .
I corrected things according to what I was able to hear when Bessie
sang. (2014, 4)

SX CUE Vinyl: fade after Bessie Smith sings: "Lordy, Lordy"

Lecture-Keepsake

RESEARCHER ARTICULATION 9: Bessie Smith, the soundtrack to the
imagination of struggling novelists, each one, just like an audience,
carrying a fragment of the record home through the uncertainty of
darkness. Each fragment designed to be a follow-spot of light which
illuminates a research-journey: past eureka-moment-Post-it-notes;
doodle-maps of daydream-thoughts; notebook lists of things to say;
the Day-Glo-colored research facts in photocopied articles; the piles
of books (the ones to love, the ones to leave); magazines (best lines
and quotes torn out for their pertinence); and must-be characters
with ballpoint veins, who sleep between the blue-feint lines (between
the margin and the spine), who *always* whisper loudest when they
think that thought's abandoned them. Peter Turchi writes:

RESEARCHER ARTICULATION 10: "To ask for a map is to say: 'tell me
a story'" (2004, 11).

RESEARCHER ARTICULATION 9: But to rewrite the map is to rewrite
the record. The record is a witness: a witness is a measurement of a
distance in space, or time. Look what happens when we meet on the
journey of change, the record our witness, which acts as a measurement of the distance between where we are now—and how far we
have come.

SX Cue Vinyl: Ma Rainey's "Prove It on Me Blues." We hear the first verse
of the song, then

RESEARCHER ARTICULATION 6 sings, or hums along, then:

LX3: fade out in time with song fade.
Fin.

Post-Script

SX Cue Bass Track: 4

Citation-as-Poetry

> RESEARCHER ARTICULATION 11: Within a linguistic universe, the poet and the scholar share a skill and a challenge: to distil large-scale paradigms, complex concepts, or experiences into elegant, striking, memorable language. As an artist-scholar engaged in practice-steeped inquiry, I've been reflecting upon how I can synthesize both of those roles; the result is citation-as-poetry: an expression of the journey of engagement with key academic ideas, using poetry.
>
> RESEARCHER ARTICULATION 12: My practice-based process sets its compass toward justice. It traverses what Sara Ahmed in *Queer Phenomenology* observes as the "spatiality of . . . desire" (2006, 1). It follows the "trace, the glimmer[s] . . . and specks" of Jose Esteban Muñoz's "Ephemera as Evidence" (1996, 10) in search of the river of what Marina Abramovic terms "Liquid Knowledge" (2016, paragraph 10). Upstream, it finds Mihaly Csikszentmihalyi's flow state (2002) and there—via Ann Cvetkovich's *An Archive of Feelings* (2003)—it enters the landscape of Rosi Braidotti's nomadic thinking (2011); here, it tunes into Audre Lorde's "concert of voices" (1980, 31) and sings a queer pitch of Fred Moten's Blackness and sonic resistance (2003).

Acknowledgments

Big thanks to: 125th and Midnight—electric presences who have touched this research process: Juliet Ellis (director and filmmaker); Jason Hird (dramaturg); Jenni Molloy (composer and musician); Mat Lazenby (designer); Professor Ros Steen (vocal director); Hazel Holder (dialect coach); Tenzin Haarhaus (studio engineer, U.K.); Marie Millward (equipment, U.K.); Matthew Elliott (technician, U.K.); Brad Burgess (technician, U.S.); Ruth Steinberg (project runner, U.K.); Terry Simpson (project runner, U.K.) and Lynette Willoughby (artists' bookmaker, U.K.). Special thanks to Jason Hird, who so generously worked as dramaturg during the process of developing this piece.

The Archives Libraries and Museums Conference (ALMS), 2016
Matt Brim, Associate Professor of Queer Studies, College of Staten Island, CUNY
CLAGS: The Center for LGBTQ Studies at CUNY
Sean Edgecomb, Assistant Professor of Theater in the Department of Performing and Creative Arts at the College of Staten Island, CUNY
Matthew Elliot, Doctoral Researcher, Leeds University, England
Amin Ghaziani, Associate Professor of Sociology and Canada Research Chair in Sexuality and Urban Studies, University of British Columbia
J.H. and N.H.
The Harris Family
Mike Love
Jan Pimblett, Principal Development Officer, London Metropolitan Archives and co-organizer of ALMS, 2016
Maggie Pearson
Jane Plastow, Professor of African Theatre, Leeds University, England
Library staff, Graduate Center, CUNY
Lynda Plummer
Jeremy Poynting, Managing Editor, Peepal Tree Press, England
Donald Springett
Ros Steen, Professor Emerita, the Royal Conservatoire, Scotland
Frank Hentschker and the Martin E. Segal Theatre Center, New York
Jane Taylor, Andrew W. Mellon Chair of Aesthetic Theory and Material, University of the Western Cape, Cape Town, South Africa
Polly Thistlethwaite, Professor and Chief Librarian, Graduate Center Library, CUNY
Fiona Williams, O.B.E., Emeritus Professor of Social Policy, Leeds University
Evie Wilson-Lingbloom

NOTES

1 This essay-as-performance is intended to be read out loud. It began as a twenty-minute lecture-as-performance, set to a double-bass score; a collaboration with director, actor, and filmmaker Juliet Ellis and musician and composer Jenni

Molloy. The lecture was given at the Bishopsgate Institute, London, for "Without Borders: The Archives Libraries and Museums LGBTQ+ Conference," ALMS, 2016. At the invitation of the City University of New York's CLAGS: The Center for LGBTQ Studies, Graduate Center Library and Graduate Center PhD Theater Program, the lecture was developed into an hour-long solo piece in partnership with my company of collaborator-makers, 125th and Midnight. The lecture text (both spoken and sung) is fused with music and film: rommi-smith.co.uk/the-map-where-we-meet/.

2 LX and SX are lighting and sound codes, respectively; part of the lighting "plot" within a theater technician's performance-script. As a poet and narrativist, I'm fascinated by metaphors within theatrical terms such as state, or plot. I employ such terms with narrative and political connotations in mind. Here, the lighting plot (with plot's double-meaning of story) is utilized to politically illuminate hidden queer stories.

3 *Quare* is a reference to the work of E. Patrick Johnson, who employs this vernacular term to describe "nonnormative sexuality" (Johnson 2005, 124). I'm exploring use of the hyphenated term queer-quare to acknowledge the political use of quare by (among others) Black, Irish, and working-class scholars, but also to reference queer—to which quare is a response. In an essay that explores multiplicities of the self, I propose the working-dualism *queer-quare* as a term capable of holding the differences, choices (and also tensions and contradictions) within debates concerning self-definition.

4 Between 1970 and 1978, attendees at eight Women's Liberation Movement conferences produced the "Seven Demands," a working manifesto aimed at women's liberation.

5 Max Reddick Experience 2015.

6 The lecture-keepsake was placed in a midnight-black envelope, which was sealed and marked with the words: "do not open, yet" and placed under each theater seat. Keepsakes were intended to be cut from vintage vinyl. However, production investigations revealed the cutting method would release chlorine gas. Alternative cutting options proved vastly expensive for production budgets, so a high-quality card version was produced. Each piece of record contains a research provocation: a "clue" in the form of a stanza from a redaction-as-revelation poem. A purpose-built webpage (only accessible by those who were at the lecture and have "a piece of the record") reveals the full redaction-as-revelation poem I created especially for the lecture-as-performance. The inclusion of my business card in the keepsake envelope was designed as a prompt for feedback and dialogue.

WORKS CITED

Abramović, Marina, interviewed by D. Levy. 2016. "Walk through Walls: A Memoir by Marina Abramović—Five Decades of Groundbreaking Performance Art." *The Guardian*, November 19. www.theguardian.com/.

Ahmed, Sara. 2006. *Queer Phenomenology: Orientations, Objects, Others*. Durham, NC: Duke University Press.

Baker, Jean-Claude, and Chris Chase. 1993. *Josephine: The Hungry Heart*. London: Random House.

Baldwin, James. 1954. *Go Tell It on the Mountain*. London: Penguin Books.

Baldwin, James. 1994. *Just Above My Head*. London: Penguin Books.

Baldwin, James. 2014. *James Baldwin: The Last Interview and Other Conversations*. Brooklyn, NY: Melville House.

Blackburn, Julia. 2006. *With Billie*. London: Vintage Books.

Braidotti, Rosi. 2011. *The Portable Rosi Braidotti*. New York: Columbia University Press.

Brim, Matt. 2014. *James Baldwin and the Queer Imagination*. Ann Arbor: University of Michigan Press.

Brim, Matt, and Amin Ghaziani. 2016. "Introduction: Queer Methods." *WSQ: Women's Studies Quarterly* 44 (3–4): 14–27.

Brown, Jayna. 2008. *Babylon Girls: Black Women Performers and the Shaping of the Modern*. Durham, NC: Duke University Press.

Cixous, Hélène. 1994. *The Hélène Cixous Reader*, edited by Susan Sellers. New York: Routledge. xxvi–xxxii.

Courtney, Martin, and Wendy MacNaughton. 2017. *Focus 2017*. July 28. https://society6.com/.

Couser, G. Thomas. 1999. "Autopathography, Women, Illness, and Lifewriting," In *Women and Autobiography*, edited by Martine Watson Brownley and Allison B. Kimmich, 164. Lanham, MD: Rowman & Littlefield.

Crenshaw, Kimberlé. 1989. "Demarginalizing the Intersection of Race and Sex: A Black Feminist Critique of Antidiscrimination Doctrine, Feminist Theory, and Antiracist Politics." *University of Chicago Legal Forum* 1989 (1): 139–67. http://chicagounbound.uchicago.edu/.

Csikszentmihalyi, Mihaly. 2002. *Flow*. London: Rider.

Cvetkovich, Ann. 2003. *An Archive of Feelings*. Durham, NC: Duke University Press.

Davis, Angela. 1999. *Blues Legacies and Black Feminism*. New York: Vintage Books.

DeFrantz, Thomas F., and Anita Gonzalez. 2014. *Black Performance Theory*. Durham, NC: Duke University Press.

Du Bois, W.E.B. 1994. *The Souls of Black Folk*. New York: Dover Books.

Gordon, Avery. 2004. *Ghostly Matters: Haunting and the Sociological Imagination*. 4th ed. Minneapolis: University of Minnesota Press.

Gumbs, Alexis Pauline. 2016. *Spill*. Durham, NC: Duke University Press.

Halberstam, Jack. 2011. *The Queer Art of Failure*. Durham, NC: Duke University Press.

Hannula, Mika, Juha Suoranta, and Tere Vaden. 2014. *Artistic Research Methodology: Narrative, Power, and the Public*. New York: Peter Lang.

Harper, Phillip Brian. 2005. "The Evidence of Felt Intuition: Minority Experience, Everyday Life, and Critical Speculative Knowledge." In *Black Queer Studies: A Critical Anthology*, edited by E. Patrick Thompson and Mae G. Henderson, 106–23. Durham, NC: Duke University Press.

Heaney, Seamus. 1980. *Preoccupations: Selected Prose 1968–1978*. London: Faber and Faber.

Heyward, Dubois, and George Gershwin. 1973. "Summertime." On *Billie's Blues*. Recording. Holland: CBS.

Holiday, Billie, with W. Dufty. 1975. *Lady Sings the Blues*. London: Sphere Books.

Holiday, Billie. 2013. "Strange Fruit." On *Lady Sings the Blues*. Recording. European Union: Not Now Music.

Johnson. E. Patrick. 2005. "'Quare' Studies, or (Almost) Everything I Know About Queer Studies I Learned from My Grandmother." In *Black Queer Studies: A Critical Anthology*, edited by E. Patrick Johnson and Mae G. Henderson, 124–57. Durham, NC: Duke University Press.

Kershaw, Baz, and Helen Nicholson, eds. 2011. *Research Methods in Theatre and Performance*. Edinburgh: Edinburgh University Press.

Kleon, Austin. 2010. *Blackout Poetry*. New York: Harper Perennial.

Lewis, Sarah. 2014. *The Rise: Creativity, The Gift of Failure and the Search for Mastery*. London: William Collins.

Lieb, Sandra R. 1981. *Mother of the Blues: A Study of Ma Rainey*. Amherst: University of Massachusetts Press.

Light, Alan. 2016. *What Happened, Miss Simone?* Edinburgh: Canongate.

Lorde, Audre. 1980. *The Cancer Journals*. San Francisco: Aunt Lute Books.

Lorde, Audre. 1984. "Poetry Is Not a Luxury." In *Sister Outsider: Essays and Speeches*. Berkeley, CA: Crossing Press.

Margolick, David. 2000. *Strange Fruit*. London: Payback Press.

Max Reddick Experience. 2013. "Letter from Tallulah Bankhead to J. Edgar Hoover." Blog. http://soulbrotherv2.tumblr.com/post/68272567247/letter-from-tallulah-bankhead-to-j-edgar-hoover.

Monk, Thelonious. 1947. *Genius of Modern Music: Volume 1*. www.youtube.com/watch?v=zreou5XyNfY&list=PL4ypuAMic-GhMxBDzKH59KdFptqmD4Mr9.

Moten, Fred. 2003. *In the Break: The Aesthetics of the Black Radical Tradition*. Minneapolis: University of Minnesota Press.

Muñoz, José Esteban. 1996. "Ephemera as Evidence: Introductory Notes to Queer Acts." *Women and Performance: Journal of Feminist Theory* 8 (2): 5–16.

Nelson, Robin, ed. 2013. *Practice as Research in the Arts*. Hampshire, UK: Palgrave Macmillan.

Nepon, Ezra Berkley. 2016. *Dazzle Camouflage: Spectacular Theatrical Strategies for Resistance and Resilience*. N.p.: Creative Commons.

Obama, Barack. 2008. *Dreams from My Father: A Story of Race and Inheritance*. Edinburgh: Canongate Books.

Osthoff, Simone. 1999. *Performing the Archive: The Transformation of the Archive in Contemporary Art from Repository of Documents to Art Medium*. New York: Atropos Press.

Rainey, Gertrude "Ma" (accompanied by the Tub Jug Washboard Band). 1928. "Prove It on Me Blues." www.youtube.com/watch?v=5QptNDPGZzo.

Razaf, A., and K. Macomber. 1970. "On Revival Day." *The World's Greatest Blues Singer: Bessie Smith.* Recording. CBS.

Rich, Adrienne. 1994. "Compulsory Heterosexuality and Lesbian Existence." In *Blood, Bread, and Poetry: Selected Prose, 1979–1985.* New York: W. W. Norton.

Rich, Adrienne. 1995. *What Is Found There: Notebooks on Poetry and Politics.* London: Virago.

Rich, Adrienne. 2017. "Diving into the Wreck." *Poets.org.* www.poets.org/poetsorg/poem/diving-wreck.

Schechner, Richard. 2002. *Performance Studies: An Introduction.* 3rd ed. London: Routledge.

Sedgwick, Eve Kosovsky. 2003. *Touching Feeling: Affect, Pedagogy, Performativity.* Durham, NC: Duke University Press.

Sellers, Susan, ed. 1994. *The Hélène Cixous Reader.* New York: Routledge. xxvi–xxxii.

Sharpe, Christina. 2016. *In the Wake: On Blackness and Being.* Durham, NC: Duke University Press.

Smith, R. 2016. "Dear Billie." Unpublished Ghost-Document poem.

Soul Music, Strange Fruit. 2013. BBC Radio 4, November 26.

Sporke, Michael. 2014. *Big Mama Thornton: The Life and Music.* Jefferson, NC: McFarland.

Stern, Keith, and Ian McKellen. 2009. *Queers in History: The Comprehensive Encyclopaedia of Historical Gays, Lesbians, and Bisexuals.* Dallas: BenBella Books.

Stoever-Ackerman, Jennifer. 2010. "Splicing the Sonic Color Line." *Social Text* 28 (1): 59–85. http://socialtext.dukejournals.org/.

Turchi, Peter. 2004. *Maps of the Imagination: The Writer as Cartographer.* San Antonio, TX: Trinity University Press.

Walker, Alice. 1989. "Purple Prose: An Interview with Alice Walker." *Elle* (October): 45–50.

Women's Liberation Movement. 1970–1978. "Seven Demands." www.bl.uk/.

10

Discursive Hustling and Queer of Color Interviewing

STEVEN W. THRASHER

In journalism and academia alike, I've tried to be a queer hustler: a code-switching secret agent who uses *discursive hustling* to furtively ferry knowledge between two worlds.

Since 2014, I have shuttled back and forth between writing stories for the *Guardian* and peer-reviewed articles for academic journals, and I'm probably the first person admitted to PhD programs with a writing submission first published by *Gawker* (and writing a dissertation that began as a *BuzzFeed* story).

But in journalism and academia alike, over these past few years I have tried to imagine my readers as queer people of color. I write to them as such for three reasons. First, readers are assumed by most academic journals and mainstream publications I've written for to be white, straight, male, and cisgender; this misconception is imagined as immutable in both the present and the future (while neither is true). Second, imagining myself writing for white and/or straight readers would cast me in the role of the "native informant" (Spivak 1999), writing *about* communities of color for the white gaze, which is a dynamic I refuse to engage. Finally, even though there are white readers in my audiences, I think they will benefit from being written to as if they are queer people of color. Queer people of color have long had to adapt to reading work not written for us, which has forced us to develop creative and often renegade reading practices. White straight readers, long denied this challenging extra workload, can benefit from doing extra levels of interpretation and cultivating what Eve Sedgwick called "paranoid and reparative critical practices" of reading (2003, 128). (Similarly, while *Moonlight* was made in an all-Black world for queer people not used to seeing themselves on film, white viewers got to grapple with how to appreciate the 2016 Oscar winner for best picture when no one looked like them.)

But while I've been imagining my readers as queer people of color for years, and while I've tried to consciously understand myself as a queer writer of color for even longer than that, I've only more recently realized that creating work with both of those things in mind is contingent upon a specific technique. This technique, long unnamed to myself, must be deployed from the moment I begin conceiving of a story. I call it *queer of color interviewing*.

Although much of my initial training as an interviewer happened by going to film school at the Tisch School of the Arts, crewing on HBO's film of *The Laramie Project*, and working for NPR's StoryCorps project, those experiences on other people's projects trained me to conduct interviews (with subjects of all races and sexualities) with a straight, white audience in mind. The kinds of questions asked, the location of that questioning, the time constraints of the interviews, the modes of distribution: all of these factors framed the work with a white audience in mind. This imbued the work with whiteness (Lipsitz 1998) and heteronormativity (Warner 1993), even when the subjects being interviewed were Black and/or queer.

It took some years to decolonize my mind such that, as I have produced my own work, I have developed ways to conduct queer of color interviews, which shape my stories from their conception to their completion. Using what Roderick Ferguson coined as *queer of color critique* or *queer of color theory*—the process of centering the experiences of queer people of color (Ferguson, 2003)—this essay will explore methods for creating queer of color interviews. It will also provide an approach for a discursive hustle, not from queer communities of color to white eyeballs but in the dance between popular journalism into academia. To do this, I will present two case studies for how I've created queer of color interviews: in my reporting on the Michael "Tiger Mandingo" Johnson HIV criminalization case in Missouri for *BuzzFeed* (conducted from 2014 to 2018), and in my reporting from Orlando, Florida, on the shootings at the Pulse nightclub (conducted in 2016). I will end with a section on how queer of color interviews shade not just the creation of the journalism stories I write but pave the way for this discursive hustling between journalism and academia.

Geography: Queer Space in St. Louis

In February of 2014, Mark Schoofs, the new investigations editor at *BuzzFeed*, met me for dinner to discuss a story he had in mind that he thought I would "work on for a long time." He thought I should write about the "Tiger Mandingo" HIV story in Missouri, which I had barely heard of at the time. Over the next four years, I would write a dozen stories on the case, including two investigative stories of approximately 7,500 words each: "How College Wrestling Star 'Tiger Mandingo' Became an HIV Scapegoat" (2014) and "A Black Body on Trial: The HIV Conviction of 'Tiger Mandingo'" (2015). It has also become the basis for my doctoral research on race, HIV criminalization, gay politics, and the Black Lives Matter movement.

But when my editor initially approached me in beginning of 2014, little was known publicly about "Tiger Mandingo," which is an online screen name of a young man named Michael Johnson. In October of 2013, Johnson was charged with "knowingly" exposing at least six sexual partners to HIV and with "infecting" two of them with the virus. There had been salacious, poorly written stories about this "monster" when he was arrested. They amounted to little more, however, than recycling the prosecution's press release and whipping up hysteria around well-worn "Mandingo" tropes about predatory Black male sexuality.

Schoofs wanted me to do to what no one else had done: go to Missouri, find Johnson's friends and sexual partners, get into the jail where Johnson was being held—and interview all of them.

Pulling this off would mean refuting many ways the story had been lazily and erroneously reported thus far. No journalist had interviewed the accused or any of the accusers, employing the unethical practice (increasingly common, particularly as journalism budgets are slashed) of relying primarily upon prosecutor's talking points to source a story. This practice undermines the ability of accused people to maintain that they are innocent until proven guilty. Ironically, refuting this assumption makes it an increasingly queer practice to adhere to the legal norm of habeas corpus *and* imagining people accused of crimes as legally innocent until they are convicted.

Primarily, though, finding the "Tiger Mandingo" story meant that I would have to use a number of queer of color techniques for my reporting, culminating in creating a queer of color interview, *if* I could get it, with Johnson himself.

First, I had to think about myself as a queer of color reporter who was willing to imagine Johnson as legally innocent up to the time he might (or might not) be convicted. I also had to be willing to listen to anyone who would tell me about interactions with him. This meant I had to refute the idea that "neutral" or "objective" reporters were white, straight, cisgender, HIV negative—or that "objective" reporters existed at all. I had to confront myself as a mixed-race Black, queer, HIV-negative writer from New York and wrestle with that. I had to work with how I was coming into Missouri from the afar (which had drawbacks and benefits) and work with myself subjectively. (I also had to acknowledge that white, straight reporters seldom have to reckon with themselves so honestly.)

Then, I had to figure out where I would find the people I needed to interview. As Johnson was a student wrestler, I found the names and email addresses of his teammates easily enough, and I emailed every single one of them (and messaged them on Facebook). This resulted in some gem quotes, including from the player I asked about showering with a gay teammate. He told me that Johnson had "never showered with us—and he was the only Black guy on the team, so if he'd showered, everyone would have noticed!" This revealed the multiply formed anxiety Johnson's teammates had about his sexuality *and* race—even *before* his positive HIV status was known. I also reached out to people who had commented on Johnson's many public social media accounts. Though these were standard investigative digital reporting moves, they were made in the service of my nascent theory of queer of color interviewing. That methodology crystallized into explicitly queer of color thinking when I realized I needed to use or create accounts for every queer hookup app that I knew Michael had used (Grindr, Scruff, and the more Black-oriented Jack'd), as well hookup websites like Adam4Adam, Manhunt, and BarebackRT, the last a site explicitly for "bug chasers" and people who have sex without condoms.

I had a strong suspicion that "Tiger Mandingo" was probably being charged so harshly because he had had sex with white men. Though my hunch was ultimately proven right (four of the six accusers were white, as was the first accuser to come forward and the one who would drive the case, Dylan King Lemons), I wouldn't know this for more than a year after I began my investigation, until Johnson's trial.

So how was I to find people on websites and apps who may have known him?

One way was by finding websites that advertised interracial sex parties in St. Louis. But also, with all the apps and websites I visited, I searched out users who were seeking "BBC," "Big Black Cock," and "Mandingo" in their handles and advertisements. There were many people seeking BBC—especially on the campus of the small, nearly all-white, Christian-affiliated college Johnson had attended—but this helped me to narrow down who I approached to a manageable number.

I then approached people under the ethical terms of journalism with immediate disclosure. There was no "catfishing" (Saeedi 2012). I would begin every interaction by writing something like, "Hi, my name is Steven. I live in New York and am doing a piece for *BuzzFeed* about this 'Tiger Mandingo' story. I'm trying to find people who knew him or hooked up with him. If you did, or know someone who did, would you be willing to talk? Happy to protect the identity of my sources—thanks." Sometimes I would provide contact information for my editors and links to my work, so they could know something about me and ask my colleagues about my trustworthiness. Most people didn't respond but many did, even a few who had met Michael, slept with him, or could connect me to someone who had. And some people chatted with me in a way that was deeply informative about what life was like for queer people of color in Missouri, which provided excellent background context for my reporting.

While my practice of identifying myself and not "lurking" could be used by any journalist, there is a practice known as "Grindr baiting" (Nichols 2015), and I think straight reporters are more likely to use it. Grindr baiting was perhaps most famously utilized by the white, straight *Daily Beast* writer Nico Hines to out an athlete at the Rio Olympics (Rodriguez 2016). Grindr does make it easy to see where there are gay people anywhere, and many people who use the app post photos that are ostensibly public; but, as a queer person of color, I am used to being surveilled. I don't want my sources who are mostly private people to ever feel that they are under surveillance or that they have to speak to me lest they will be outed. (However, I will vigorously confront and track down via social media public officials who get taxpayer money to get them on the record, but that's a very different setting.)

Finding these sources meant putting myself in Michael Johnson's head and hanging out digitally where he would hang out. A straight person wouldn't (and shouldn't) necessarily be hanging in the digital spaces I was occupying. They would not be likely to know enough about barebacking to check out a bareback website. And while a white and/or straight reporter wouldn't be likely to know enough about *Mandingo-ism* (du Cille 1997, 299) as a theoretical concept, interracial pornography is very popular in the United States, and they might know enough to search terms like "Black," "Black dick" or "BBC." Still, as a Black gay man, I had access to a knowledge base from a place of empathy—and not coming strictly from the fetishizing surveillance of the white gaze—which allowed me to be inside the head of the person I was reporting on, to get closer to understanding what happened in the kinds of intimate spaces in which the story had unfolded, and to write *for other Black men*. (Interestingly, this did not create a niche readership; my stories on "Tiger Mandingo" for *BuzzFeed* have been read by more than a million people.)

I also needed to physically go to places Johnson may have visited. For help on this, I turned to St. Louis Effort for AIDS, the main HIV prevention nonprofit in St. Louis. Because of who is affected by AIDS, whenever I land in a new city to report on anything, I turn to HIV prevention workers to point me toward where work is being done around race, poverty, and medical oppression. They told me the neighborhoods to check out and the bars I should go to (and, in racially segregated St. Louis, what nights I could find Black people at which bars). They also told me about the local bathhouse. I frequented the bars, asking around for people who knew Michael. Even from those who didn't know him, I got a decent sense from bartenders and patrons about how people in Missouri felt about HIV criminalization and Black gay men. I blended in just fine at a drag performance, which had hundreds of mostly Black people in its audience. And I went to the bathhouse. I didn't go to find sources, talk to anyone, or even to write about it explicitly; but I wanted to experience what one kind of embodied gay sexuality looked like in a large city far from the coastal cities I've inhabited my whole life. (And it taught me a lot about how race plays out in St. Louis's queer sex scene.)

Only a queer person of color writing for queer people of color could have accessed and utilized this empathetic, embodied knowledge as I did. Finally, I wanted to conduct a queer of color interview with Johnson himself. I didn't get to do it until the last day of that first trip to St. Louis (and I wasn't sure it would happen at all). Given all the negative press that had been printed about him, Johnson had little reason to trust any journalist. I was hoping, as one Black gay man to another, to convince him that I wanted to get to know him as a whole person.

But anything to do with prison is queer; it creates space, time, and relationships that are out of sync with dominant notions of straight life—even for a reporter. I had been unable to speak to Johnson by phone. I had written him a letter, but I knew he couldn't really read. I heard through someone who had contact that he wanted to speak with me, but I couldn't confirm this independently. The only way I could really communicate with him was to fly to Missouri and hope we'd get to speak, not knowing if I was blowing the lump sum of money I got for the story on a trip that wouldn't pan out.

There is a shame in jail buildings that is not incongruous with queerness, that extends to everyone who even visits. At the St. Charles Correctional Center (as at all jails), I had to give up a lot of personal information about myself to people who treated me like a criminal. I don't believe that a white straight reporter would experience this with the same level of anxiety I did as a Black gay reporter trying to connect with someone known as "Tiger Mandingo." For days, the commanding officer in charge played a game with me, always asking for one more piece of information than he had asked for the previous day (which, if he'd just given all the requirements to me at once would not have been a problem). When I finally met the commanding officer face to face—a portly man in a white uniform that brought to mind the character Boss Hawg from *The Dukes of Hazzard*—he made it clear to me that he controlled the Black body I wanted to speak to. (Johnson's lawyer told me sometimes the jail would send the wrong Michael Johnson up to speak to her.)

The waiting for Michael Johnson, the not knowing if the interaction I so deeply longed for would happen or not, was not unlike cruising. Queer theorist José Esteban Muñoz's belief that "[q]ueerness is a structuring and educated mode of desiring that allows us to see and feel beyond the quagmire of the present" is helpful when trying to talk to someone in jail. As a reporter, you wait for hours or days to talk to your subject, as your subject waits months or years for freedom. Gratification is delayed, if it is to come at all.

And then, I finally got to interview Michael Johnson. There were many constraints on us. We were being recorded by the jail. We couldn't discuss things that could further incriminate him. But we were able to talk to each other in a heartfelt way. Never having met before, we both came from differently surveilled worlds that were similar enough that each of us knew what "Mandingo" meant to the other. Michael wanted people to care about his story and to know what was happening to him was an injustice, and I wanted readers for my work, so there was much that was transactional about our exchange. I was keenly aware of how queer it was that I was hypermobile and could investigate many deeply intimate aspects of incarcerated Michael Johnson, his "Tiger Mandingo" persona, and his sexual interactions with others while he was locked up; to that end, I tried to reveal some things about myself, including that I was also gay, in a small gesture of making myself seem vulnerable and relatable to him. I found that we could just talk to each other with some ease because of this, short-handing certain info in the little time we had—in a way a white and/or straight reporter never could. (Over the past five years, it has grown into the one of the most queer and intense relationships I have, even though we speak infrequently and see each other even less often.)

Reflecting on this interview with Johnson (and several more which were conducted between 2014 and 2017), I have found that there are three elements for a queer of color interview that exceed queer of color theory in their specificity: the interview needs to be conducted by a queer interviewer of color, conducted with a queer interviewee of color, with an imagined queer audience of color in mind. (On this last point, the actual audience can be *anyone,* but the interview must be conducted between queer people of color and written with queer people of color in mind.)

Integral to publishing a story with a queer of color interview at its heart was who was editing me. The story was commissioned by Mark Schoofs, a white gay journalist who won a Pulitzer for writing about AIDS in Africa in the 1990s and who has been writing and editing about

HIV for decades. He edited it with Saeed Jones, the Black queer poet who was *BuzzFeed* LGBT's first editor. Mark is older than I am and Saeed younger, and the intergenerational conversations with these white and Black gay men about HIV, gay sex, and race in America shaped the story as queer in a way editing from straight and only white editors wouldn't have. Particularly in stark relief against the salacious news stories written about Johnson as far away as Australia—which imagined his HIV diagnosis to pose a mortal threat worldwide to an audience of white heterosexual readers, even though the likelihood of being exposed to HIV is relatively small for white heterosexuals compared to Black queer men—the questions my gay editors asked me, and their frames of analysis, made for a very different way of forming the story. I was not on offense in trying to explain this to them, as I have been in the majority of my writing career when my editors were white heterosexuals. We worked in concert to conceive of a story for a general audience but with a queer of color subjectivity in mind, rooted in the queer of color jailhouse interview.

Over the years, this ethos has guided our continued coverage of the Johnson case. In 2015, Johnson was convicted of one count of HIV transmission and four counts of exposing or attempting to expose others to transmission and was sentenced to 30.5 years in prison; he would have gotten out in 2044. However, in 2016—in part due to our reporting in *BuzzFeed*—Johnson's supporters began to raise $25,000 to hire an attorney and successfully appealed his case; a Missouri appeals court ruled Johnson's prosecutor had engaged in prosecutorial misconduct for failing to disclose evidence and overturned the conviction. Then, facing a new trial in 2017, Johnson took a no-contest "Alford" plea deal for ten years and was approved in 2018 for parole about eighteen months before it was scheduled to begin. He is scheduled to leave prison in 2019 instead of 2044, after having served six years.

Ethnography: Queer Time in Orlando

Around 2 A.M. on June 12, 2016, late into a Saturday night that had become a Sunday morning, I returned to my home from a party hosted by the gay poet Adam Fitzgerald. Scrolling through Twitter as I got into bed, I saw that something awful was happening at a gay nightclub in

Florida, on its Latin Night. I found the Orlando Police Department's scanner online and, as everyone was asleep in the United States and in England, found a *Guardian* editor working in Australia. We worked together through the night on the news, and I went to bed at 6:00 A.M., only to be awakened at 6:30 and told to write an opinion piece before getting myself on the first flight I could to Orlando. I'd feel sleepy and confused for the next seven days.

Time and space are inseparable things, impossible to consider independently, of course. But if my reporting in Missouri made me rethink "queer space" in regards to making the queer of color interview, my reporting in Orlando made me understand and explore queer time.

"Queer uses of time and space develop, at least in part, in opposition to the institutions of family, heterosexuality, and reproduction," Jack Halberstam writes in *In a Queer Time and Place: Transgender Bodies, Subcultural Lives*. "They also develop according to other logics of location, movement, and identification" (2005, 2). People are not queer necessarily on a tidy schedule and in easily locatable spaces.

Halberstam also notes how "[q]ueer time perhaps emerges most spectacularly, at the end of the twentieth century, from within those gay communities whose horizons of possibility have been severely diminished by the AIDS epidemic." The threat of AIDS forced gay men to live against the concept of *futurity* (Edelman 2004)—the framing of politics as dependent upon the future of the Child—and to find meaning in life (and pleasure) without it. And so, queer time resides in the pleasure of the now, perhaps, or while "cruising for utopia" in the moment right after this, as Muñoz argued—but not in future of one's progeny.

But Halberstam writes about queer time mostly in terms of explicitly queer sexual subcultures and in terms of conventional literature, such as Michael Cunningham's novel *The Hours*. Halberstam doesn't deal with queer time in journalism, something I will deal with in this section. Halberstam's interpretation of how Robert Reid-Pharr and Samuel Delany problematize "the elevation of white male experience (gay or straight) to the level of generality and the reduction of, say, Black gay experience to the status of the individual" (2005, 4) will also help me with something else: understanding the temporal and spatial choices made by media and LGBT organizations run by white people (gay and straight) in Orlando in response to the slaughter of queer people of color. That many of the killed (and those close to them) were working-class service workers rendered them queer not just to straight people because of their sexuality but to gay politicos for being poor. And, understanding their queerness meant adjusting to queer time.

But national media and organizations did *not* embrace queer time. My first morning in Orlando, I arrived near the Pulse to find the same kind of media "scrum" I had seen near the burned-down Kwik Trip gas station in Ferguson and the burned-out CVS in Baltimore. There, I encountered the same fleets of white cable satellite trucks crewed by the same white (and presumably straight) men operating on TV time. There was really nothing to do there except create a backdrop from a distance of the scene of the crime. The only people to interview were government officials and people seeking attention.

I told my editors that I thought that the real story was about queer people of color, and I wasn't seeing them downtown or in any gayborhood Orlando might have. While they were supportive of this, none of my *Guardian* editors were gay or people of color, and they would never have thought of this angle; two even expressed shock that this might be significant, but trusted my instinct.

I then went to the Parliament House, the aging gay resort in a bleak industrial section of Orlando, far from its downtown and theme parks. With the closure of the Pulse, Parliament House now housed the largest gay club in town, and many if not most people who worked at one place also worked at the other. I had stayed at a hotel by the airport my first night, but when I went to the Parliament House and discovered it was only $100 for three nights' accommodation, I knew I had to write my story from there.

I was one of only two reporters who stayed there (the other was also gay, but white), and though others passed through, no one stayed for very long; as a result, I had the queer of color story largely to myself. I learned a lot about who had died, who they were, where and how they worked, and how they lived by sleeping at this rundown motel over time; this allowed me to create an ethnography of the community. I ate in the motel's seedy restaurant and a young waiter told me, on the verge of tears, that although he knew at least ten and maybe fifteen people who had been killed (they hadn't all yet been identified), he couldn't go to the citywide memorial because he was a shift worker and he wasn't allowed to take the time off or he would lose his job.

This was when I first started considering the deceased existing in a queer time of service workers. Some of them worked at local Disney and Universal theme parks, but almost all of them worked in the service economy that supported Orlando tourism in some way. This meant that they had to get up before Disney-bound tourists, make sure those Mouseketeers had fun, feed them, and put them to bed before they could have some themselves.

At Parliament House and Southern Nights (the other big club, post-Pulse), I found communities of queer people of color—but they didn't start to congregate until around midnight. Congregating for dancing and drag shows, they'd party until 3 or 4 A.M., before catching a few hours of sleep and getting up to take care of people en route to Disneyland all over again. At Southern Nights, I watched drag queens raise thousands of dollars for the injured.

It was at Parliament House's Hip Hop night where I made out with a beautiful brown young man who was in a state of shock about the events. It's also where I met queer Latina activist Paulina Helm-Hernandez on the dance floor. Well accustomed to queer time and space, she came to meet queer people of color when and where they were gathered. And here, around 2 A.M., I saw Angelica Sanchez, a drag queen who had survived Pulse just a few nights earlier, give her first performance since—a drag routine that will live in my heart forever.

Many of the organized mourning activities that drew media and organizations were in Orlando's central business district, in spaces and at times where queer people weren't likely to be found. The time to report about, observe, and interview queer people of color was on the dance floor of the Parliament House in the middle of the night. I was the only reporter there, and Paulina was one of few organizers present.

I got a sense of the Parliament House and queer life in Orlando not just in those wee hours, but around the clock. When I filed a story at 3 A.M.and went for a walk on the beach behind the motel—excited that the temperatures dropped to the 80s—I learned to be leery. I needed to navigate tweaking men openly masturbating (not such a big deal) as well as what I thought was a crocodile splashing in the water (a much bigger deal, given one had recently eaten a baby at a nearby Disney resort).

During the daytime, as I worked on my laptop in my first-floor room, I kept getting knocks on the big glass window that overlooked the pool. At first, I thought the men (who seemed high on meth) were cruising me. But it wasn't until I talked to a man I couldn't wave off that I understood he was offering me money and thought I was "working"—and not as a journalist. (Understanding the code, I closed my curtains.)

Then, there was the young sex worker who approached me while I was writing outside on a patio table. Dark-skinned, painfully thin, and genderfluid, he kept trying to get *me* to pay *him*. I gave him a few dollars for bus fare, declined his offer for a $5 blowjob, and talked to him about running out of the Pulse the night of the shooting. He seemed to take the violence in stride compared to the routine violence of his life getting around in Orlando without a car and hustling to make ends meet.

The timing of my interview with him—in the afternoon, during a rainstorm, far from the city center—helped me understand how racially segregated queer people of color are in Orlando from the city's formal, white-faced LGBT leaders. The timing of the ill-fated Latin Night at Pulse and the Hip Hop night at the Parliament House educated me on the same. The coworkers of those killed at Pulse I met at Parliament House, and their friends who gathered around midnight, were more accessible to a queer person of color like me in general, but they were only *practically* accessible to me because I gave in to queer time. And I think the white bros of the satellite trucks, who needed someone to give them a succinct soundbite in front of the club live on the six o'clock news, were never going to find these people, were never going to explore the edge of the city in the middle of the night.

Discursive Hustling

After using queer time and space to land the queer of color interview and shape my story as a journalist, the next step is to discursively hustle that knowledge into the academy.

Just what is the queer act of *discursive hustling*?

Let me rewind a bit to explain by beginning, as James Baldwin (2017) might have, in the Black church. Or rather, in a specific Black church, on a Sunday morning in New Orleans's Ninth Ward in late October 2007. The neighborhood was still reeling from Hurricanes Rita and Katrina, and I had spent the previous week collecting oral histories in it for NPR's StoryCorps project, camped out in one of the local churches. When they caught wind that I sang in a gospel choir back in New York, the members of the church commandeered me to come to church on Sunday morning and to sing a solo with their choir.

Shortly before the services began, the church musicians arrived. They had all been up all night playing jazz in clubs around the city, and they still smelled strongly of cigarettes. The organist had booze on his breath, mildly mitigated by the smell of mouthwash, and in song after song, they tore that church up like it was a juke joint. (I joined them for Jerry Calvin Smith's "This Morning When I Rose.")

That band embodied two old sayings about music in the church. First, the tunes they rocked articulated how gospel music is just Motown or R&B with the word "baby" replaced with "Jesus." Second, they showed how R&B and Motown tunes create a kind of religious hustling of the Good Word out of the church into the wider secular world, while gospel music is a kind of secular hustling of rhythm into the church. And often, the hustling of the secular-into-the-religious and the religious-into-the-secular is done by the *very same people*, who jam all night long in Satan's lair until the sun rises before slugging down some coffee, gargling some mouthwash, and picking up their music makers in the house of the Lord without missing a beat or changing clothes.

The shuttling back and forth between these two worlds, especially when the hinge between them is embodied as Black men who have to navigate such different spaces, can be a very queer thing.

It is writing both as a journalist for mainstream publications as an academic (where I work in universities and write for scholarly journals) that I view myself as a queer hustler. In navigating both of these worlds, I have found that academia can look down upon journalism with as much pious disdain as the Black church sometimes scoffs at secular music; similarly, many a journalist can have as much antagonism towards a professor they feel is safely hidden in the ivory tower as a bluesman can have contempt for a pastor they consider out of touch. And yet, journalism and academia are continuously informing each other, just as the musical genealogies of Motown and the Baptist church did in the twentieth century—often by queer hustlers who slip back and forth between these worlds.

In some ways, my model for discursive hustling is based on the Grammy-winning gospel composer Andrae Crouch, who also arranged megahits for Diana Ross, Stevie Wonder, and Michael Jackson. But musically hustling church into Diana's Motown tracks or Jacksonian "Man in the Mirror" beats into a choral arrangement isn't *entirely* queer. For a Black man like Crouch, the slipping back and forth between a sanctuary and a studio might be a queer act; however, it's not especially queer for a Black man to be in the worlds of gospel or R&B.

It is, however, *extremely* queer for a Black man to be in academia *or* in journalism, both of which practically have "whites only" signs over their doors. Even as a majority of babies born in the United States are not white (Cohen 2016), and "majority-minority" status is only decades away, an annual survey of the American Association of Newspaper Editors (2015) has found that print journalism jobs have been about 87 percent white for the past decade; similarly, the National Center for Educational Statistics (2013) found that 84 percent of full university professors are white (with 56 percent of those professorships being accounted for just by white men).

So, the mere act of trying to work in journalism *or* academia (let alone *both*) for Black gay people like myself is itself a queer, nonnormative, somewhat rebellious act. Unless I were to engage in the likely foolhardy task of trying to blend in with my white straight peers (which I don't), I am never going to blend into a newsroom or a faculty (other than at an historically Black college or university) the way a Black person might within a Black band or church choir.

In primarily white newsrooms or universities, there's a feeling that at any time, I could be thrown out. Often treated with suspicion in media and academia alike (for my race and sexuality, but also because I have a foot in both worlds), I have decided to embrace feeling like a thief. To that end, I hustle as much knowledge as I can out of both settings, whisking it from one world into the other. I try to steal everything I learn in universities and share that knowledge I learn in popular media with people who will never get to be inside of the universities I infiltrate. At the same time, I try to infect academic jargon with the communication tools I practice in mainstream media, so that my academic research may become more widely accessible to more kinds of people.

And in recognizing that I will never fit in so well in *either* world, I try to take solace in the slippage between them. In his book *Sexual Discretion: Black Masculinity and the Politics of Passing* (2018), Jeff McCune writes of the "downlow brothas" not as a pathologized villains, but as Black men negotiating the "downlow" as a discursive space. In negotiating this space, McCune writes:

> [T]here is an intentional slippage between "discreet" (showing good judgment in conduct) and "discrete" (individually distinct), as particular commitments to normative gender muddies the ability to mark a clear distinction between these terms. For those who are under repeated surveillance, they often dance between the discreet and discrete, sometimes embodying both in one moment—signaling the collapse of these terms, especially for those who are very clear that they are sexually distinct, but also sexually protective. (2014, 8)

In creating queer of color interviews, I similarly try to show the good judgment of centering the stories of queer people of color *and* the individually distinct nature of queer stories of color, because a commitment to telling good stories in general (as a journalist or scholar) muddies an ability to mark a clear distinction between the two.

In this essay, I have shown how to create queer of color interviews by interviewing queers of color within queer time and space. I have then argued that the queer knowledge I have gained in academia should be used to inform creating these interviews, and that the knowledge produced should be hustled back into the academy, into a mutually informative circle of exchange. Finally, I am noting that queer of color interviews don't just inform the work of the queer scholar or journalist of color; they also empower us *as* queers working in primarily white and heteronormative institutions.

Acknowledgments

At *BuzzFeed*, I am grateful to Investigations Editor Mark Schoofs for commissioning my work on "Tiger Mandingo," as well as to LGBT Editor Saeed Jones, Investigations Assistant Talal Ansari, Deputy Investigations Editor Ariel Kaminer, Executive News Editor Shani Hilton, and

Editor-in-Chief Ben Smith for developing and editing various iterations of my reporting over three years. At the *Guardian* U.S., I am grateful to Features Editor Jessica Reed for commissioning my feature on queer people of color in Orlando, as well as to reporters Ed Pilkington and Jessica Glenza for their aid in our team coverage from Florida. At NYU's American Studies program, I am grateful to Julie Livingston, Lisa Duggan, Andrew Ross, Nikhil Singh, Jennifer Morgan, and Philip Brian Harper, and I'm especially thankful to Gayatri Gopinath for being the first person to tell me that my reporting represented "queer of color" theory in action. The term "discursive hustling" is a riff of Elena Gonzalez's phrase "recursive hustling," which developed in an email conversation among her, Kevin Murphy, Molly McGary, and me in preparation for a panel on Publicly Engaged American Studies Scholarship at the 2016 American Studies Association annual conference. Finally, I indebted to Amin Ghaziani and Matt Brim, who came up with the term "queer of color interview" and wanted me to develop it for this essay.

WORKS CITED

American Society of Newspaper Editors. 2015. "Percentage of Minorities in Newsrooms Remains Relatively Steady; 63 Percent of Newspapers Have at Least One Woman among Top-Three Editors." July 28. http://asne.org/.

Baldwin, James, and Steve Schapiro. 2017. *The Fire Next Time*. New York: Taschen.

Cohen, D'ver. 2016. "It's Official: Minority Babies Are the Majority among the Nation's Infants, but Only Just." Pew Research Center, June 23. http://pewrsr.ch/.

duCille, Ann 1997. "The Unbearable Darkness of Being: 'Fresh' Thoughts on Race, Sex, and the Simpsons." In *Birth of a Nation'hood: Gaze, Script, and Spectacle in the O.J. Simpson Case*, edited by Toni Morrison and Claudia Brodsky Lacour, 293–338. New York: Pantheon.

Edelman, Lee. 2004. *No Future: Queer Theory and the Death Drive*. Durham, NC: Duke University Press.

Ferguson, Roderick. 2003. *Aberrations in Black: Toward a Queer of Color Critique*. Minneapolis: University of Minnesota Press.

Halberstam, Jack. 2005. *In a Queer Time and Place: Transgender Bodies, Subcultural Lives*. New York: NYU Press.

Lipsitz, George. 1998. *The Possessive Investment in Whiteness: How White People Profit from Identity Politics*. Philadelphia: Temple University Press.

McCune, Jeffrey. 2014. *Sexual Discretion: Black Masculinity and the Politics of Passing*. Chicago: University of Chicago Press, 2014.

National Center for Education Statistics. 2013. "Race/Ethnicity of College Faculty." Fall. http://nces.ed.gov/.

Nichols, James Michael 2015. "Reporter Uses Grindr at CPAC Gathering to Track Down Gay Men." *Huffington Post*, March 3.

Rodriguez, Matthew. 2016. "*Daily Beast* Editor Nico Hines Used Grindr at 2016 Rio Olympics—It's a Homophobic Mess." *Mic*, August 11.

Saeedi, Goal Auzeen. 2012. "'Catfish' and the Perils of Online Dating." *Psychology Today*, December 10.

Sedgwick, Eve Kosofsky 2003. *Touching Feeling: Affect, Pedagogy, Performativity.* Durham, NC: Duke University Press.

Spivak, Gayatri Chakravorty. 1999. *A Critique of Postcolonial Reason: Toward a History of the Vanishing Present.* Cambridge, MA: Harvard University Press.

Thrasher, Steven W. 2014. "How College Wrestling Star 'Tiger Mandingo' Became an HIV Scapegoat." *BuzzFeed*, July 7.

Thrasher, Steven W. 2015. "A Black Body on Trial: The HIV Conviction of 'Tiger Mandingo.'" *BuzzFeed*, December 1.

Warner, Michael, ed. 1993. *Fear of a Queer Planet: Queer Politics and Social Theory.* Minneapolis: University of Minnesota Press.

11

Like Inciting a Riot

Queering Open Education with EqualityArchive.com

SHELLY EVERSLEY AND LAURIE HURSON

"The learning process is something you can incite, literally incite, like a riot" (Lorde and Rich 1981, 727). Audre Lorde described this process in a conversation with Adrienne Rich about teaching. For both Lorde and Rich, teaching is learning. They understood the riotous potential of learning, of something Lorde also described as "the transformation of silence into language and action" (Lorde 2007, 40). The two became colleagues and collaborators while teaching in the City University of New York's SEEK Program, an open admissions investment that has made college education possible for thousands of the city's working-class people of color. The program began, in part, as a result of Black and Latino student uprisings in the late 1960s ("Second Chances" 2012). In those turbulent times, the students were demanding access to higher education; the teachers who welcomed them were committed to learning as an opportunity to change the social order. For Lorde and Rich, the learning they would incite was also framed by the rise of Black studies and women's studies programs as well as social equality and peace movements, including activisms for gay liberation and women's equality and their various affinity groups. Learning was (and still is) inseparable from politics. It demands risk: "How do you deal with things you believe, live them not as theory, not even as emotion, but right on the line of action and effect change?" (Lorde and Rich 1981, 734). Their poems, essays, and activist pedagogies provide some answers to this question; their examples inspire our commitment to learning.

When we imagined and built EqualityArchive.com, we also wanted to incite a riot. We wanted to create an opportunity to change the social order, an opportunity for learning about the people, history, and issues around the fight for self-identified women's gender equality in the United States. These commitments could help us organize a vivid offering at the intersections of theory, lived experience, and practice—a feminist praxis for a generation trained to seek information online (Eversley and Hurson 2017). We hoped that by assembling various parts of feminist knowledge in uncomplicated multimodal forms, we could inspire action. And, following Lorde's and Rich's commitment to learning, we understood our project needed to be open access, available for free to any curious person interested in learning.

Our method is queer. As collaborators, our creative and intellectual relationship requires an openness to change and to transformation. As queer, our process welcomes the kinds of multiplicity, misalignments, and silences Matt Brim and Amin Ghaziani associate with "how we study the social construction of sexuality and the sexual construction of the social" (2016, 16). To build a digital archive about gender equality is also to explore the messiness and interconnectedness of sexuality, sex, and of the constructs that shape not only thought, but also action. When we decided to focus on self-identified women's gender equality, we understood we would be confronting various and often contested perspectives on how to think about gender identity, about equality, and about the United States and its borders. Lorde and Rich remind us to "never close our eyes to the terror, the chaos" (1981, 730), so with eyes open we launched EqualityArchive.com. Our process, like our project, is dialogic.

SE: When we first started talking about building the archive, I referenced the Equal Rights Amendment website. It is loaded with so much important information about the constitutional amendment that is only one state shy of ratification. "Equality of rights under the law shall not be denied or abridged by the United States or any state on account of sex," could be part of the U.S. Constitution in our lifetime. And then I started to wonder how many people know this, how could we create a digital learning and activist community around sex and gender equality embedded in the material world, and responsive to the multiple ways people seek reliable information online, whether on computers, smart phones, or tablets.

LH: When you shared your vision for Equality Archive with me I immediately wanted to be part of a project that would publish perspectives and histories that are often marginalized and obscured in crowd-sourced, digital information sources. In our initial conversation the platform you envisioned would be easy to navigate and accessible to young people by providing media-rich resources about intersectional and academic ideas in a contemporary and digestible format. The combination of information legibility and multimodality was possible by building Equality Archive with the flexible and easy-to-use WordPress web framework. WordPress met our needs because it was functionally and ideologically aligned with the visions for this project. WordPress also facilitated our collaboration by allowing us to build and design EqualityArchive.com in the way that we describe our vision as a "theater for history and social justice with the goal to provide a forum for curious people" (Equality Archive 2016). Since WordPress connects easily to the open web through API integrations and other plugins, we could incorporate various types of content that young people engage with such as videos, audio clips, and image galleries. Because it is an open-source framework, WordPress situated us within a networked community that values free/libre resources, provides peer support, shares framework information, and updates often (WordPress.org 2018a). In the same way that epistemological lineage matters, thinking below the level of our web framework, we chose to host the project with Reclaim Hosting, which is designed to help educators create projects that are owned and controlled by the scholars who create them.

SE: You set the course for our commitment to open-source technology. In so many important ways, the radical trust associated with some of the most transformative open source collaboratives—like *Wikipedia* and WordPress—have disrupted traditional academic models of knowledge and of learning. Instead of the old, vertical hierarchies of learning, Equality Archive celebrates the kinds of intersections and assemblages that emerge from collaborative processes. When a teacher, scholar, activist, or artist contributes an entry, our collective reviews it for factual accuracy. This version of "peer review" reflects our smaller-scale version of the kinds of crowd-sourced checks and balances integral to an open-source project like *Wikipedia*. It shifts the structure and the orientation of more traditional models of thinking and learning.

LH: Absolutely. Our small-scale but robust method of peer-review allows us to push the boundaries of what is considered "academic" and therefore trustworthy. The collective peer review ensures that the entries provide relevant, well-sourced information while also embracing the dynamic media-centric nature of the web. In this way, the multimodal, openly accessible entries on Equality Archive challenge traditional notions of academic publishing as the means for sharing knowledge. As universities and learning institutions embrace free and open sources of knowledge as part of the movement toward Open Education Resources (OER), Equality Archive provides faculty and students with myriad opportunities to teach, learn, and explore these open resources. Equality Archive offers resources that could be integral for faculty looking to engage with and develop critical and digital pedagogies that embrace discovery and community (Stommel 2014). By presenting entries that highlight often overlooked topics and voices, Equality Archive works to queer the OER movement itself, adding to the catalog and expanding the boundaries of open knowledge. By incorporating many voices in the creation, review, and content of the entries, the Equality Archive strives to embody feminist collectivity and collaboration.

SE: Exactly. Equality Archive is a collective project. It belongs to no one and to everyone. New contributors are always welcome. We seek feminist artists, teachers, writers, or activists whose knowledge would communicate the layers, intersections, and disputes about gender equality in the United States that could help us learn, and, we hope, use knowledge in the service of social justice. That's why every entry also includes an opportunity to get involved. Embedded in each entry is at least one opportunity to connect with a social or political organization committed to gender justice. By including access to opportunities to get involved, we hope the curious visitor can recognize the connections between thought and action, between what they think and how they imagine the world.

LH: Yes, and by providing curious people with information and opportunities to act. Equality Archive entries aim to connect visitors with chances to participate by presenting multiple entry points for interaction with the content. By providing multiple mediums including text, images, videos, audio clips, and links, Equality Archive attempts to address the variety of ways in which people learn, across engagement styles, levels of ability, and literacy. Equality Archive hopes to cultivate a culture of increasing information literacy, linking visitors to well-researched and established information sources at a time when mainstream media is often contested and inflammatory. Just like any skill, developing the ability to find and assess sources can be fostered over time, and Equality Archive hopes to play a role in this ongoing progression. Recognizing that people understand and process information in various ways, the content on EqualityArchive.com is networked through a taxonomy of categories and tags, both organizational features of WordPress, in order to allow visitors to navigate the site in a way that follows their flow of thought and interest.

SE: Sara Ahmed's description of a queer phenomenology, one that positions "the question of the 'orientation' of 'sexual orientation' as a phenomenological question" (2006, 1), really resonates in our method. Ahmed calls attention to the lines of thought that would orient us toward a "compulsory heterosexuality" (EqualityArchive.com), and that would orient knowledge to perceive only one option for human sexuality. If Equality Archive's nonlinear, intersectional assemblage can offer a disruption to a singular phenomenology, to a "straight" line of thought, then maybe it can offer alternative lines of orientation, of perception, transforming what we know and also our own relationship to knowledge. Our mission is to advance multiple lines of thinking, in multiple registers, all at the same time. This is how we would like to incite a riot since we think of gender inequality as a heteronormative knowledge form. If people find themselves oriented toward sexism and misogyny because of a straight phenomenology that facilitates it, then our ambition is to advocate for queering knowledge. In this way, Equality Archive seeks to resist the phenomenology of misogyny. Its ambition is to be out of line, as it were.

LH: Our project challenges linear and canonical knowledge in favor of nonlinear, open knowledges from the borders and margins. Reacting to the epistemological violence (Teo 2010) inflicted by traditional academic knowledge production, Equality Archive presents new possibilities for knowledge creation, learning, and action. Opposing a linear progression of entries, the information on Equality Archive is organized into a linked network of content. Relying on hyperlinks to connect information, which is the foundational feature of the web 2.0, Equality Archive entries connect voices and ideas to one another and also move beyond the platform, connecting to the open web by linking to outside sources and allowing outside sources to link back and reference Equality Archive entries. As the archive grows, new entries are "bound in to the structure of the web by other users discovering the content and linking to it" (O' Reilly 2012).

In the spirit of taking action and building the connections between Equality Archive and the open web, we have facilitated several *Wikipedia* edit-a-thons to develop these linkages (*Wikipedia* 2017). During one particular event, participants searched for underdeveloped *Wikipedia* entries on topics that were well documented in Equality Archive. When insufficient *Wikipedia* entries were found, participants edited *Wikipedia* to add information to these entries and linked back to the Equality Archive as the secondary reference source (standard practice for *Wikipedia* editing). Creating these linkages connects Equality Archive to *Wikipedia*, the largest repository of information in the world, so that even more people have the chance to visit and learn from the open knowledge our archive offers. Linking to Equality Archive as a source on *Wikipedia* puts the marginalized voices and ideas presented on the platform into conversation with more traditional sources on the web.

By developing these links to connect information we acknowledge how reading and engagement with information has changed. Current readers, thinkers, and visitors constantly jump between sources, so we aim to make Equality Archive as accessible as possible by creating opportunities for discovery. This practice acknowledges the dominance of Google's page rank system, which ranks sources based on the number of links to and from a site, while also resisting this system and the dominance of certain sources by attempting to inject our links into these rankings. Google's page rank system often supports algorithmic bias (Noble 2018), returning results that are skewed by race, sex, and class. Equality Archive fights this bias by constantly developing the platform so that individuals can find content that contains feminist and queer ideas, voices, and histories that speak to their experiences so they can begin to form new phenomenologies and ways of knowing.

SE: It's been an important part of our feminist praxis to explore cyber-feminisms (Daniels 2009) and the transgressive potentials to experiment with the range of theories and practices surrounding gender identity and digital culture. We also have been thinking a lot about class identity as an important question of access, which like language, ability, and race affect how individuals use digital tools. As the project grows, we will continue to learn and adapt.

LH: For sure. Aside from addressing and cultivating informational literacy, our project certainly has more work to do in addressing how visitors can use Equality Archive, especially by thinking through various levels of ability. In the future we should consider creating audio clips for each entry, optimizing the site for screen-readers, and providing translations so we can forge better connections with more kinds of curious people from around the world.

SE: And the seeming rise of web 3.0 is another challenge: should we publish Equality Archive on a blockchain platform? We know the internet is always changing. Our queer method requires that we pay attention and prepare for its adaptations and its multiple forms. Right now, most people think about cryptocurrencies when they try to discern what blockchain technology is, and while financial markets are a big part of the ecosystem of web 3.0, also known as blockchain, there is so much more in development. Blockchain offers peer-to-peer digital storage. In this web 3.0 model, private networks like Facebook, Google, or Uber can no longer dominate public infrastructures. These infrastructures would no longer have control over a person's online activities—for instance, networks and mobile phone providers would not be able to surveil and own our information. This is what decentralization means for web 3.0 and blockchain technology. It also claims end users will own and control their data, that data breaches will dramatically decline, and that end users will have unrestricted access to information regardless of geography or because of any other social and demographic factors (Zago n.d.).

As teachers and learners committed to open education and queer phenomenologies, we have to pay attention to new developments in ethical and sustainable models for publishing and distributing reliable information. Our political climate demands it. For instance, some blockchain publishing platforms are now advocating commitments to press freedom and accountability in the face of global changes in technology, economics, and politics. Their interest in these new developments in open access, especially censorship-resistant open access, along with permanent non-erasable archiving, suggests truly innovative and disruptive potentials (Zalatimo 2018). And when nonprofit organizations on web 3.0 build platforms that recognize the increasing need to protect end users' privacy as well as their right to free access to information ("Civil Constitution" n.d.), it is important that we pay attention—especially since our ambition to change the way people think is also a confrontation with the status quo.

LH: Theoretically, the foundational principles of decentralization and transparency inherent to blockchain do coalesce with Equality Archive's commitment to decentralized knowledges and collective and transparent knowledge production. Blockchain and web 3.0 infrastructures offer possibilities to change the way we create, publish, and share information. Creating a web that gives people ownership over their data and unrestricted access to information would be a welcome move away from the capitalist control of data and levels of surveillance we have seen recently (Zuboff 2014). The potentialities presented by web 3.0 hold promise for what the web could ultimately become.

Changes to the web raise questions about infrastructure, development, community support, and critical mass adoption of new frameworks for creating and sharing information. Most foundationally, it is critical for Equality Archive to work with the affordances of web 2.0 and also consider the possibilities that blockchain and web 3.0 offer. How can we strike a middle ground, reaching curious visitors and providing them with information while also pushing them to engage with the web in new ways? Contending with these possibilities will allow Equality Archive to embrace new phenomenologies while remaining accessible to all visitors across varying levels of ability, learning style, and method of engagement. And beyond making our platform accessible, it is equally important to fight the algorithmic bias that will continue to silence the voices Equality Archive attempts to highlight and uplift.

WORKS CITED

Ahmed, Sara. 2006. *Queer Phenomenology: Orientations, Objects, Others.* Durham, NC: Duke University Press.

Brim, Matt, and Amin Ghaziani. 2016. "Introduction: Queer Methods." *WSQ: Women's Studies Quarterly* 44 (3–4): 14–27.

Church, Zach. 2017. "Blockchain, Explained." http://mitsloan.mit.edu/ideas-made-to-matter/blockchain-explained.

"Civil Constitution." n.d. https://civil.co/constitution/.

Daniels, J. 2009. "Rethinking Cyberfeminism(s): Race, Gender, and Embodiment." *WSQ: Women's Studies Quarterly* 37 (1–2): 101–24.

Equality Archive. 2016. "About." http://equalityarchive.com/about/.

Eversley, Shelley, and Laurie Hurson. 2017. "Equality Archive: Open Educational Resources as Feminist Praxis." *Feminist Media Histories* 3 (3): 154–58.

Lorde, Audre. 2007. "The Transformation of Silence into Language and Action." In *Sister Outsider: Essays and Speeches*, 40–44. Berkeley, CA: Crossing Press.

Lorde, Audre, and Adrienne Rich. 1981. "An Interview with Audre Lorde." *Signs* 6 (4): 713–36.

Noble, Safiya Umoja. 2014. "Social Influences on Technology: Safiya Noble at TEDx-UIUC." *TEDx Talks.* www.youtube.com/watch?v=UXuJ8yQf6dI.

Noble, Safiya Umoja. 2018. *Algorithms of Oppression: How Search Engines Reinforce Racism.* 1st ed. New York: NYU Press.

O'Reilly, Tim. 2012. "What Is Web 2.0? Design Patterns and Business Models for the Next Generation of Software." In *The Social Media Reader*, edited by Michael Mandiberg, 32–52. New York: NYU Press.

"Second Chances: The CUNY Seek and College Discovery Story." 2012. CUNYtv, March 19. www.youtube.com/watch?v=TtGbYi4KtlE.

Stommel, Jesse. 2014. "Critical Digital Pedagogy: A Definition." *Hybrid Pedagogy*, November 18. http://hybridpedagogy.org/.

Teo, Thomas. 2010. "What Is Epistemological Violence in the Empirical Social Sciences?" *Social and Personality Psychology Compass* 4 (5): 295–303.

Wikipedia. 2017. "Wikipedia: Meetup/NYC/Baruch/Equality Archive Edit-a-thon." March 10. https://en.wikipedia.org/.

Wikipedia. 2018. "Gender Bias on Wikipedia." June 24. en.wikipedia.org/.

WordPress.org. 2018a. "About Us: Our Mission." https://wordpress.org/about/.

WordPress.org. 2018b. "Codex: Main Page." https://codex.wordpress.org/.

Zago, Matteo Gianpietro. n.d. "Why the Web 3.0 Matters and You Should Know About It." *Medium.* https://medium.com/.

Zalatimo, Salah. 2018. "Blockchain in Publishing: Innovation or Disruption?" *Forbes Tech*, May 3. www.forbes.com/.

Zuboff, Von Shoshana. 2014. "A Digital Declaration." *Frankfurter Allgemeine*, September 15. www.faz.net/.

PART IV

Historicizing/Resisting

12

Dyke Methods

A Meditation on Queer Studies and the Gay Men Who Hate It

JANE WARD

In the late 2000s, when I was writing *Not Gay: Sex between Straight White Men* (2015), mainstream LGBT political discourse was dominated by aspirations for legal rights and bio-evolutionary legitimacy (Duggan 2004; Spade 2015). The political future of lesbian, gay, and bisexual people seemed to hinge on the biological origins of same-sex desire, and research projects that could provide evidence of these origins generated considerable excitement (Jordan-Young 2011; Walters 2014; Whisman 1995). Queer and feminist scholars were experiencing pressure to redefine interdisciplinarity as a partnership with neuroscientists and others who might deepen our understanding of the hormonal and genetic causes of "same-sex" desire—as if "same-sex" were a transparent concept. It seemed like no one was paying attention to sociologist Vera Whisman, who, in her prescient 1995 book *Queer by Choice*, made the compelling case that "born this way" arguments typically serve gay men—politically and culturally—in ways that they do not serve queer women. And if people *were* thinking about the gendered implications of the sociobiology of sexual orientation, they were listening to evolutionary psychologists like Lisa Diamond (2008), who explained women's sexual fluidity as a congenital condition, an evolutionary adaptation.

It was in this context that I wrote *Not Gay*, a book about sex practices that, to my mind, begged for attention to the limitations of sociobiological accounts. Several sociologists have conducted empirical studies of sexual contact between straight-identified men (Anderson 2008; 2010; Carrillo and Hoffman 2016; Reynolds 2015; Silva 2018). There was no urgent need for more empirical research on this subject. What had not yet been examined, however, were the cultural narratives circulating around straight white men's homosexual encounters and the rhetorical and material conditions that allowed white men's sex practices to circumvent the pathologizing gaze applied to men of color on the down low (Snorton 2014). Drawing on an eclectic archive of cultural materials and the tools of cultural studies, *Not Gay* investigated the stories people tell about why and how straight white men might behave homosexually. I drew on a broad theoretical and methodological repertoire—a synthesis of queer studies, cultural studies, sociology, and feminist theory. I wrote in a feminist tradition invested in exposing the myth of scientific objectivity by locating myself, and my utopian feminist longings, within the story of the research (Reinharz 1992). I followed the lead of critical race ethnographers by simultaneously studying up, down, and sideways as a white feminist dyke asserting her right to make claims about the meaning of homosexual contact between straight white men (Twine and Warren 2000). The entire book was infused with the queer impulse to forget my disciplinary training (in sociology), to draw on lowbrow and eclectic archives that make new ways of thinking possible, and to see what desire, humor, and rage might yield if allowed to run through my writing, unleashed and directed at straight white men (see Halberstam 2011).

I watched many hours of porn. I spent months trying to acquire the rights to reprint original photos of male sailors eating garbage out of each other's anuses during a navy initiation ceremony. I wrote in cabins in the woods where I laughed and cried at my own excited response to the opportunity to subject straight white men's sexual encounters to a queer, feminist analysis. The book was both a feminist "fuck you" to the persistent normalization and idealization of straight white men's bodies and sex practices, and an unexpected chamber in which my empathy for straight white men deepened.

Not Gay was read by far more people than I ever anticipated. Due to some savvy marketing on the part of NYU Press and the apparent salaciousness of the subject matter, the book received an unusual amount of media attention, with coverage by *New York* magazine, *Forbes*, *Cosmopolitan*, the *Guardian*, *Newsweek*, the *Huffington Post*, *Vice*, and *Salon*, and a number of reporters in Europe, Latin America, and the Middle East. A *Gawker* reviewer described news of the book's release as having "penetrated the internet" (Juzwiak 2015). The first printing of the book sold out within a few weeks of being published. Exemplifying the power of celebrity and social media, Amazon sales of the book skyrocketed following an Instagram shout-out from the actor James Franco, shown in a photo holding the book in his dressing room.

I was happy with the book's success, but became a bit anxious as I started to read the internet comments that we are all warned never to read. If one of *Not Gay*'s basic arguments can be summed up in a sentence, it is that sometimes straight people engage in homosexual sex for heterosexual reasons, and therefore it is not especially useful—from a queer political perspective at least—to claim *all* homosexual encounters as signals of a repressed gay or bisexual identity. As I learned from the many hundreds of comments I read online, one particular demographic was especially outraged by this claim: white gay men. Within this avalanche of criticism of *Not Gay*, an unexpected archive of white gay men's reflections on "the broader problem with queer studies" had fallen into my lap. White gay men characterized the book as the latest example of an alarming trend within queer scholarship. They explained that rather than offering useful, empirical evidence of the legitimacy and fixity of gay identity, *Not Gay* made false claims about male sexual fluidity without actually interviewing men, and in so doing, promulgated dangerous queer ideas vulnerable to cooptation by the religious right. Positing *Not Gay* as evidence of the proliferation of elitist, feminist-inflected, queer pseudoscience at odds with the lived experiences of the gay general public, critics depicted a significant divide between "average gay men" and "Queer Theorists," the latter of whom they named as frivolous and out-of-touch feminists "obsessed with intersectionality."

Here, my aim is to use these responses as data, so to speak, to examine white gay men's resistance to queer, feminist methods of inquiry— particularly work produced from a dyke standpoint—and to consider what this resistance tells us about the generative possibilities of dyke-centric queer methods. But first, what *are* queer methods? While limited sustained attention has been paid to the details of queer research practice, those who have engaged the subject suggest that queer methods are:

1. intersectional (queer projects are designed to investigate the ways that imperialism, settler colonialism, white supremacy, poverty, misogyny, and/or cis-sexism give shape to queer lives and queer resistance) (Nash and Browne 2010);

2. intimate, reflexive, and/or collaborative, often anchored within the extant subcultural and political affiliations of the researcher (Ward 2008);

3. infused with the erotic, or marked by a conscious recognition of sex practices, bodies, and desires and their place within the presumably asexual realm of research (Newton 2000);

4. interdisciplinary, or comprised of humanistic approaches concerned with the particularities of cultural representation and discourse, social science approaches concerned with behavioral patterns, and hybrid methodologies (Brim and Ghaziani 2016; Nash and Browne 2010);

5. focused on fluid or "messy" categories, shifting classifications, and people and practices often illegible within prevailing disciplinary schemas (Ahmed 2006).

Queer methods can certainly offer us new research techniques, such as including an expansive list of genders on one's survey questionnaire. But queer methodology is also more than this; it is a praxis aimed at undoing prevailing assumptions about epistemic authority, legitimate knowledge, and the very meaning of research. If queerness is a willful orienting of oneself toward improper objects (Ahmed 2006) and a feeling of being "pulled" toward as yet unknown gendered and sexual possibilities (Muñoz 2009), then queer methods, too, are fluid and evolving, capable of transforming to keep pace with the ever-changing shape of antiqueer epistemic violence.

Hence, to pair the terms "queer" and "methodology"—the former defined by its celebrated failure to adhere to stable classificatory systems or be contained by disciplinary boundaries, and the latter defined by orderly, discipline-specific, and easily reproducible techniques—produces something of an exciting contradiction, a productive oxymoron. And to place dyke subjectivity at the center of queer studies—a field with many of its early roots in gay men's theorizations of their own history, art forms, and erotic attachments—is to push the queer project even further in the direction of counternormative research practice.

Perhaps it goes without saying that not all lesbian, gay, and bisexual people are excited by the contradictions and subversive possibilities posed by queerness as an intellectual project. A growing number of LGBT people view themselves as respectable citizens who are no different from their straight neighbors and are delighted by the ways that their homo- or bisexuality has become an increasingly normalized and inconsequential feature of their lives (Ghaziani 2011; 2014; Walters 2014). Queer studies projects that illuminate and critique LGBT people's investments in white supremacy and other forms of structural violence (Haritaworn, Kuntsman, and Posocco 2014), homonormativity (Duggan 2004), homonationalism (Puar 2007), and misogyny (Ward 2000) pose a direct challenge to the political worldview of many lesbian, gay, and bisexual people, who are likely to feel alienated from, and unrepresented by, the critical methodologies characteristic of queer studies. In this vein, I want to consider the ways that white gay men's alarmed commentary about *Not Gay* might signal not only their dislike of my particular book but also the way that the field of queer studies is viewed—by white gay men in particular—as a rogue discipline helmed by dykes and contaminated by intersectionality.

Social Constructionism and Intersectionality: More Dangerous for Gay People Than the Religious Right

The week that *Not Gay* was published, a handful of gay critics who had not yet read the book explained that they didn't like its premise. They argued that to allow men who have sex with men (MSMs) to identify as straight (and not gay or bi) is to collude in their internalized homo- or biphobia; it is to fail to recognize the power of the closet. Exemplifying the *I-haven't-read-it-but-I-don't-like-it* response were some remarks made by the popular white gay columnist Dan Savage:

> The men Jane Ward studied might not be gay—gayness could be ruled out in some cases—but straight-identified, married-to-women guys who have sex with other men are likelier to be bisexual, closeted or not, than they are to be straight, fluidity or otherwise. I'm going to get the book and read it with an open mind, of course, but the summary pushed out by NYU Press doesn't inspire confidence. (2015)

In interviews with journalists, I tried to respond to these concerns by explaining that the book was not about a special subset or subculture of

men who have sex with men; it was about the culture of white heterosexual masculinity more broadly, and how it produces a striking number of opportunities for *all* white men to touch each other's anuses and
penises and to understand these encounters as nonsexual. I explained
that if people *read* the book, they would see that it was not a sexological
study of individual men's desires but a cultural studies investigation of
the practices of heteromasculine institutions, like college fraternities and
the military, that compel and justify intimate bodily contact between
men as part of the process of producing heteromasculinity. I continued
that I was not so interested in statistics about how many men had sex
with men or whether they were (born) gay, bi, or straight. Instead, my
book was about the cultural narratives that have been used to justify and
dismiss well-documented cases of sexual contact between straight white
men in bathrooms, biker gangs, the military, and fraternities.

The critiques continued to roll in. Hundreds of mostly gay male but
also bi-identified online commenters made some version of the same
predictable, essentialist claim that any man who has ever made sexual
contact with another man—or even has *the capacity* for this kind of
contact—needs to be understood as bisexual or gay because "words have
meaning" whether or not promoters of poststructuralist, queer, feminist
studies are willing to acknowledge reality. Many of the critiques centered squarely on the illegitimacy of queer and feminist methods, which
gay men described as "weak" or "flimsy" but also incredibly dangerous.
Gay critics described queer methods as damaging to LGBT people, as
damaging as the political rhetoric of the religious right. Here's a sample
of readers' comments posted in 2015 from one interview with Graham
Gremore, published on the popular gay website *Queerty*:

> Ugh—Jane Ward strikes again with another volume of pop pseudo-
> science heavily marketed to the press with best click bait titles ever! Un-
> fortunately, most empirical sociologists cringe because she is notorious
> for employing weak methodology shaped by the most extreme post-
> structuralist/queer theory. . . . Ward is a hardcore social constructionist
> who rejects any biological explanations for human behavior, especially
> when it comes to gender and sexuality. For her, there is no reality to
> sexual identities outside of a very extreme anti-capitalist, anti-normative
> politics, which the vast majority of people, gay and straight, would reject

as nonsense. . . . Ward, just like the religious right, is motivated by a kind of faith-based denial of science—her faith being in Queer Theory—and allows her own ideology to trump the lived experiences and narratives of the vast majority of LGBT people.

. . . She keeps chalking this up to a heteronormative culture, but what she really should be talking about is the homophobic culture and how that drives so many bi-oriented men into a life of forced heterosexual behavior. Good lord . . . I'd rather read Rick Santorum's prayer journal than this woman's "research." Pass.

. . . Here's the truth about Queer Theory and everything affiliated with that nonsense: It's all bullshit. Basically, Queer Theorists like this idiot want to impose queerness on everything and anything they can. . . . As per morons like this dumb broad, gayness and bisexuality were created in Germany in the early 1900s, prior to that, there's never been gayness . . . which is bullshit. . . . Here's the question this dumb bitch along with those who think like her fail to answer: If sexuality is as fluid as they claim, then reparation therapy is in fact effective. . . . This is where none of these theorists . . . will go. Because then they have to endorse that Michelle and Marcus Bachmann are in fact correct in their premise and thus endorsed by these academics.

Commenters portrayed a sharp divide between "average gay men" and "Queer Theorists," the latter cast as social constructionist dupes who needed to get out of the ivory tower and interview average gay men about the realities of homosexual sex. Here, implicit charges of queer elitism—in which queer scholars deploy "nonsensical" methods that the gay majority would reject—are expressed in and through misogyny. The ivory tower queer scholar may be part of an intellectual elite, but she is also simply a dumb bitch. Gay male critics posited themselves as simultaneously smarter than the queer theorist, but also oppressed by her, her anticapitalist and antinormative politics understood to be as threatening to the prosperity and assimilation of gay men as the political work of Rick Santorum, Michele Bachmann, and other representatives of the religious right.

Those of us engaged in queer scholarship might be tempted to imagine that heteronormativity is the major source of resistance to our work. And yet in many cases, queer research—especially when it is substantively intersectional and/or focused on the cultural, ethnoracial, and historical variability of same-sex encounters—finds its fiercest opposition from homonormative corners. While the biological sciences and the quantitative social sciences are well positioned to produce clear-cut, legitimizing data to be used in support of claims for normalization and equal rights, humanistic and cultural studies methods, by contrast, often produce work that illuminates the mutability of sexual desires and subjectivities. Pushing beyond narratives of congenital homosexuality and singular gay oppression, queer studies projects also examine sexual agency and willful queerness, as well as interrogate the complicity of white, cis gay, and lesbian people in the conditions of suffering experienced by people of color, women, bisexuals, and trans people. From the vantage point of white gay men, queer studies *does* share something in common with the political agenda of the religious right: both projects pose a challenge to the biological essentialism now at the heart of gay rights claims, and both destabilize narratives of gay oppression, albeit with very different political aims. Gay men, it seems, feel attacked from all sides.

Hate Male: Gay Male Panic and the Lesbianification of Queer Studies

I reflected on gay men's sexism almost twenty years ago in my first published essay, "Queer Sexism: Rethinking Gay Men and Masculinity" (2000). I wrote it when I was twenty-four years old and spending a lot of time being called "fish" by gay male friends while we drunkenly danced together in the bars. Fast forward to 2015 and I found myself in receipt of dozens of outraged, mansplaining emails from gay male readers of *Not Gay*, each wanting me to know that I did not and could not understand male homosexuality because I am a woman, a feminist, and a "political lesbian" with a bias against white men. They took issue with my argument in *Not Gay* that straightness is not most productively defined as the absence of homosexual sex but as a fetish for heteronormativity and a deep feeling of being at home within heterosexual culture. They railed against my hardly original suggestion that we understand queerness not as a sexual identity organized around desire for "same-sex" bodies but as a collective, subcultural desire for gender and sexual transgression.

And they hated my method: my choice of white men as the subject of the study, my decision to be a dyke who writes about men, my feminist and critical race theoretical orientation, and my archive itself (cultural case studies instead of interviews with men). One email from a gay man named Adam stated:

> I actually went out of my way to find you on the net, and I've concluded one thing. You are bigoted, ignorant, and self-entitled with no redeeming qualities. Your little vendetta against hetero males of European decent is childish, sexist, and racist. Your left wing radicalism is hardly hidden, and completely nonsensical. . . . And yes, I'm aware you only point out white males in attempt to somehow demonize or defame them, due to your internally racist nature. Oh, and please stop claiming to be a representative for gay males. It's quite embarrassing. My sexuality is not a soapbox for you to preach your idiocy from.

Another email from a gay man named Jonathan read:

> You don't know what you're talking about because you aren't us. Your book is insulting and ignorant. Something Ann Coulter would write. Or at least love. But when you're talking about the men we sleep with, the ones you call straight, we know a bit more than you. Because they are more like us than you. To say that being straight is "wanting to be straight" would apply to most of us gay men. We all wanted that. You are not one of us. Please stop—Signed, All Gay Men

Another email from a gay man named Steve declared:

> It seems to me that the subtitle of your new book perhaps should have been, "Universalizing from my political lesbian subjectivity to little relevant consequence." Sorry, but plenty of us reject the trendy bisexual assault on gay male identity that your book is just a part of. . . . Well, you're entitled to your own subjectivity. Congratulations on your political lesbianism. (Pat on the head.) But you aren't entitled to my subjectivity or any other gay man's. No, sorry, but being gay wasn't a political choice for most of us and the label isn't meaningful only as a political identity, no matter how aggressively you try to erase any consideration of expe-

riences that challenge your self-absorbed ideological imposition to the contrary. Good luck trying to bully gay men into your social constructivist extremism.[1]

Mirroring the comments on *Queerty*, the emails characterized me as a dangerous enemy to all gay men, on par with conservatives like Ann Coulter. Again, it was not just my book that was the problem—it was what my book represented: the "trendy bisexual assault" on gay male identity, proffered by self-absorbed dyke bullies leading the queer charge with their social constructionist extremism. The emails from white gay men also conveyed a sense of white gay male vulnerability and fragility, a feeling of being under attack and in need of closing gay ranks and defending gay territory. *Not Gay*—a book in which I had consciously decentered gay men, even within the book's title—seemed to produce anxiety and outrage in gay men in large part because I had dared to state that the book wasn't about them.

The emails from gay men expressed anger not only that a lesbian had written a book about men's homosexual practices, but also that lesbians might have a different (more "political," more "socially constructed") experience of homosexuality, and that this *lesbian* experience was perhaps being privileged within queer studies. The emails held the telltale signs of backlash—not against me, but against the lesbianification of queer studies. Were dykes taking over queer studies? Were they daring to speak not just about themselves but also about the meaning of queerness generally? Were feminist dykes trying to force gay men to think differently about the tenuous lines between gay, bi, and straight? Were dykes suddenly licensed to speak in ways that men could not? Perhaps this fear was best expressed by the same *Queerty* reader who referred to me as a "dumb broad" above. He posted another comment in the same thread in which he bemoans, "If a cisgender male were to present [Ward's arguments] as fact, feminists would be neutering him. Except . . . it's not a right wing zealot saying it. . . . She relies on post-structuralist jargon a la Judith Butler for cred. Again I say, dumb broad."

Also telling was Jonathan's email, in which he asserted that "most gay men" want, or have wanted, to be straight (and in which he signs off as "All Gay Men"). Responses like Jonathan's alluded to the widely popular narrative that no one would ever "choose" to be gay because doing so would mean a life of discrimination, and hence, we must all be born this way. Many gay men's responses to the book seemed to take for granted that being straight is always a better life circumstance than being gay, and from this premise, they argued that to allow straight men to have sexual contact with men and retain their straight status was to let them unfairly have their cake and eat it too. It was to give them a gift—the gift of heteronormativity—that they did not deserve. It was a gift that had not been made available to gay and bisexual men. The vexed tone of so many of the responses to *Not Gay* seemed detached from an empathic concern for straight-identified men who were perhaps suffering in the closet. Instead, reminiscent of the actress Cynthia Nixon being forced by gay men to revise her statement that she "chose" to be a lesbian (Walters 2014; Ward 2015), I felt the weight of gay men's righteous demand that I identify any and every man engaged in homosexual sex as either bisexual or gay. Otherwise, the critics seemed to be saying, the entire political argument upon which modern gay rights claims are based would crumble. Here again, the absence within gay rights discourse of even a very basic queer and/or feminist understanding was striking. Utterly invisible was the possibility that straightness had been so damaged by sexism and the gender binary that it could be more miserable, especially for women and genderqueer people, than being queer. Queer and feminist ideas and methods may be flourishing within the academy, but responses from the "average gay men" who read *Not Gay* (or read the media coverage) made alarmingly clear that the interventions we are making in the academy have had little impact on gay men more broadly.

Gay male commenters on Amazon and elsewhere warned other gay men not to buy the book, proclaiming that the book's cover—an image depicting two tan, muscular, and shirtless young white male surfers sitting together on top of a truck, their hands almost touching—was bait to attract unsuspecting gay male readers, who would encounter my feminism with no forewarning. An Amazon reviewer calling himself "Hu(man)" suggested in 2015 that readers not purchase the book but "borrow [a] library copy to sample how disparagement of white men currently masquerades as research in sociology." There is no doubt that some part of the story of gay men's uptake of *Not Gay* had to do with the book's marketing. University presses are increasingly interested in crossover books that reach both academic and popular audiences, and books about sex are particularly likely to be marketed with this goal in mind. Some of the snarky responses to the book by gay male readers suddenly made more sense to me when I looked up the Kindle edition of *Not Gay* on Amazon and was shown several examples of similar items purchased by people who bought *Not Gay*. All of those "similar items" were gay porn, both videos and novels. The possibility that gay men bought the book imagining that it would be a smutty novel about straight frat boys fucking each other helped to make sense of 2015 Amazon reviews like, "Fun until I hit the academic jargon early in the first chapter" and "The first two pages were somewhat intriguing. . . . Then it's just a snooze fest."

Similarly, in the first months after *Not Gay* was published, I received calls from a reality TV producer interested in producing a show about straight men who have sex with men, an invitation to appear on the daytime talk show *The Doctors* (so that I could counsel wives about the normalcy of their husbands' homosexual experiences), and a request to help a *Playboy* journalist track down straight men who would be willing to talk about their desire for sex with men. The book had fallen into the hands of many people who had absolutely no interest in the queer, feminist, critical race critique at its heart. And yet, somehow, I sympathized with them. They just wanted to make trashy TV or get off on porn, and each interview with me (in the case of the TV producers) and each effort to actually read the book was a complete buzzkill.

Dumb, Dangerous, and Mentally Ill: Gay Men Diagnose Me

And speaking of buzzkills . . . When I think about gay men's desire to keep lesbian feminism out of gay eroticism, I am reminded of "no open-toed shoes" policies and other ways of denying lesbians (and transwomen) access to gay bars and clubs. The presence of lesbians in the bar was purportedly a palpable turnoff, an erotic buzzkill for gay men cruising one another. Lesbians were and are no strangers to being depicted by gay men as boring, overly serious (i.e., political), nagging, and asexual. While all feminists could be said to be killjoys (see Ahmed 2010), lesbian feminists have arguably perfected the art form. I raise this cultural and political divide to consider its intellectual corollary—to suggest that the more critical, feminist, and intersectional queer studies becomes, the less fun and hot it is for many white gay men (and the hotter it becomes for dykes).

I want to be very clear that *Not Gay* received thoughtful, productive criticism from many quarters, including from brilliant gay male scholars, and I have learned considerably from that feedback. But, by contrast, the *other* criticism—coming largely from disgusted and self-righteous gay men—conveyed an overwhelming lack of understanding of the book's basic theoretical aims and an even more overwhelming knee-jerk resistance to feminist and queer methods. For as much as gay men were put off by my use of (my own) dyke sexuality as a foil to gay male sexuality—a practice feminist scholars call reflexivity and gay male readers referred to as "unnecessary personal anecdotes"—they were happy to try to imagine the personal reasons that a lesbian feminist like me would write a book about what they understood as their own turf: sexual contact between men. Gay male commenters described me as "someone who wets her panties at the prospect of brojobs" (*Queerty*), "dumb as a doorknob and locked in her tide of intersectionality" (*New York* magazine), and a "ridiculous . . . lesbian women's studies professor trolling man2man sex ads for over a decade. This woman has mental issues" (*Huffington Post*). A gay man using the name "Lawrence Topping," the author of the following 2015 Amazon review of *Not Gay*, addressed my mental health most directly. His review reads:

> I'm a retired, gay/male clinical therapist, and I read this book. A profile. I believe the author, sometime in her youth, suffered an assault or was a victim of one of the many forms of abuse, at the hands of a straight, white male. I also believe she, subsequently, never effectively resolved this traumatic experience and, as a result, she carries its emotional damage with her wherever she goes, whatever she does. . . . And, now, she's written a book. This emotional disorder (PTSD) is evidenced by her biased outlook on the subject matter and, especially, through her unnecessary personal anecdotes.

Reflecting a long tradition of pathologizing both lesbianism and feminism as dangerous maladaptations to individual trauma, here my research was dismissed by a gay male therapist as the product of emotional damage.

Other gay male critics pointed to my lesbian ignorance of how penises work and my ostensibly blind faith in the possibility that sexual arousal can be shaped by social and cultural circumstances. For instance, a review of *Not Gay* published on *Gawker*, titled "That's Not How Dicks Work" and written by a white gay man (Juzwiak 2015), quoted the following passage from my book: "This investment in heteronormativity is itself a *bodily desire*; in fact, I believe it is *the* embodied heterosexual desire, more powerful than, say, a woman's yearning for male torsos or penises or a man's longing for vaginas or breasts" (Ward 2015, 35; emphasis in original). To this suggestion, the author of the review responded:

> Yeah, but that's not how dicks work. . . . By and large, men are more simple than she describes—I guarantee you that no straight dude has ever identified as someone who enjoys heteronormativity more than pussy or tits (that's another example of Ward arbitrarily choosing to impose *what men really mean* over what they project while still taking "straight" for an answer). The reason that many of us feel "born this way" is because your dick gets hard at *what your dick gets hard at*. (Juzwiak 2015; emphasis in original)

There was much I wanted to say in response: that getting off on "pussy and tits" is often the same thing as getting off on heteronormativity; that clits and dicks get hard at what they get hard at but that doesn't mean that bodies, by themselves, are the only stimuli making us hard; and that the popularity of the dismissive claim that "men just aren't that complicated"—most frequently used to silence women who want to hold men accountable for their behavior—is itself very telling. But each individual piece of criticism from gay men, and each reply I might have wished to give in return, was drowned out by the overwhelming chorus of gay male misogyny. It was difficult to take any one critique seriously when each sounded so similar to the others—from the guy who called me a "dumb broad" to the guy who offered "congrats on your political lesbianism" to the guy who informed me "that's not how dicks work." To digest it all, I began reading the hate mail to public audiences while giving lectures at universities and doing readings in bookstores. And I was, of course, met with love and solidarity by many feminist gay men who were as horrified by the responses as I was. "Oh God," they would say. "I'm *so* sorry. What's wrong with gay men?!"

The Urgency of Dyke Methods

What *is* wrong with gay men? While the characterization of queer studies as dangerous, self-absorbed, nonsensical, and frivolous is often presented as a gender-neutral disciplinary critique, the frequency with which it is leveraged by gay men against queer women—for example, Judith Butler and her minions—tells another story, a story of sexist backlash against queer theorizing that decenters gay men. Consider, for instance, this comment from "Jacob23," published in 2015 on *Queerty* in response to Graham Gremore's interview with me about *Not Gay*:

> 100 years ago, academics in these fields would be dedicated to studying and resolving major social problems afflicting human society. Today, they are writing about how the gendered anus is represented in hetero-normative discourse on *Dancing with the Stars*. These people are not only a waste of space, but they draw away talent and energy of people who could actually improve the condition of the world. BTW, here's a sample of some of Jane Ward's other "scholarly works." . . . She seems obsessed with taking down heterosexuality, smearing gays as r@cists, promoting transgenderism, and using children to experiment with queer theory.

While the first part of the comment might be described as an expression of uninformed but reasonable curiosity about the value of examining popular culture, the second half of the comment makes crystal clear the conservative political investments never lurking too far behind these concerns. In this view, research that critically examines heterosexuality and racism, that promotes the rights of trans people, or that advocates for queer approaches to parenting constitutes a trendy obsession, an insult to real science. Again and again, queer intellectual projects are waved away as silliness, feminized through accusations that queer scholars—like uppity women everywhere—are making things too complicated, overly personal and particular. Real men, real gay men, aren't that complicated, their desires and erections are easily explained by straightforward science.

White gay men's response to *Not Gay* also suggests that these sorts of rancorous methodological critiques of queer, feminist work may also be triangulated with psychic impulses—in this case, gay men's thwarted sexual desire for heteromasculinity. *Not Gay* is a book that decenters gay men in its theorization of sexual subjectivity; but perhaps more infuriating for some gay readers, it is a book that describes erotic exchanges between men that are intensely desired by, but ultimately unavailable to, many gay men. The news that straightness desires straightness is indeed bad news for queers who fetishize heterosexual masculinity (and femininity). The virulence running through the above responses to *Not Gay* may, in fact, reflect the ways in which erotic disappointment is routed through various channels, including methodological critique.

As I pat myself on the head and reflect on my status as a stupid bitch with no business writing about gay men, I am reminded that the feature of queer-dyke scholarship most lambasted by gay men is one of its most fundamental contributions: as an anti-essentialist and interdisciplinary project, it provides us with the tools to think about queer and hetero forms of sexualities—their boundaries and meanings—without gay men (or any other essentialized gender category) at the center of our thinking. Dyke methods are not about making a commitment to balanced ideas and crass versions of LGBT inclusivity; they are about investigating—with the dyke's intersectional and interdisciplinary tools, and through the dyke's analytic lens—all matters of gender and sexuality, including those that involve dicks.

NOTE

1 All of these emails were sent to me in 2015.

WORKS CITED

Ahmed, Sara. 2006. *Queer Phenomenology: Orientations, Objects, Others*. Durham, NC: Duke University Press.

Ahmed, Sara. 2010. "Feminist Killjoys (and Other Willful Subjects)." *The Scholar and Feminist Online* 8 (3). http://sfonline.barnard.edu/.

Anderson, Eric. 2008. "'Being Masculine Is Not about Who You Sleep With . . .': Heterosexual Athletes Contesting Masculinity and the One-Time Rule of Homosexuality." *Sex Roles: A Journal of Sex Research* 58 (1–2): 104–15.

Anderson, Eric. 2010. "I Kiss Them Because I Love Them: The Emergence of Heterosexual Men Kissing in British Institutes of Education." *Archives of Sexual Behavior* 41 (2): 421–30.

Brim, Matt, and Amin Ghaziani. 2016. "Introduction: Queer Methods." *WSQ: Women's Studies Quarterly* 44 (3–4): 14–27.

Carrillo, Hector, and Amanda Hoffman. 2016. "From MSM to Heteroflexibilities: Non-Exclusive Straight Male Identities and Their Implications for HIV Prevention and Health Promotion." *Global Public Health* 7 (7–8).

Diamond, Lisa. 2008. *Sexual Fluidity: Understanding Women's Love and Desire*. Cambridge, MA: Harvard University Press.

Duggan, Lisa. 2004. *The Twilight of Equality: Neoliberalism, Cultural Politics, and the Attack on Democracy*. New York: Beacon Press.

Ghaziani, Amin. 2011. "Post-Gay Collective Identity Construction." *Social Problems* 58 (1): 99–125.

Ghaziani, Amin. 2014. *There Goes the Gayborhood?* Princeton, NJ: Princeton University Press.

Gremore, Graham. 2015. "'Bro-Jobs' Author Talks Straight Man-on-Man Sex and 'Repressed Homosexual Desire.'" *Queerty*, August 6. www.queerty.com/.

Halberstam, Jack. 2011. *The Queer Art of Failure*. Durham, NC: Duke University Press.

Haritaworn, Jin, Adi Kuntsman, and Silvia Posocco, eds. 2014. *Queer Necropolitics*. New York: Routledge.

Hsieh, Mason. 2015. "Dear Straight Men, Come Out Already." *Huffington Post*, July 30. www.huffingtonpost.com/.

Jordan-Young, Rebecca M. 2011. *Brain Storm: The Flaws in the Science of Sex Differences*. Cambridge, MA: Harvard University Press.

Juzwiak, Rich. 2015. "That's Not How Dicks Work: On Not Gay and 'Straight' Men Who Have Gay Sex." *Gawker*, August 12. http://review.gawker.com/.

Muñoz, José Esteban. 2009. *Cruising Utopia: The Then and There of Queer Futurity*. New York: NYU Press.

Nash, Catherine J., and Kath Browne. 2010. *Queer Methods and Methodologies: Intersecting Queer Theories and Social Science Research*. London: Routledge.

Newton, Esther. 2000. *Margaret Mead Made Me Gay: Personal Essays, Public Ideas*. Durham, NC: Duke University Press.

Puar, Jasbir K. 2007. *Terrorist Assemblages: Homonationalism in Queer Times*. Durham, NC: Duke University Press.

Reinharz, Shulamit. 1992. *Feminist Methods in Social Research*. Oxford: Oxford University Press.

Reynolds, Chelsea. 2015. "'I Am Super Straight and I Prefer You Be Too': Constructions of Heterosexual Masculinity in Online Personal Ads for 'Straight' Men Seeking Sex with Men." *Journal of Communication Inquiry* 39 (3): 213–31.

Savage, Dan. 2015. "Not Gay Men Who Have Not Gay Sex with Other Not Gay Men." *The Stranger*, July 27. www.thestranger.com/.

Signal, Jesse. 2015. "Why Straight Men Have Sex with Each Other." *New York Magazine*, August 5. http://nymag.com/.

Silva, Tony. 2018. "'Helpin' a Buddy Out': Perceptions of Identity and Behavior among Rural Straight Men That Have Sex with Each Other." *Sexualities* 21 (1–2).

Snorton, C. Riley. 2014. *Nobody Is Supposed to Know: Black Sexuality on the Down Low*. Minneapolis: University of Minnesota Press.

Spade, Dean. 2015. *Normal Life: Administrative Violence, Critical Trans Politics, and the Limits of the Law*. Durham, NC: Duke University Press.

Twine, France Winddance, and Jonathan Warren, eds. 2000. *Racing Research, Researching Race: Methodological Dilemmas in Critical Race Studies*. New York: NYU Press.

Walters, Suzanna Danuta. 2014. *The Tolerance Traps: How God, Genes, and Good Intentions Are Sabotaging Gay Equality*. New York: NYU Press.

Ward, Jane. 2000. "Queer Sexism: Rethinking Gay Men and Masculinity." In *Gay Masculinities*, edited by Peter Nardi, 152–75. Thousand Oaks, CA: Sage.

Ward, Jane. 2008. *Respectably Queer: Diversity Culture in LGBT Activist Organizations*. Nashville, TN: Vanderbilt University Press.

Ward, Jane. 2015. *Not Gay: Sex between Straight White Men*. New York: NYU Press.

Whisman, Vera. 1995. *Queer by Choice: Lesbians, Gay Men, and the Politics of Identity*. New York: Routledge.

13

Haunted by the 1990s

Queer Theory's Affective Histories

KADJI AMIN

Through case studies of key texts across the history of queer inquiry, this chapter analyzes the temporality, affectivity, and politicality of the term *queer* in its academic usages. My goal is to lay bare a method: that, inarticulate and opaque, which orients what objects, processes, and relations "count" as *queer* within queer studies. For if *queer* is a singularly mobile and mutable term, capable of adjectivally modifying a range of phenomena—from sex practices, to social formations, temporalities, affects, diasporas, and inhumanisms—it is, nevertheless, not equally capable of being applied to *anything* nonnormative or boundary-crossing. The method that orients what may be felicitously named *queer* is, I propose, fundamentally *affective*: it is a matter of sensing some resonance between one's object of study and the inchoate cluster of feelings that inhabit and animate the term *queer*. These feelings, I propose, must be understood as historical in origin. Specifically, I argue that, despite the frequency with which queer inquiry has described itself as uncommitted to its pasts and definitionally attuned to questions of immediate political urgency, it remains affectively haunted by the historical and political moment of the U.S. 1990s in which it emerged. Ultimately, I propose that the future of the field of queer studies—as well as its relevance for scholarship on prior historical periods, racialized populations, and areas outside of the United States—requires a reckoning with the field's affective haunting by the inaugural moment of the U.S. 1990s. This reckoning may take the form of a *re-* rather than a *de*historicization. That is, whereas queer scholars have tended to gesture toward the unbounded future as the domain in which *queer* can have a renewed life by becoming other to what it has been so far, it may be more efficacious to engage *queer's mul-*

tiple pasts—including those prior to its explicit deployment as a political and theoretical term in the 1990s—in order to differently animate *queer*'s dense affective histories. I close by offering *attachment genealogy* as a method of exposing, fragmenting, and reworking *queer*'s historical inheritances to enable *queer* to do different work in new contexts.

Queer and Now

Before elaborating on the significance of the 1990s, I want to begin with a text that marks an important moment in queer studies scholarship, the introduction to the 2005 special issue of *Social Text* edited by David Eng, Jack Halberstam, and José Esteban Muñoz titled "What's Queer about Queer Studies Now?" Published as a field intervention that markedly highlighted the work of "a younger generation of scholars," this special issue, as described in its introduction, sought to foreground the question of "the political utility of queer" in its assessment of "what's queer" about contemporary queer studies scholarship (Eng, Halberstam, and Muñoz 2005, 1). The antennae of political utility, in turn, orients the editors to identify the target of queer critical intervention as a series of "late twentieth-century global crises" which they describe, quoting Walter Benjamin, as "historical emergencies" (1). Their list of the "emergencies" to which this special issue responds includes:

> the triumph of neoliberalism and the collapse of the welfare state; the Bush administration's infinite 'war on terrorism' and the acute militarization of state violence; the escalation of US empire building and the clash of religious fundamentalisms, nationalisms, and patriotisms; the devolution of civil society and the erosion of civil rights; the pathologizing of immigrant communities as 'terrorist' and racialized populations as 'criminal'; the shifting forms of citizenship and migration in a putatively 'postidentity' and 'postracial' age; the politics of intimacy and the liberal recoding of freedom as secularization, domesticity, and marriage; and the return to 'moral values' and family values' as a prophylactic against political debate, economic redistribution, and cultural dissent. (2)

The editors' list is significant in several ways: it unambiguously affirms *queer* as a term capable of intervening in a social and political field conceived more broadly, for queer studies, than in the past; it centers within the field large-scale processes—such as militarization, racialized criminalization, and shifting forms of migration—whose link to the humble object of "queer sexuality" is, though not insignificant, at least not immediately foregrounded; and it therefore attenuates *queer*'s reference to sexuality. This list is also indicative of the special issue's important and generative role as a both a platform and a mission statement for the centering of issues of race and global geopolitics in the field. While this expansion of the field of queer scholarship is undoubtedly energizing, readers may well wonder what makes it cohere. What makes *queer* gravitate to these points of intervention and not others? Why not, in fact, *everything*?[1] For the editors of this special issue, what coheres this field of intervention is, on the one hand, a concern with the exigencies of the "now," and, on the other, an understanding of *queer* as "a political metaphor without a fixed referent" (1). The latter, much quoted, formulation is important, for the "fixed referent" which the authors affirm *queer* to be lacking is clearly the referent of sexuality, or, even more narrowly, gays and lesbians. Freed of its historical debt to same-sex sexuality, *queer* is defined as *that which flies wherever the demands of political urgency might call it*. Above all, this is a powerful statement for the cutting-edge relevance of the field.

Queer theory has long celebrated *queer* as an almost infinitely mobile and mutable theoretical term that, unlike *gay and lesbian* or *feminist* need not remain bound to any particular identity, historical context, politic, or object of study and that, for that very reason, promises a cutting-edge political intervention. Hence, while what they designate as the scope of queer scholarship may be new, Eng, Halberstam, and Muñoz's implication that *queer* not be constrained to its historical reference to same-sex sexualities, cultures, and movements and their understanding of *queer* as definitionally oriented toward urgent political interventions is not. This is, in fact, something that the editors acknowledge in their citations of Judith Butler's "Critically Queer" and Michael Warner's "Introduction" to *Fear of a Queer Planet*, two foundational texts in early 1990s queer theory. In "Critically Queer," published in the first volume of the *GLQ* in 1993, Judith Butler argues, in what has become a field-defining statement:

> If the term 'queer' is to be a site of collective contestation, the point of departure for a set of historical reflections and futural imaginings, it will

have to remain that which is, in the present, never fully owned, but always and only redeployed, twisted, queered from a prior usage and in the direction of urgent and expanding political purposes and perhaps also yielded in favor of terms that do that political work more effectively. (Butler 1993, 19)

Somewhat tautologically, perhaps, the relevance of *queer*, as a term, is described as contingent on its constant *queering*—we see here, already, the proposition that *queer* can never be never *queer enough*; that is, that the future of queer scholarship depends on always queering and being queerer than what came before.[2] Here, also, we find the claims, which Eng, Halberstam, and Muñoz echo and sharpen, that *queer* must always be "queered from a prior usage," never allowing its meaning or field of reference to settle, and that what guides this constant queering movement is none other than "urgent and expanding political purposes." Wherever political urgency calls, queer must follow. While this may sound like a declaration of *queer*'s infinite adaptability and limitless futurity, Butler ends on a less sanguine note, evoking the possibility of *queer*'s eventual demise, its potential need to be "yielded in favor of terms that do that political work more effectively." This clause, tacked on to the sentence almost as an afterthought, is in fact an important recognition of the temporality, the timeliness of *queer*, as well as the possibility that we may have to abandon it. In the 1993 foreword she pairs with her 1991 essay "Queer and Now," Eve Sedgwick muses, "I suppose this must be called the moment of Queer," which seems immediately to evoke the worry that "[i]n the short-shelf-life American marketplace of images, maybe the queer moment, if it's here today, will for that very reason be gone tomorrow." This worry proves fleeting, however, and Sedgwick steps back from the abyss to issue the reassuring and redeeming claim "that something about *queer* is inextinguishable" (Sedgwick 1993, xii). Butler, by contrast, seems to recognize that the politicality of *queer* is a product of historical conditions; and that, under different circumstances, *queer* might become a term unsuited for the aspirations with which history, in the U.S. moment of the early 1990s, had freighted it.

Insofar as early 1990s queer theory was, in part, a bid to bring some of the energy, in-your-face defiance, political urgency, and transgressiveness of on-the-ground queer activism into the academy, its early appeal was inseparable from its affective connection to a range of events outside of the academy.[3] If *queer* offered itself up, at this time, as a name for a set of theoretical interventions around the relations between sexuality, normativity, and the political, it was because of the current and recent cultural contests it invoked: the genocidal Reagan administration's unresponsiveness to the AIDS crisis; the associated resurgence of violent homophobia; a newly performative, in-your-face, and media-savvy form of activism in groups like ACT UP, the Lesbian Avengers, and Queer Nation; highly publicized battles over the state funding of queer artists like Robert Mapplethorpe and David Wojnarowitz; and the ongoing legacy of the "sex wars" that roiled feminists and birthed a vocal feminist sex-radicalism during the 1980s.[4] *Queer* was not only a term explicitly mobilized within a series of highly charged political and cultural conflicts; it was a term that seemed to carry within it the loaded transgression and charged sense of struggle around sex and sexual cultures that was cropping up, seemingly everywhere, and taking a multitude of inventive cultural forms during the 1980s and 1990s. This was the sense in which *queer* was of the "now," and the early 1990s was, indeed, "the moment of Queer" (Sedgwick 1993, xii). Born of a desire to fuck up the "normal business in the academy" by carrying into scholarship the political charge and current urgency of sexual politics, queer theory was, as Heather Love reminds us, *never intended to age* (Love 2013; Warner 1993, xxvi).

That was then, this is now. The introduction to "What's Queer about Queer Studies Now?" is a field statement about how queer studies can have a future that stays true to its originary charge of political urgency and "nowness" in a much-changed landscape for sexual politics and cultures. The sentence that ends with the call for an understanding of *queer* as "a political metaphor without a fixed referent" begins by invoking "[t]he contemporary mainstreaming of gay and lesbian identity—as a mass-mediated consumer lifestyle and embattled legal category," staking the issue of the renewal of queer studies on the crisis of gay and lesbian culture's loss of its transgressive political charge (Eng, Halberstam, and Muñoz 2005, 1). In 2005, gay marriage was the civil rights issue of the day, and *queer*, in the mainstream mass cultural arena, is more likely to invoke consumer culture–centric popular television shows such as *Queer Eye for the Straight Guy* and *Queer as Folk* than images of mass protest, the shock of transgression, or a sense of life-or-death urgency. At the same time, racialized homophobia and transphobia continue to have a deadly and enervating, though highly uneven, impact across populations and geographies. What future for queer studies when *queer* is no longer the term of *the now* and when its historical link to same-sex sexuality is no longer sufficient to guarantee its politicality? Eng, Halberstam, and Muñoz respond by definitionally centering *queer*'s meaning around its charge of political urgency, which was an affective product of the moment of the 1990s, rather than its historic reference to same-sex sexuality. At a moment when "gay and lesbian" no longer describes a radical and transgressive political constituency, however, this taxes queer studies with pushing itself to remain continually on the move, forever in search of that object, diagnosis, or scene of intervention that will make good on the political promise that inaugurated this field-that-was-not-meant-to-be-a-field. Robyn Wiegman has argued that fields founded on aspirations for social justice must "perform inexhaustibility continuously" (2012, 122). Given its central anti-identitarian claim, that is, the much reiterated definition of *queer* as, paradoxically, *undefined*, but as emphatically *not* synonymous with same-sex sexuality, queer studies is perhaps unique in having been founded on the "durational strategy" and "aspirational horizon" of being always *elsewhere* than where it was before (Jagose 2015, 34).

Queer anti-identitarianism and indefinition, however, produce their own problems. The use of *queer* as a false umbrella term that, in practice, most often refers to gay white men has often been exposed and critiqued. For Hiram Pérez, the transparent subject of much queer theorizing problematically replicates the "race-neutral objectivity" of "the university's ideal bourgeois subject," and for Jasbir Puar, this ideal state of "freedom from norms" draws on the values of autonomy, individualism, and choice enshrined within liberalism (Pérez 2005, 172; Puar 2007, 22–23). In a linguistic analysis of the term *queer*, Mel Chen critiques the ways in which anti-identitarian field statements by David Halperin and Michael Warner tend to mystify *queer*'s indefinition and idealize its mobility (Chen 2012, 64 and 68–69). Biddy Martin has prominently critiqued the ways in which the value accorded to queer mobility implicitly denigrates a static "feminine" domain of enmeshment in kinship and reproduction (Martin 1994). These critics and others have amply demonstrated that it is both dangerous and disingenuous to obfuscate the subject of queer anti-identitarianism and to idealize *queer*'s definitional openness. Less discussed is the worrisome harmony between *queer*'s much trumpeted mobility, flexibility, adaptability, and portability and the demands for accelerated obsolescence and flexible and mobile labor that characterize late capitalism.[5] Might queer studies resist the demand that it constantly sell a new product that satisfyingly reproduces the cutting-edge cachet of its founding moment, as well as the implication that to fail to do so is to be, simply, dead? "What's queer about queer studies *now*?" we hear . . . and *now*? . . . and *now*?

I want to propose that queer mobility and indefinition function within queer studies as both a disciplinary norm and a front. A disciplinary norm because queer studies has become a field paradoxically defined by its lack of a defined object of study and by its quasi-infinite mobility of reference. A front because, whereas field statements affirming *queer*'s inexhaustible definitional mobility claim to open up queer theory as an antidisciplinary mode of inquiry that is capable of radical transformations and becomings, they actually work to secure it as a field that need not be accountable to its own history (which now spans, in its named institutional form, more than two decades) because it is already beyond it. A front, moreover, because little queer scholarship actually uses *queer* in an entirely dereferentialized manner. To avow, however, the tacit consensus that queer scholarship does in fact reference sex, gender, and sexuality would be pin the field down, exposing it as defined not by whatever is most radical, urgent, and cutting-edge, but rather by the ordinary vicissitudes of the politics of gender, sex, sexuality in social context. If this is the case, then how can we get out of the bind produced by the requirement that *queer* retain its originary charge of transgression, avant-garde novelty, and political potency by always meaning something new without, for that matter, restricting the imaginative and politicized expansion of queer inquiry that is the most valuable legacy of Eng, Halberstam, and Muñoz's special issue?

Queer's Affective Histories

We might begin by zeroing in on, rather than running away from the current problem of *queer*'s affective deflation. In an astute analysis, Chen ascribes *queer*'s deanimation both to its loss of affectivity, as the term has been partially reclaimed from its status as an insult, and to its stultifying fixation into a noun and identity category. According to Chen, *queer*

> has been both re-animated and de-animated. While it continually reanimates in new formations—thanks particularly to queer of color, transnational, disability, and trans scholarship—it has also achieved nominal fame as an identity; but it has simultaneously coalesced, gotten sticky, inertial, lost its animation and its drive in the context of the United States. (2012, 83)

In concluding by arguing that *queer*'s future is contingent on its capacity to overcome its current inertia and stickiness by being modified by something else, Chen ultimately seeks to reanimate *queer* by giving it a future that diverges from its past. However, at the same time, Chen offers a linguistic history of *queer* that precedes the 1990s, including Gloria Anzaldúa's theorization of *mestiza queer* during the 1980s—a "first" that is not usually taken up as a foundation for queer theory—and E. Patrick Johnson's account of the African American vernacular term *quare*, seeming to imply that reanimation could proceed through an excavation of the alternative historicities that swarm within and beside *queer*, rather than only by the term's future movements. Indeed, Chen relates the term's loss of both animacy and affectivity to its loss of historicity, analyzing how *queer* as "a nominal category can seem to 'forget' its history" (2012, 77). Could *queer* be rendered lively, then, by an engagement with its *multiple* pasts, by a reanimation of its dense affective historicity, and not only by a future of continual modification by something else?

I want to propose that, instead of continuing to celebrate queer mobility and indefinition, we ground *queer* in its various contexts, histories, genealogies, and inheritances. For these contexts are the source of *affective histories* that influence, without it being acknowledged, what meanings adhere to *queer*, how this term is deployed, and what happens when it takes on life in new contexts. Rather than regarding *queer*'s stickiness as a problem to be overcome by ever more mobility, I propose that we account for *how* the associations *queer* has accrued in its travels—within mostly U.S. and Anglophone political and academic discourses—assure that *only certain* forms of nonnormativity, *only particular* sex acts seem to attach to it.[6] We need to understand what coagulation of historical affects gives body to *queer* and to attend to what becomes of these affective histories when *queer* travels to novel historical, geopolitical, conceptual, and demographic locations.

Avowing the affective histories of *queer*—which often display themselves less through explicit claims than in affective dispositions toward and away from certain terms—would require our willingness to admit that *queer* is not endlessly open-ended, polyvalent, and reattachable. Instead, it is a term *sticky* with history, one that bears the impression, in its characteristic gestures, dispositions, and orientations, of its travels in time and space. For Sara Ahmed, "stickiness" describes the ways in which terms accumulate affectivity through histories of use: "signs become sticky through repetition; if a word is used in a certain way, again and again, then the 'use' *becomes* intrinsic; it becomes a form of signing" (Ahmed 2004, 91; emphasis in original). Ahmed's understanding of how emotions and historicity are intimately conjoined might usefully be brought to bear on scholarship on the affectivity of the term *queer*. In *The Cultural Politics of Emotion*, she demonstrates that figures and key terms that seem inherently laden with emotion often conceal the history—of circulation, repetition, and association with other terms—that has resulted in their accumulation of affective value. In other words, historicity makes figures and terms "sticky"—particular emotions, particular proximate terms become bound to them, while others become blocked, sliding inconsequentially past. This is how terms can get "stuck," becoming difficult to resignify, redeploy in novel circumstances, or project into new constellations of association. The discipline of queer studies has worked hard to keep *queer* slick rather than sticky, unbound, detachable, and able to reattach itself to an endless array of new objects and methods.[7] Nevertheless, I would argue that the very polyvalent richness of *queer*—the fact that it remains a highly charged term that can evoke, simultaneously and contradictorily, injury, negativity, utopianism, transgression, defiance, righteousness, superiority, radicalism, hipness, and rage, but most often some combination, some metonymic attraction between a series of those terms—indicates that *queer* is *not* slick but rather the stickiest of terms. It has been *made* sticky not only by its career, its course within mostly U.S.-centered academic conversations, but also by its historical emergence in precisely the U.S.

scene of the 1990s that contemporary queer studies often seems so eager to forget and to move beyond.[8] Forgetting this history is useful to the field, precisely because it permits us to refuse to define or to historicize *queer*, to say we are holding it open to indefinite becomings, all the while making implicit and explicit arguments that draw both their conviction and their appeal from *queer*'s affective charge, that is, from its disavowed historicity.

To investigate and contend with the historicity of *queer* would mean both remembering the contexts of *queer*'s academic emergence during the 1990s and excavating the alternative historical imaginaries that teem within *queer*. The task of unpacking the legacy of the 1990s, however, seems particularly urgent. For, I suspect that however far contemporary queer studies travels in topic, methodology, and scope from the concerns of early 1990s queer theory, it remains haunted by the electric 1990s convergence, under the banner of *queer*, of same-sex sexuality, political urgency, and radical transgression.[9] This accounts for certain contradictions of queer inquiry during a contemporary juncture in which neither the political urgency nor the transgressive effects of *queer* can be taken for granted.

The Agencies of Historicity

This is not to say, however, that *queer* has become detached from political radicalism. I would argue, to the contrary, that it remains haunted by the political and transgressive charge of the early 1990s moment, and that this haunting orients it toward particular political and intellectual projects in the present. One symptom of this haunting is the fact that, as I write this, *queer* is likely to carry a *nostalgic* charge. For many self-identified queer subjects as well as queer scholars, *queer* signals a disidentification with the contemporary mainstreaming and assimilationism of gay and lesbian politics and culture and, as Lucas Hilderbrand has written regarding the significance of queer AIDS activism for those of us who came of age after it, a "nostalgia for a previously radical queer community" (2006, 303). In a significant shift, *queer* has gone from being *of* the "now" to being *a rejection* of the "now." Indeed, if Muñoz's *Cruising Utopia: The Then and There of Queer Futurity* is such a visionary and timely book, it is because it theorizes contemporary queers' disaffection with the present and yearning for a more radical time and place. Declaring "the present is not enough," Muñoz boldly identifies queerness with the utopian longing for a different futurity that does not proceed, in an inevitably linear fashion, from the fallen state of the present (Muñoz 2009, 17). As he repeatedly specifies, the present that is not enough is that "of neo-liberal ideology and the degrading of politics brought about by representations of queerness in contemporary popular culture": it is contemporary queer normalization within the fold of neoliberalism that has ruined the present (7). But the "Then" of the book's subtitle is not only the future. *Cruising Utopia* seeks to reactivate the past through a "queer utopian memory" that is ultimately oriented toward helping us glimpse a more expansive futurity (35). Finding the radical political charge of the queer early 1990s flagging in the present, scholarship that we might characterize as *radically nostalgic* seeks to reanimate, and indeed to intensify this charge by characterizing, as *queer*, a *utopian longing* that draws hope for the future out of the radical aspects of various pasts. *Queer*'s affective historicity is reanimated and transformed through multiple temporal torsions, imbuing *queer* with an intensified utopianism that draws its energy from the pangs of nostalgia and loss.

By contrast, most scholarship on homonormativity and homonationalism—in its trenchant critiques of the incorporation of homosexuality into neoliberal governmentality and a defanged multicultural diversity that consolidates familiar gender, racial, and geopolitical hierarchies—is far from utopian. Nevertheless, I am interested in how, in the sheer *energy* of its critique, scholarship on homonationalism and homonormativity seems still to be animated by the now-injured aspiration that queer sexuality *ought to* attach to radical politics and to an anti-assimilationist stance toward the institutions of the state. That is, it seems to me that what drives the prominence of critiques of homonormativity and homonationalism in contemporary queer studies is a historical disappointment—of those political and anti-assimilationist energies that continue to reverberate in *queer*, even as some versions of queer sexuality have become absorbable into a neoliberal politics of lifestyle choice and anodyne diversity.

The energy of queer work on homonormativity and homonationalism, as well as the readiness with which it disidentifies with normalized gay and lesbian subjects, betrays its continuing animation by *queer*'s affective histories and, as a result, its unwillingness to give *queer* up to its deanimated and defanged contemporary uses. On a linguistic level, we see this desire to preserve and redirect the politically potent affective histories of *queer* in a bifurcation in the term's meaning and uses. In scholarship on homonormativity and homonationalism, terms such as "queer liberalism" or the "disciplinary queer" subject position *queer* as an affectively neutral and deradicalized descriptor for privileged gay and lesbian subjects absorbed into techniques of neoliberal global governance (Eng 2010; Puar 2007, xxvii). At the same time, another *queer* is often preserved as the carrier of *queer*'s affective histories and of the political aspirations of the field of queer studies. This *queer* refers either to authentically oppressed and truly contestatory queer political subjects, or, in a dereferentialized form, to those processes or forces that exceed the systems of governance or power being diagnosed and critiqued. But what is it about *queer* that allows it to be the name for that which *exceeds* power, even as it simultaneously designates those gay and lesbian subjects who are the contemporary *agents* of state power? Through this bifurcation in the meaning of *queer*, *queer*'s affective histories may be preserved against the failure of contemporary gay and lesbian politics to make good on them.

Attachment Genealogy as Method

I am interested in how much work in contemporary queer studies responds to *queer*'s present failure to make good on past aspirations that continue to inhabit it with a renewed utopianism that relocates the affective energies of *queer* onto objects and analytics—from transnationalism to affect to assemblages—deemed more politically and theoretically promising than mere same-sex sexuality. Despite *queer*'s disappointments, we cannot seem to allow it to fail, for that would not only threaten the future of the field of inquiry that bears its name, but also the possibility of using queer studies as a resource for the renewal of contemporary queer political imaginaries. As a result, queer scholars deploy *queer*'s lush connotations, bifurcating from the denotative use of *queer* as an umbrella for LGBT to exploit instead some connotative sense of *queer* that appears better suited to forward the transgression

and political potency with which *queer* became laden around the early
1990s. My hypothesis, then, is that what queer studies has institutionalized, more than an object of study or method, is a set of historical
emotions generated within U.S. queer culture and politics around the
early 1990s, and indeed, that these historical affects propel the inchoate
method that animates what objects may be claimed as *queer*.

This may be unwelcome news for scholars whose entry-points to
queer are elsewhere than the U.S. 1990s and who seek to make queer
scholarship relevant outside of this narrow context of institutional
emergence—I am thinking particularly of queer scholarship on non-
U.S. areas, prior historical periods, and racialized populations. My argument, to be clear, is not that queer studies needs to confine itself either
to the historical time and place of *queer* or to the "object" of same-sex
sexuality. To the contrary, I am arguing that any redeployment of *queer*
outside its narrow context of emergence that seeks to keep *queer*'s affective histories intact by preserving the 1990s convergence of same-sex
sexuality, political urgency, and radical transgression might go further
still. For, one reason why queer scholarship on Asia, Africa, and Latin
America, as well as on earlier historical periods, tends to be marginalized within the field as a whole is because it examines sites in which
queer operates in markedly different ways from what has been canon-
ized within queer studies. In their introduction to a 2016 special issue
of *GLQ* on queer studies and area studies, Anjali Arondekar and Geeta
Patel incisively critique the tendency of queer scholarship to mine the
global South for examples rather than epistemologies, failing to attend
to how key "concepts as loss, margin, normative, and nonnormative"
emerge from a U.S. political context (Arondekar and Patel 2016, 152).[10]
Recent U.S. politics and histories inform not only the conceptual apparatus of queer studies, but also the very affective method by which new
subjects, politics, practices, and concepts are claimed as queer in the first
place. Finding a "match" between a historical or area studies example
and one of *queer*'s affective connotations—such as shame, camp irony, or
radical opposition—can offer a gateway from sexuality studies to queer
studies scholarship, a wider audience, and a certain theoretical cachet,
but at the cost of reinscribing *queer*'s U.S. affective histories at the center
of work on new contexts. In order to make good on the expansion of
the terrain of queer scholarship since the "What's Queer about Queer

Studies Now?" special issue, we might instead rework *queer*'s affective historicity to allow *queer* to do new kinds of work with different objects and archives in a range of historical, cultural, and geographic contexts. This may mean allowing *queer* to come not only *to mean* but also *to feel* differently than it does now.

I propose *attachment genealogy* as a method that focuses on analytically queer forms of nonnormativity that clash with *queer*'s current affective and political connotations in order to excavate the historical attachments that inform *queer*'s aversion to these particular objects. The ambition of such a method is to at once bring into view and to multiply the historical and social conditions that shape what is possible, imaginable, and sensible under the sign of *queer*. Attachment genealogy begins with the experience of scholarly unease. For the field of queer studies, an object that produces unease is one that exposes, fragments, and reworks *queer*'s own affective histories. When a scholarly object or archive rubs against the grain of, rather than satisfyingly echoing, one of *queer*'s affective dispositions, our discomfort is the sign that we might profitably perform an attachment genealogy. The first step is to locate the source of the rub—what affective field disposition does the object fail to satisfy? Attachment genealogy then traces backward to locate and fill out the specific context (usually from the United States and historically recent) from which that field disposition emerged. The scholar is then freed to perform the final step of attachment genealogy, that of elaborating the alternative scholarly priorities and feeling states the object generates in order to both conceptually and affectively reorient queer scholarship. In this way, rather than being mined for case studies that are legitimated as queer by virtue of their coherence with the conceptual apparatus and feeling states of queer scholarship, history, geography, and race might be valued for the divergent queer epistemologies and affective histories they generate. The method of attachment genealogy, which I put into practice elsewhere,[11] systematizes the attentiveness to the emergence of theory and feeling alike from specific contexts and histories that is exemplified in the richest and most thoughtful new queer scholarship.

When we use queer studies to think more historically about distant times, racialized populations, and non-U.S. contexts in general, we are not using *queer* as a mobile and reattachable theoretical term without a history. The transformative and intellectually generative effects that may come from recontextualizing *queer* are not the sign that *queer* has yet again elastically adapted itself to a new object; rather, they are the product of *queer*'s dense affective histories undergoing chemical reactions with new contexts. Avowing its affective histories would allow queer studies to begin the work of recontextualizing itself within new racialized and geopolitical landscapes. The outcome of such a process could not be predicted in advance. It might, however, generate a mutation in the field habitus of queer studies that could retrain its felt relations to its objects, aims, and methods of study. This process might be seen as a condition of possibility rather than as a burden or a drag. Because if *queer* is to have life, if it is to be driven to do new things and grapple with new problems, it is through the force and the course of its ongoing affective history. This is how, in Ahmed's terms, emotions, as the flesh of time, may also "open up futures" (2004, 202).

Acknowledgments

I thank Robyn Wiegman and Heather Love, as well as two anonymous readers, for their generative feedback on this chapter.

NOTES

1 Heather Love has discussed this introduction in relation to what she calls "Queer Theory's Everything Problem," that is, the field's "universalizing ambitions" and implicit dismissal of sexuality as "small-scale, private, trivial." I thank her for generously allowing me read and cite this unpublished paper (Love 2013).

2 As Love puts it in her reading of this passage, "the work of 'queering' is never done" (2007, 18).

3 Others have written about some of the institutional reasons for queer theory's early appeal. For example, Annamarie Jagose (2015) has illuminatingly argued that queer theory's rapid uptake during the early 1990s in the U.S. academy owed much to its unique strategic response to criticisms, during the 1980s, of the problems inherent in fields based on identity.

4 Indeed, much queer scholarship produced during the 1990s and early 2000s focused precisely on this set of issues. For an argument in favor of considering the 1980s "sex wars" as part of a feminist genealogy of queer studies, see Love's introduction to her special issue of *GLQ* on "Rethinking Sex" (Love 2011). Gayle Rubin (2011) offers a fuller account than I can here of the context of sexual politics in the 1980s and 1990s.

5 In "The Molecularization of Sexuality: On Some Primitivisms of the Present," Jord/ana Rosenberg (2014) argues that the ontologization of *queer* as sheer pro-

ductivity, particularly by scholarship on new materialisms, reproduces the logics of finance capital. Still, we lack a full-scale exposé of the relation between the queer discourse of fluidity, flexibility, and mobility and the demands of neoliberal capital.

6 Jagose demonstrates that though gay barebacking, anal fisting, and erotic vomiting have been deemed worthy of queer theoretical interest, orgasm has not. She uses this observation to critique the reification, in queer scholarship, of certain sex acts as both queer and political based on the marginalized sexual identities of those who perform them (Jagose 2013, 175–215).

7 Brad Epps critiqued the "fetish of fluidity" in queer theory as early as 2001.

8 For example, Tim Dean advocates in favor of "affirmatively forgetting" both the context and the fetishized authors of queer theory's U.S. emergence in the 1990s so that *queer* might do new work in other languages and geopolitical contexts (2012, 428).

9 Although I concur with Christopher Castiglia and Christopher Reed that queer theory was institutionalized at the cost of the history of 1970s–1980s U.S. gay culture in general and of the AIDS crisis in particular, I disagree strongly with their monocausaul focus on *only* these particular historical sites as *the* sites of relevance for queer studies (Castiglia and Reed 2012).

10 Arondekar and Patel's specific examples are drawn from Chauncey and Povinelli 1999.

11 I put the method of attachment genealogy to work in my book *Disturbing Attachments: Genet, Modern Pederasty, and Queer History* (2017).

WORKS CITED

Ahmed, Sara. 2004. *The Cultural Politics of Emotion*. New York: Routledge.

Amin, Kadji. 2017. *Disturbing Attachments: Genet, Modern Pederasty, and Queer History*. Durham, NC: Duke University Press.

Arondekar, Anjali, and Geeta Patel. 2016. "Area Impossible: Notes toward an Introduction." *GLQ: A Journal of Lesbian and Gay Studies* 22 (2): 151–71.

Butler, Judith. 1993. "Critically Queer." *GLQ: A Journal of Lesbian and Gay Studies* 1 (1): 17–32.

Castiglia, Christopher, and Christopher Reed. 2012. *If Memory Serves: Gay Men, AIDS, and the Promise of the Queer Past*. Minneapolis: University of Minnesota Press.

Chauncey, George, and Elizabeth Povinelli. 1999. "Thinking Sexually and Transnationally: An Introduction." *GLQ: A Journal of Lesbian and Gay Studies* 5 (4): 439–49.

Chen, Mel. 2012. *Animacies: Biopolitics, Racial Mattering, and Queer Affect*. Durham, NC: Duke University Press.

Dean, Tim. 2012. "Queer Theory without Names." *Paragraph* 35 (3): 421–34.

Eng, David. 2010. *The Feeling of Kinship: Queer Liberalism and the Racialization of Intimacy*. Durham, NC: Duke University Press.

Eng, David, Jack Halberstam, and José Esteban Muñoz. 2005. "Introduction: What's Queer about Queer Studies Now?" *Social Text* 23 (3–4): 1–17.

Epps, Brad. 2001. "The Fetish of Fluidity." In *Homosexuality and Psychoanalysis*, edited by Tim Dean and Christopher Lane, 412–31. Chicago: University of Chicago Press.

Hilderbrand, Lucas. 2006. "Retroactivism." *GLQ: A Journal of Lesbian and Gay Studies* 12 (2): 303–17.

Jagose, Annamarie. 2013. *Orgasmology*. Durham, NC: Duke University Press.

Jagose, Annamarie. 2015. "The Trouble with Antinormativity." *differences: A Journal of Feminist Cultural Studies* 26 (1): 26–47.

Love, Heather. 2007. *Feeling Backward: Loss and the Politics of Queer History*. Cambridge, Mass.: Harvard University Press.

Love, Heather. 2011. "Introduction: Rethinking Sex." *GLQ: A Journal of Lesbian and Gay Studies* 17 (1): 1–14.

Love, Heather. 2013. "Queer Theory's Everything Problem." Paper presented at the Thinking Feminism at the Limits conference, Institute for Research on Women and Gender, March, Columbia University, New York.

Martin, Biddy. 1994. "Extraordinary Homosexuals and the Fear of Being Ordinary." *differences: A Journal of Feminist Cultural Studies* 6 (2–3): 100–125.

Muñoz, José Esteban. 2009. *Cruising Utopia: The Then and There of Queer Futurity*. New York: NYU Press.

Pérez, Hiram. 2005. "You Can Have My Brown Body and Eat It, Too!" *Social Text* 23 (3–4): 171–91.

Puar, Jasbir. 2007. *Terrorist Assemblages: Homonationalism in Queer Times*. Durham, NC: Duke University Press.

Rosenberg, Jord/ana. 2014. "The Molecularization of Sexuality: On Some Primitivisms of the Present." *Theory & Event* 17 (2). muse.jhu.edu/article/546470.

Rubin, Gayle. 2011. "Afterword to 'Thinking Sex: Notes for a Radical Theory of the Politics of Sexuality.'" In *Deviations: A Gayle Rubin Reader*, 182–93. Durham, NC: Duke University Press.

Sedgwick, Eve Kosofsky. 1993. *Tendencies*. Durham, NC: Duke University Press.

Warner, Michael. 1993. "Introduction." In *Fear of a Queer Planet: Queer Politics and Social Theory*, vii–xxxi. Minneapolis: University of Minnesota Press.

Wiegman, Robyn. 2012. *Object Lessons*. Durham, NC: Duke University Press.

14

Making Lesbian History Possible

A Proposal

SARAH SCHULMAN

To forbid something is to make it unforgettable.
—Adam Phillips

At the OutHistory.org conference in New York in May 2016, I heard
two of my favorite historians, Marcia Gallo and Nan Alamilla Boyd,
confirm that the problem of "identity categories" has become a significant obstacle to researching, documenting, and analyzing the history of
lesbian lives, politics, culture, experiences, and feelings. Both of these
fascinating scholars use oral history as a foundational practice for their
work, which to date has focused on the 1950s and 1960s. They found
that in talking to those who produced and lived these histories, the word
lesbian was complex, problematic, had divergent meanings, and was a
source of both attraction and refusal. This problem of the elusiveness of
"identity categories" is one reason that documentation of lesbian history
from the 1970s onward has been seen as a kind of swamp into which few
trained and seasoned historians wish to sink.

Certainly these confusions pervade most of our social institutions
and conversations. While many of us rely on our definitions to ground
our perspectives, and some of us rely on negating definitions to do the
same, it is clear, from the not-functional divisions of books for Lambda
Literary Awards to the endless list of letters at the end of queer organizational mission statements, that we need definition. And yet the current
cataloging system has become obstructive. The focus on what categories
mean, and why we do or do not want to be in them, has brought some
essential documentation and grappling with historic events, emotions,
and actions to a screeching halt. For lesbian history in particular, there

are so many reasons to abandon ship: no other movement in American radicalism has been so mocked; the subjects, themselves, promise grief to the enterprising scholar. And, I think, most importantly, the psychological, emotional, and relational complexities, conflicts, and deprivations are a necessary but very difficult centerpiece of events and how they unfold.

What Is to Be Done?

A few weeks after the conference I read a gorgeously written biography of the iconic and reclusive painter Agnes Martin by art historian Nancy Princenthal, winner of 2016 PEN/Jacqueline Bograd Weld Award for Biography. The author was respectful of all Martin's dimensions, eccentricities, impulses, and shifts in feeling and ideas. She recorded conflictual statements and claims by Martin about her own life and experiences without judgment, embracing these complexities as an organic part of her creative imagination and emotional lens. Nuance, complexity, contradiction, vagueness, ambivalence, confusion, and dislocation were all seen as elements worthy of record and relevant to understanding her life and, more importantly, her artwork, and their interconnections.

There was one arena, though, in which variation, levels, and counterindication were deemed too difficult to articulate: Martin's emotional and sexual feelings and actions toward women. Even though there was a clear resonance between how Martin lived and described, or withheld and obscured, her emotional and sexual interiority and exteriorization with the ways she lived and made art, the author enthusiastically delved into art practice, while sidelining desire and the emotions of erotic feeling. Yet Princenthal's reasoning was not the usual blindness or ick-factor when it comes to a historic figure's sexuality. Instead, she evoked the problem of identity categories as the reason to sideline these themes in the artist's life. Princenthal documents instances in Martin's life where the artist said that she was "not a lesbian," "not a woman," and that she was "a man." Certainly that is all-important, and can bring a lot to understanding Martin's lived erotics and repressions. Instead the author uses this information to downplay the role and importance of Martin's relationships, and nonrelationships, with women.

Right away, on page 11 of *Agnes Martin: Her Life and Art* (Thames and Hudson, 2015), Princenthal writes:

> Martin's romantic attachments, if that is the right term—she was not given to sentiment and preferred living alone—were largely with other women. But she refused the label lesbian (as she did the term feminist when it was applied to her). In her life, as in her work, renunciation was as important as embrace.

But, what about the renunciation *of* embrace? Isn't that also filled with meaning and therefore with history? The "romantic," which I would define as the spark of opening, are experiences that can come to dominate an imagination: artistic, political, intellectual, emotional, and certainly sexual. Both the recognition of open-heartedness, of connection, of the pleasure of knowing each other, as well as the refusal to allow the real to develop, the shutting down, the rejection of pleasure—all of these experiences are significant in the lives of human beings, and particularly of artists. They produce aesthetics. Artistic voice, after all, expresses the contested and resists repression. Repression, similarly, is a resonant key to the question of lesbian, queer, bisexual, and trans existence, even in our contemporary moment: repression of information, of feeling, of knowledge, of existence, of potential and risk. And when examining a self-described "hermit" like Agnes Martin, aloneness also has a specificity in lesbian, queer, bisexual, and trans life, whatever those words mean to you.

Whether Martin was a lesbian, a woman, and/or a man does not mean that feelings, desires, longings, refusals, experiences, conversations, silences, actions, and repressions with women are not deeply and fundamentally relevant to her history. And the content of those experiences, and refusals of experience, are more important than the question of Martin's sexual or gender category.

Later, on page 51, Princenthal drops, in an aside, that when Martin went to live and work in New Mexico in the 1940s, she found a culture in Taos where noted collector and *saloniste* Mabel Dodge Luhan (though married to a Native American man) was "among the many women at the time in Taos (and Santa Fe) to have had romantic relationships with other women, as did O'Keeffe." My eye falls on the word *many*. And of course the name *O'Keeffe*. Where can I read *that* book? Or does this not matter because the word *lesbian* is not operational?

At this point I would like to make a radical proposal: that we temporarily forget about who calls themselves a lesbian, why, or why not. Instead, I propose that we look into the emotional, psychological, economic, political, intellectual, artistic, sexual, daily, and life-long experiences of women who allowed or refused the embrace. The conversations that did happen and did not. The words permitted, and those uttered without permission. The invitations refused and accepted. The fears. The imaginations, erotic and projected. The walks in the woods, the fucking, the pleasure of the company acknowledged and refused. The meals, the conversations, how and what conversations provoked, the actions, the artworks, the articles, books, tears, orgasms realized/failed/imagined/ remembered, caresses, tendernesses, the refusals of tenderness, kisses that were and should have been, and how this moved the earth, the culture, the society, or even just one or two people's small lives. I propose that we call this whatever we want to call it, but that we not let it fall by the wayside, because when those of us creating queer history and culture display a reluctance to go deeper and transcend the artifice of restrictive thinking, the mainstream representations are handed a convenient model of hesitant obscuration. Lesbians give each other meaning in private, and it is too easy to keep the secret. It doesn't have to be clean, neat, safe, compartmentalized, or expected. Show it all and let the chips fall where they may. Princenthal mentions that among the women who had romantic attachments to other women in Taos was Betty Parsons, who later opened a gallery in New York. Princenthal writes that when Parsons's gallery represented Agnes Martin (along with other clients like Jackson Pollock), Agnes and Betty lived together in Betty's studio in New York City for a year. Nothing further. She quotes from different sources, some saying that a sexual relationship between the two would have been impossible. Others, like Betty's assistant Jack Tilton, felt sure that they did allow the embrace. Certainly that a lesbian gallerist was the first person who showed the work of Agnes Martin implies some kind of openness, some kind of love. And it is fair to imagine that had there been no Betty Parsons, it is possible that no man ever would have shown Martin's work. But despite the living together, despite the testimony of Tilton, despite the investment in each other's dreams and visions, Princenthal just isn't sure. "In the long interview conducted with Parsons for The Archives of American Art in 1969," Princenthal writes, "Agnes Martin's name does not come up." But that is so lesbian, to pretend we never loved, to erase the attraction, to deny the opening because of complexities of historical, emotional, and psychological reasons that I wish our historians would help us articulate and unravel.

Princenthal goes on to discuss some other "friendships," one with artist Lenore Tawny of whom Martin wrote: "There is an urgency that sweeps us up, an originality and success that hold us in wonder."

An elusive Greek woman artist, twenty years younger, with one name, Chryssa, is alluded to in Martin's *New York Times* obituary as the reason she left New York to live alone on a New Mexico mesa. But Princenthal thinks that was instead a relationship of professional assistance on Martin's part. Yet, I would say to Princenthal that if lesbian artists don't help each other, it is hard to know who is going to help us. And if we love someone's work, there is more possibility for . . . romance. Without the lesbian identity, there was still the romance. As Agnes Martin wrote, "When you're in life-drawing, you're really thinking of all the women you've ever seen, and all the gestures they've ever made. That's what brings life into the drawing. . . . It's just your real self."

The punch line: decades past, I had a lesbian literary agent named Diane Cleaver, who died over twenty years ago. Diane was very old school. "I'm out," she once told me. "But I am not out and about." At her memorial service, the only person who said the word "lesbian" was a straight writer. Diane once told me that Betty Parsons and Agnes Martin were lovers, but that Betty dumped Agnes for Greta Garbo, and this was the catalyst for Agnes's great depression.

This could easily be untrue, of course. Not being a historian, I have no way of confirming or denying. But being an artist, I was able to embed this piece of wish/knowledge into a scene in my novel *The Cosmopolitans*, where Earl, the Black, gay working-class protagonist, stumbles home from a day at the meatpacking plant. He runs into a good-looking Black actor, Frank, now employed as a chauffeur for a beige Bentley parked outside of Betty Parsons's gallery, carrying a mysterious passenger. Miss Parsons emerges, slips into the back seat, and Frank drives the shining chassis away. "Who was that?" asks a young Irish girl on the way to run her mother's errands. "That was Frank," the smitten Earl replies.

"That was not Frank," a drag queen from the adjacent Hotel Albert corrects him. "Honey, that was Greta Garbo. *Dot vas Ninotchka*."

Second punch line: I was in residency at the Yaddo artist's colony and shared the summer with an eighty-three-year-old painter named Buffie Johnson. Buffie was blind at this point but still painting "spheres." She told me that she had had three husbands, one of whom died of AIDS, and two girlfriends, Jane Bowles and Patricia Highsmith. "Wow, Buffy," I said. "They both were so difficult, they must have been tough girlfriends. Were they really that bad?" "Oh," she assured me in her Katharine Hepburnesque upper-class trill. "They were horrible."

Anyway, I once visited Buffie at her home on Greene Street, where her front door was a sculpture made by Louise Nevelson (who also said she was not a lesbian, lived with a woman for the final twenty-six years of her life, and who—after Nevelson's death—sued her family for "palimony"). Buffie told me about the time, when she was young, that Georgia O'Keeffe came to her studio. "She looked at my paintings and said, 'Ah those are. . . .'" And then Buffie faltered, "What word did she use? What words did she use? It was a twenties word . . . ah yes, *keen*. She said my paintings were *keen*."

But now that I learn from Princenthal that not-lesbian O'Keeffe had women lovers like *many* women in Taos and Santa Fe, and I know that not-lesbian Buffie did too, I start to wonder about who told Georgia O'Keeffe to go check out young Buffie Johnson, and why O'Keeffe bothered to support this unknown woman painter. And I, based in my own artist's life, *know* it had something to do with the lesbiannesss of these not-lesbians, which is also a force of history and of culture. The romance, the special surprise of openness, and what it produces, whether we want it or not, is worth noting.

WORKS CITED

Princenthal, Nancy. 2015. *Agnes Martin: Her Life and Art*. New York: Thames & Hudson.
Schulman, Sarah. 2016. *The Cosmopolitans*. New York: Feminist Press.

ABOUT THE EDITORS

Amin Ghaziani is Professor of Sociology and Canada Research Chair in Sexuality and Urban Studies at the University of British Columbia. He is the author or co-editor of four books: *The Dividends of Dissent, A Decade of HAART, There Goes the Gayborhood?*, and *Sex Cultures*. His work has appeared in the *American Sociological Review, Annual Review of Sociology, City & Community, Social Problems*, and *Theory and Society*, among other outlets. Ghaziani's research has informed public commentaries about urban sexualities in the *American Prospect, British Vogue, New Yorker, Time*, and *Vice* magazines, BBC Radio 4, *Bloomberg Business*, CBC radio, *Chicago Tribune, Financial Times, The Guardian, Los Angeles Times, Monocle Daily*, NPR, *New York Times, Toronto Globe & Mail*, and *USA Today*.

Matt Brim is Associate Professor of Queer Studies at the College of Staten Island, City University of New York. He is author of *James Baldwin and the Queer Imagination*, as well as an open access online study guide for the HIV/AIDS activist documentary film *United in Anger: A History of ACT UP*. His work has appeared in the *Journal of Homosexuality, WSQ: Women's Studies Quarterly*, the *Journal of Modern Literature*, and the *Gay and Lesbian Review*. His next book, *Poor Queer Studies*, is forthcoming from Duke University Press.

ABOUT THE CONTRIBUTORS

Kadji Amin is Assistant Professor of Women's, Gender, and Sexuality Studies at Emory University and a 2015–16 Mellon Postdoctoral Fellow in "Sex" at the University of Pennsylvania. He is the author of *Disturbing Attachments: Genet, Modern Pederasty, and Queer History*.

Petra L. Doan is Professor of Urban and Regional Planning at Florida State University. She conducts research on transgender experiences of the city and explores the relationship between urban planning and the wider LGBTQ+ community. She has edited two books: *Queerying Planning: Challenging Heteronormative Assumptions and Reframing Planning Practice* and *Planning and LGBTQ Communities: The Need for Inclusive Queer Space*. She also has published a number of related articles in *Gender, Place, and Culture, Women's Studies Quarterly, Environment and Planning A*, the *Journal of Planning Education and Research, Progressive Planning*, and the *International Review of Urban and Regional Research*.

Shelly Eversley teaches literature, feminism, and black studies at Baruch College, City University of New York, where she is Associate Professor of English. She is the author of *The "Real" Negro: The Question of Authenticity in Twentieth-Century African American Literature*, as well as several essays on literature, race, and culture. She is editor of *The Sexual Body* and *The 1970s*, both special issues of *WSQ*, a journal from the Feminist Press. She is also editor of the forthcoming book *Black Art, Politics, and Aesthetics in 1960s African American Literature and Culture*, and is writing a new book titled *Black Listed: African American Literature and the Cold War Politics of Integration*. She is founder of EqualityArchive.com.

Jessica Fields is Professor of Sociology and Sexuality Studies at San Francisco State University and author of *Risky Lessons: Sex Education and Social Inequality*. With Laura Mamo, Nancy Lesko, and Jen Gilbert, she leads the Beyond Bullying Project, a community-based storytelling project funded by the Ford Foundation that aims to understand and interrupt ordinary hostility in high schools to LGBTQ sexualities. Fields is currently writing her second book, *Problems We Pose: Feeling Differently about Qualitative Research.*

Patrick R. Grzanka is Associate Professor of Psychology at the University of Tennessee, Knoxville, and the editor of *Intersectionality: Foundations and Frontiers* (2nd ed.). His new book traces the "born this way" wars—debates about the nature, origins, and mutability of sexual orientation—in science, law, and the emotional lives of sexual and gender minorities.

Marcus Anthony Hunter is Scott Waugh Endowed Chair in the Division of the Social Sciences, Associate Professor of Sociology, and Chair of the Department of African American Studies at University of California, Los Angeles. He is the author of *Black Citymakers: How "The Philadelphia Negro" Changed Urban America* and co-author of *Chocolate Cities: The Black Map of American Life* with Zandria F. Robinson. Hunter's research and commentary on urban black life and inequality has been featured in journals and news media such as CSPAN's *BookTV*, the *Du Bois Review, City & Community, Sexuality Research & Social Policy*, the *Washington Post*, and the *New York Times.*

Laurie Hurson is the architect of EqualityArchive.com and a PhD candidate in Environmental Psychology at the Graduate Center at the City University of New York. She works in instructional technology, digital pedagogy, and faculty development as a Hybrid Coordinator at Baruch College, CUNY, and a Teaching and Learning Fellow at the Graduate Center, CUNY. She is also the Coordinator for Planning and Development of OpenCUNY.org, a student-run, open-source, participatory digital platform for the Graduate Center community.

E. Patrick Johnson is the Chair of African American Studies and Carlos Montezuma Professor of Performance Studies and African American Studies at Northwestern University. A scholar/artist, Johnson performs nationally and internationally and has published widely in the areas of race, gender, sexuality and performance. He is the author of *Appropriating Blackness: Performance and the Politics of Authenticity*, *Sweet Tea: Black Gay Men of the South—An Oral History*, and *Black. Queer. Southern. Women.—An Oral History*, as well as editor of several volumes.

Heather Love is the author of *Feeling Backward: Loss and the Politics of Queer History* and the editor of a special issue of *GLQ* on Gayle Rubin ("Rethinking Sex") and the co-editor of a special issue of *Representations* ("Description across Disciplines"). She has written on topics including comparative social stigma, compulsory happiness, transgender fiction, spinster aesthetics, reading methods in literary studies, and the history of deviance studies. She is currently completing a book on practices of description in the humanities and social sciences after World War II.

Jenni Molloy is a critically acclaimed jazz double bassist and composer, known for her live recording *Bach ReLoaded Trio +*. She has collaborated internationally on numerous theater, poetry, and improvised music projects. An in-demand jazz bassist, Jenni is also a Goju Ryu martial artist, and runs the Tsuyoi Kokoro Dojo in Leeds.

Kevin L. Nadal is Professor of Psychology at John Jay College of Criminal Justice and the Graduate Center at the City University of New York. Nadal is a former executive director of CLAGS: The Center for LGBTQ Studies and president of the Asian American Psychological Association. He is the author of many books, including *That's So Gay! Microaggressions and the Lesbian, Gay, Bisexual, and Transgender Community*.

David P. Rivera is Associate Professor of Counselor Education at Queens College, City University of New York and former board chair of CLAGS: The Center for LGBTQ Studies. His research and practice focus on cultural competency development and issues impacting the marginalization and wellbeing of people of color and oppressed sexual orientation and gender identity groups, with a focus on microaggressions.

Zandria F. Robinson is Associate Professor of Sociology at Rhodes College and the author of *This Ain't Chicago: Race, Class, and Regional*

Identity in the Post-Soul South and co-author of *Chocolate Cities: The Black Map of American Life* with Marcus Anthony Hunter. Her scholarly work has appeared in *Annual Review of Sociology* (with Marcus Anthony Hunter), *Contexts*, and *Issues in Race and Society*; her creative nonfiction work has appeared in *Rolling Stone, Oxford American*, and *Hyperallergic*.

Sarah Schulman is a novelist, nonfiction writer, playwright, screenwriter, journalist, AIDS historian, and the author of eighteen books. A Guggenheim and Fulbright Fellow, Sarah is a Distinguished Professor of the Humanities at the College of Staten Island, City University of New York, and serves on the advisory board of Jewish Voice for Peace.

Rommi Smith is the inaugural British Parliamentary Writer-in-Residence and the inaugural Poet-in-Residence for Keats' House, London. John Barnard Doctoral Research Scholar at the University of Leeds, Smith is a Visiting Scholar at the City University New York (CUNY). Her scholarly work has been presented at the Royal Academy, Segal Theatre New York, the Schomburg Center for Research in Black Culture, Harlem, and the Archives Libraries and Museums LGBTQI+ Conference. She has won commissions by companies including Paines Plough and Pentabus and broadcast media including BBC Radio 3, 4, and 5. Smith's writing is published by Peepal Tree Press, Bloodaxe, Seren, the Forward Foundation, and Oberon Modern Plays. Her website is rommi-smith-co.uk and she tweets at @rommismith.

Steven W. Thrasher is the inaugural Daniel H. Renberg Chair in Media Coverage of Sexual and Gender Minorities at Northwestern University's Medill School of Journalism, the first ever journalism professorship to focus on LGBTQ subjects and scholarship. He was named to the Hall of Fame of the American Sociological Association's journal *Contexts* in 2017. From 2014 to 2018, he was a doctoral fellow in American Studies at New York University and writer-at-large for the *Guardian*, while he also contributed writing to the *New York Times, New York Review of Books, Esquire*, BuzzFeed, the *Journal of American History*, and *Radical History Review*. Thrasher has been named Journalist of the Year by the National Lesbian and Gay Journalists Association for his writing in the *Village Voice* and *Out* magazine, and his research on blood science and HIV criminalization has been supported by grants from the Alfred P. Sloan, Gannett, and Ford Foundations. He tweets @thrasherxy.

Jane Ward is Professor of Gender and Sexuality Studies at University of California Riverside, where she teaches courses in feminist, queer, and heterosexuality studies. She is the author of *Not Gay: Sex between Straight White Men* and *Respectably Queer: Diversity Culture in LGBT Activist Organizations.* Ward is currently working on a book titled *The Tragedy of Heterosexuality: How Misogyny Doomed the World's Most Cherished Union and Hid the Wreckage.*

INDEX

AAPF. *See* African American Policy
Forum
Aberrations in Black (Ferguson), 149
Abramovic, Marina, 224
academia: empiricism, 193; with "scholar,"
meaning of, 199–200; whiteness and,
244
academic freedom, 191
ACT UP. *See* AIDS Coalition to Unleash
Power
Adam4Adam, 233
addiction, drugs, 63
administration, queering leadership and,
197–201
African American Policy Forum (AAPF),
182–83
African American studies, 33–34
African American women in the South.
See *Black. Queer. Southern. Women.—
An Oral History*
After Method (Law), 28
Agnes Martin (Princenthal), 296
Ahmed, Sara, 13, 224, 252, 285, 291
AIDS Coalition to Unleash Power (ACT
UP), 3, 169, 281
AIDS/HIV. *See* HIV/AIDS
Ainsworth, Claire, 135
Alaskan women, in PAR workshops, 68
Albuquerque, 112
Alexander, Bryant Keith, 51
Allen, Jafari, 40n4, 70
*All the Women Are White, All the Blacks
Are Men, But Some of Us Are Brave*
(Hull, Bell-Scott, and Smith), 19, 160n1

Alyson Publications, 159
Amazon, 269–70, 271–72
American Association of Newspaper Edi-
tors, 244
American Indian women, in PAR work-
shops, 68
American Psychiatric Association, 125, 198
American Psychological Association,
138n1
Amin, Kadji, 31, 292n11
Andrus Family Fund, 199
Annual Review of Sociology, 166
anti-identitarianism, 282–83
Anzaldúa, Gloria, 90–91, 284
"apparent incommensurability," 5, 29
An Archive of Feelings (Cvetkovich), 224
archives, 150, 151, 216; EqualityArchive.
com, 248–55; of queer chocolate cities,
177–83
Archives of Flesh (Reid-Pharr), 150, 151
Arcus Foundation, 199
armed forces, U.S., 89
Arondekar, Anjali, 40n4, 289, 292n10
Arseneau, Julie, 89
Asian/Pacific Islander women, 68
Atlanta, 103
attachment genealogy, as method, 288–91
Austin, 105, 114
"axiom of additivity," 9

Bachmann, Marcus, 265
Bachmann, Michelle, 265
Badu, Erykah, 174
Bailey, Marlon, 14

Playing in the Dark (Morrison, Toni), 161n8
playscripts, 208
Plummer, Ken, 8, 10, 14–15, 39n4
plurality, gender, 13
poet, as diviner, 215
poetry: blackout, 216; citation-as-poetry, 224
political struggle, 36, 69
politics, 213, 285
Pollock, Della, 46, 53–55
populations: cross-dressers, 126–27, *128*, 133–34, 135; HIV/AIDS and marginalized, 65; intersex, 127, *128*, 139n4; migration and, 103; same-sex households and city, 103–5; sexual reassignment surgery, 126; transsexuals, 125–26, *128*; U.S. Census, 103–6, 116n1. *See also* gayborhood studies; medical model, for counting transgender population
porn, 235, 260, 270
Portland, 105
post-positivism, 84–85, 98
poverty, 63, 65
Povinelli, Elizabeth, 292n10
praxis: CRT and, 196; essay-as-performance and, 209; queer methods as, 262
The Price of the Ticket (Baldwin), 143
Pride parades, 113, 163
Primo, David, 5
Princenthal, Nancy, 295–99
prison. *See* incarceration
"profeminists," 52
progress narrative, 79
"Prove It on Me Blues" (Ma Rainey), 212, 223–24
Provincetown, 105
psychology, role of, 89
Puar, Jasbir, 282
Pulse nightclub, 231, 238–42

qualitative methods, 203
quantification: Foucault and, 88; LPA, 95–96; of subject, 16

quare, 59n1, 284; connotations, 172; methods with oral history as performance, 55–59; role of, 226n3. *See also Black. Queer. Southern. Women.—An Oral History*
"Queer and Now" (Sedgwick), 280
Queer as Folk (television show), 281
"queer," as term, 278–84
queer black literacy, 160n3; pedagogies of, 157–60, 160n2
Queer by Choice (Whisman), 259
Queer Eye for the Straight Guy (television show), 281
queering measurement, transgender community and: in context, 121–25; cross-dresser estimates, 126–27, *128*, 133–34, 135; gender-flux category, 133–35; intersex expanded, 135; intersex population estimates, 127, *128*, 139n4; medical model, 125–30; toward more fluidity, 131–36; population counts expanded, 135–36; population estimates (2014) using traditional methods, *128*; traditional methods for counting population, 125–27; transsexual definition expanded, 131–33; transsexual estimates, 125–26
queering methodology, 16–18
queering methods, queer methods and, 14–16
"Queer Method" conference (2013), 4, 30, 39n3
queer methods: in context, 3–5, 8–10; dualisms, rejection of, 12; impermeable categories, rejection of, 11–12; interest group politics, rejection of, 12–13; principles, 11; queering methodology and, 16–18; queering methods and, 14–16; queer pedagogy and, 19–22; renaissance, 3–4, 22–23; research practices, 261–62; responses to, 33; unchanging categories, rejection of, 10–11; world-making and livability, 5–8

www.ingramcontent.com/pod-product-compliance
Lightning Source LLC
Chambersburg PA
CBHW032101040426
42336CB00040B/626